# Barriers to Effective Civil Society Organisations

This book provides an insight into the historical changes and present-day circumstances that have influenced, and continue to influence, the development and future of civil society.

Civil society organisations (CSOs) play a crucial role in international development, however their impact on policy and practice is limited by a range of shifts across their political, social and financial landscapes. *Barriers to Effective Civil Society Organisations* is divided into three parts addressing each of these shifts in turn, and places particular emphasis on civil society actors linked not only by political constraints, but also by ethnic and cultural diversities that are crucial markers of political and social identity. This book draws on case studies from across Latin America, Africa, MENA and Ireland to highlight how CSOs in these countries are shaped by, and react to, shifting challenges. Reflecting on solutions for the sector, the authors provide an understanding of the various 'self-accommodation' policies and techniques employed by CSOs in order to continue their services and increase their credibility across global contexts.

Aimed at researchers, policymakers and CSO/NGO workers looking to better understand the current state and future of the sector from the perspective of emerging scholars working in these regions, and in the Global South in particular, this innovative book is a celebration of the important work of CSOs and a reaffirmation of their right to sit at the policy table.

**Ibrahim Natil** is a Lecturer at Dublin City University, Ireland.

**Vanessa Malila** is a researcher at the Humanitarian Academy for Development. She was previously a Research Follow in the School of Journalism and Media Studies at Rhodes University, South Africa.

**Youcef Sai** is an independent researcher with a PhD in Education from Trinity College Dublin.

## Routledge Explorations in Development Studies

This Development Studies series features innovative and original research at the regional and global scale. It promotes interdisciplinary scholarly works drawing on a wide spectrum of subject areas, in particular politics, health, economics, rural and urban studies, sociology, environment, anthropology, and conflict studies.

Topics of particular interest are globalization; emerging powers; children and youth; cities; education; media and communication; technology development; and climate change.

In terms of theory and method, rather than basing itself on any orthodoxy, the series draws broadly on the tool kit of the social sciences in general, emphasizing comparison, the analysis of the structure and processes, and the application of qualitative and quantitative methods.

**Political Financing in Developing Countries**
A Case from Ghana
*Joseph Luna*

**Dilemmas of Regional and Local Development**
*Edited by Jerzy Bański*

**Security, Development and Violence in Afghanistan**
Everyday Stories of Intervention
*Althea-Maria Rivas*

**Economic Development in Ghana and Malaysia**
A Comparative Analysis
*Samuel K. Andoh, Bernice J. deGannes Scott and Grace Ofori-Abebrese*

**Rethinking Multilateralism in Foreign Aid**
Beyond the Neoliberal Hegemony
*Edited by Viktor Jakupec, Max Kell and Jonathan Makuwira*

**The Informal Economy Revisited**
Examining the Past, Envisioning the Future
*Edited by Martha Chen and Françoise Carré*

**Barriers to Effective Civil Society Organisations**
Political, Social and Financial Shifts
*Edited by Ibrahim Natil, Vanessa Malila and Youcef Sai*

# Barriers to Effective Civil Society Organisations

## Political, Social and Financial Shifts

**Edited by**
**Ibrahim Natil, Vanessa Malila and Youcef Sai**

LONDON AND NEW YORK

First published 2021
by Routledge
4 Park Square, Milton Park, Abingdon, Oxon OX14 4RN
605 Third Avenue, New York, NY 10017

*Routledge is an imprint of the Taylor & Francis Group, an informa business*



*British Library Cataloguing in Publication Data*
A catalogue record for this book is available from the British Library

*Library of Congress Cataloging-in-Publication Data*
Names: Natil, Ibrahim, editor. | Malila, Vanessa, author. | Sai, Yousef, editor.
Title: Barriers to effective civil society organisations : political, social and financial shifts / edited by Ibrahim Natil, Vanessa Malila and Yousef Sai.
Description: Abingdon, Oxon ; New York : Routledge, 2020. | Includes bibliographical references and index.
Identifiers: LCCN 2020012346 (print) | LCCN 2020012347 (ebook) | ISBN 9780367512583 (hardback) | ISBN 9781003053040 (ebook)
Subjects: LCSH: Civil society–Developing countries–Case studies. | Civil society–Ireland–Case studies. | Non-governmental organizations–Developing countries–Case studies. | Non-governmental organizations–Ireland–Case studies.
Classification: LCC JC337 .B38 2020 (print) | LCC JC337 (ebook) | DDC 300.9172/4–dc23
LC record available at https://lccn.loc.gov/2020012346
LC ebook record available at https://lccn.loc.gov/2020012347

ISBN: 978-0-367-51258-3 (hbk)
ISBN: 978-0-367-51259-0 (pbk)
ISBN: 978-1-003-05304-0 (ebk)

Typeset in Times New Roman
by Taylor & Francis Books

# Contents

# Illustrations

## Figures



## Tables

# Contributors

**Ibrahim Natil** is a lecturer at Dublin City University, teaching politics and business at the Centre for Talented Youth, CTY Ireland at Dublin City University (DCU). Dr Ibrahim Natil is the winner of the Robert Chamber best overall paper, selected by DSA Ireland. He is also a research fellow at the Institute of International Conflict Resolution & Reconstruction (Dublin City University). He is the Co-convener of NGOs in the Development Study Group, DSA-UK. He is an international development consultant and has worked for many civil society organisations. He has managed more than 56 human rights, women's and youth empowerment and peace-building programmes since 1997. He is a leading co-editor of the book: *The Power of Civil Society in the Middle East and North Africa: Peace-building, Change, and Development* (Routledge 2019). He has also authored more than 20 academic papers/chapters on a wide range of peacebuilding, human security, conflict resolution, civil society, international relations and political violence topics. He has also published a number of blogs/pieces for audiences beyond the academic.

**Vanessa Malila** has a PhD in media and communications from the University of Leeds. The research for her contribution was carried out while she was Head of the Advocacy and Impact Programme at the Public Service Accountability Monitor at Rhodes University, South Africa. She is currently Research & Development Officer at the Humanitarian Academy for Development, working on understanding humanitarian, development and aid in the global context. She began her career as an academic specialising in media and citizenship in the South African context. In 2016, she moved to the civil society sector, working as a researcher for a South African NGO. Her areas of specialisation include understanding the relationship between the media and civil society, the roles of journalism in promoting good governance, citizenship, the role of the media, civil society and citizens in development, and research ethics.

**Youcef Sai** is a researcher in Islamic studies, with a PhD in Education from Trinity College Dublin. He has published widely in the field of Islamic education and Muslim schools in Ireland, including *Islamic Education in Ireland: Insights and Perspectives* (Oxford: Peter Lang, 2020).

**Ola Alkahlout** is currently a PhD researcher in her final year at Coventry University. Her research examines the global and regional issues regarding the application of *Zakāt* in Qatar (2017–2019). She lived in Gaza and completed her BSc in Maths and Computer Science at Al-Azhar University, Gaza, Palestine. She then enrolled in a master's degree course in Islamic Banking, Finance, and Management at the University of Gloucestershire.

**Ahmed El Assal** is a researcher and practitioner with ten years of experience in the international development sector, with a focus on governance and development issues. Ahmed holds an MA in Governance, Development, and Public Policy from the Institute of Development Studies (IDS), University of Sussex. Ahmed's research interests focus on state–society relations, civil society and social movements, human rights, gender and democracy.

**Rikio Kimura** is a professor at the College of Asia Pacific Studies of Ritsumeikan Asia Pacific University in Japan. He holds a Doctor of Education from the University of Sussex. He worked for an international development NGO in Cambodia from 1997 to 2007. His research interests include NGO, social enterprise, community development, adult learning, pedagogy and Cambodia.

**Amr Marzouk** is a PhD candidate at the University of Rotterdam. He holds an MSC in criminology from Durham University. Amr's research work focuses on issues related to social movements, cyberspace policies and criminology.

**Mohsen Moheimany** holds a PhD degree in political science and international relations from Dublin City University. He is a researcher and journalist with a primary area of interest in Iran's politics and civil society. He has a background of editing and writing for the Iranian and international media. Apart from reports and interviews on Iran's current issues, he is working on a book titled *NGOs, Policy Networks and Political Opportunities in Hybrid Regimes.* He received his BA in political science from the University of Tehran and an MA in public policy from the University of Nottingham.

**Alireza Najafinejad** is an Assistant Professor of Political Science at Golestan University in Iran. He holds a PhD in politics and government from University Putra Malaysia. His areas of interest include Middle East politics and human rights in Islam. His BA is in political science from Mashhad University and his MA is also in the same field from Karaj Azad University. He has experience of working with the Iranian local government, media and political parties.

**Chris O'Connell** is a Postdoctoral CAROLINE Fellow in the School of Law and Government at Dublin City University (DCU). His research interests centre on alterative and sustainable models of development, and their political realisation. Chris holds a PhD in Political Science from DCU, where his thesis examined civil society influence on the policies of left-wing governments in Latin America, with a particular focus on environmental policy. Other research interests include the political economy of development in Latin America and the politics of 'post-neoliberalism'; human and environmental rights; and the Sustainable Development Goals and Agenda 2030. His current research is supported by funding from the Irish Research Council and the European Union, and focuses on the relationship between climate change, vulnerability and human exploitation in Peru and Bolivia.

**Mohammed Yachoulti** graduated from Mohammed Ben Abdellah University, Faculty of Arts & Human Sciences, Fez, Morocco with a BA degree in English literature, an MA in Gender Studies and a Doctorate in Linguistics & Gender Studies. Currently, he is an associate professor at the Faculty of Arts & Human Sciences, Moulay Ismail University of Meknes, Morocco. He is interested in gender, social movement and migration studies. His publications include "Moroccan civil society after the 2011 constitutional reforms: The case of the women's movement", "Moroccan women's resistance to *Al-hogra* in the aftermaths of Arab Spring", "Syrian refugees in Morocco: Realities and prospects", "Women of February 20th Movement in Morocco: A new feminist consciousness" among others. He has also participated in many national and international conferences and workshops on gender, civil society and migration

# 1 Introduction

*Ibrahim Natil*

Civil society organisations (CSOs) play an increasingly important role in generating the political, economic and social developments that shape our daily life in our contemporary and global society. A CSO is as an independent actor that assists "people to claim their rights in promoting rights-based approaches, in shaping development policies and partnerships and in overseeing their implementation" (Busan Global Partnership Forum for Effective Development Cooperation, 2011; UNDP, 2013: 123; OECD, 2011: 10). They are governed by ordinary citizens on a voluntary basis, without significant government control or representation, and are considered by some as a form of the "participatory democracy" process where active citizens have the power to decide on change (Aragones and SánchezPagés, 2009: 56–72). There are many types of CSO involved in delivering aid, including faith-based groups, trade unions, professional associations and internationally affiliated organisations with branches in many different countries. Furthermore, they have been active contributors to relief, development and empowerment of civil society despite social, cultural, economic and political shifts and challenges (Hanafi and Cuhadar, 2010: 211).

There are, however, many aid actors, workers and governments in southern countries, referred to as non-governmental organisations or 'NGOs' and their role in international aid and development cooperation is also significantly important (UNDP, 2013: 123). 'NGO', however, is a term, included under a broader category of 'CSOs'. 'NGO' is sometimes used interchangeably with 'CSO', but NGOs should be more accurately understood as a subset of CSOs involved in development cooperation (OECD, 2011: 12). Organisations, such as trade unions or professional associations, for example, often avoid characterising themselves as NGOs, preferring to label themselves CSOs. Moreover, not-for-profit universities and research institutes are also defined as CSOs. They include a diverse set of organisations, ranging from small, informal, community-based organisations to the large international non-governmental organisations (INGOs) working through local CSOs across southern countries (UNDP, 2013: 123). Although the Development Assistance Committee (DAC) of the Organisation for Economic Co-operation and Development (OECD) have traditionally used the term 'NGO', however, they have adopted the definition of CSOs:

> [CSOs] can be defined to include all non-market and non-state organisations outside of the family in which people organize themselves to pursue shared interests in the public domain. Examples include community-based organizations and village associations, environmental groups, women's rights groups, farmers' associations, faith-based organizations, labour unions, co-operatives, professional associations, chambers of commerce, independent research institutes and the not-for-profit media.
>
> (OECD, 2011: 10)

Additionally, CSOs have proven that they are capable of delivering a model of services managed by professional teams. CSOs have been considered crucial stakeholders in mobilising and empowering society as key drivers of political, economic and societal change processes. They deliver actions in the fields of women of empowerment, civic engagement, community development, human rights, community peacebuilding, conflict resolution, health and sports. CSOs also aim at increasing engagement of marginalised and vulnerable groups in public dialogue, activism and community peacebuilding (Natil, 2014: 82–87).

CSO activists and/or ordinary citizens attempt to challenge ineffective, inefficient and insufficient public policies while they still have some influence over processes of change (Paffenholz, 2010). However, some of the barriers facing civil society influence are defined as the ability of this sector to cope with and operate within shifting conditions, restrictive political environments, and despite the complexity of the sociocultural and economic context. CSOs have the capacity to drive innovation and provide humanitarian relief in the face of natural disasters, war and other crises around the world. Repressive regimes in some countries, however, have been found to control CSOs by imposing a system of dominating financial channels (Weeden, 2015).

CSOs work and cooperate with a number of international organisations and foreign donors to implement participatory civil society activities (Wildeman, 2019). Foreign aid remains, however, essential for effective civil society and development programme implementation (Baliamoune Lutz, 2016: 320–341). This significant contribution of civil society organisations is reflected in their ability to engage in development and change process, and to contribute to the introduction of long-term changes in attitudes and prejudices and to promote the rights of vulnerable groups, while fostering tolerance by applying lessons learnt from other conflicts in the world (Paffenholz and Spurk, 2010: 66–76). With a diverse range of organisations, objectives and activities that target local, national and international issues, the CSO sector is an expansive terrain characterised by dynamic relationships between agents of action, the causes they serve and the communities that benefit from their activities. Occupying the ground between business and government, the CSO sector faces a number of regulatory and financial challenges that affect its overall health and sustainability. Civil society activists are increasingly witness to poor public freedom, socio-political deadlock, narrow civic space owing to controlled political systems and harsh economic life (Natil, 2019).

In short, this book seeks to address the following questions: To what extent has civil society actually succeeded in achieving its own objectives despite the shifting landscape? What is the role of civil society in accommodating the changes? How did civil society organisations (CSOs) overcome challenges in these societies? By assessing contexts and engaging policymakers with rigorous empirical research in a systematic way, CSOs can work to overcome both the internal and external challenges they face. This book aims to bring about a heightened awareness of the challenges faced by CSOs, as well as highlight the potential for greater policy engagement for poverty reduction. The main contribution of the book is to undertake new research, particularly around informed practice on the ground, and present recommendations to policymakers, practitioners, stakeholders and donors on ways of providing more conducive spaces for CSO contributions on specific policy issues. This book provides insights into a field neglected by research, and stimulates others to research this growing area of research. It also introduces the lessons learnt by civil society in responding to political shifts, social constraints and foreign aid changes, despite the existence of social conservatism, conflict, violence and the absence of democracy. It concludes with some implications and offers direction for future research in the field of CSOs in non-Western and Western contexts.

This book will be highly influential as it contains in-depth understandings and evidence of particular CSOs, outlining the problems and challenges that exist. This provides a platform which is part of the solution towards increasing the policy influence and social impact of the work of CSOs in a shifting global landscape. By presenting up-to-date empirical research, this chapter will help to increase the legitimacy and effectiveness of CSOs. CSOs are currently engaging in various contexts, which is important for different target groups, including scientists, researchers, national-level policymakers, donors, NGO staff and the beneficiaries themselves. Each of these groups have different communication needs. The book explores various factors which influence the civil society sector. It will focus on challenges facing CSOs' societal contributions, current operational practices and strategies for future development.

It is without doubt that there have been significant changes to the CSO sector in recent years and this book explores the factors, circumstances and historical changes that influence the development and activities of CSOs, as well as the organisational, financial and political challenges facing the sector today. Remarkably, although considerable research has highlighted the weaknesses and limitations of civil society, rather less attention has been paid to its power in dealing with the exceptional circumstances and dynamics characterising some undemocratic and democratic societies in which CSOs find themselves. Therefore, the volume offers new insights into how CSOs in these countries not only are shaped by but also react to shifting challenges by considering papers from different parts of the world to promote cooperation within societies. CSOs, for example, have been challenged at all levels by violence, social context, and the conditions, requirements and shifts of international donors (Hanafi and Cuhadar, 2010: 211).

In order to best examine the barriers faced by CSOs and how they overcome these, the book focuses on three themes/shifts – political, social and foreign aid – and, by examining specific case studies on Cambodia, Iran, Egypt, the Palestinian territories, Ireland, Malwai, Tanzania, Zambia, South Africa and Mozambique and Morocco, aims at improving our understanding on the shifts of CSOs in various societies. Particular emphasis is placed upon the different challenges faced by civil society actors from different locations around the world that are linked not only to political constraints but also to ethnic, linguistic and cultural diversities, as well as religious salient differences that are crucial markers of social and political identity. The purpose of this book is to explore the lessons learnt by civil society in responding to political changes, social constraints and foreign aid shifts. Despite the existence of social conservatism, conflict, violence and the absence of democracy and exclusive political systems in a number of countries, CSO civic engagement and community participation challenge the political, social and financial constraints in Latin America, Africa, MENA and Ireland.

In this volume, new research by young scholars provides contributions that are innovative and different as they mainly stem from their experiences and fieldwork. Contributions provide examples of the way CSOs are currently engaging in various contexts, which is important for different target groups, including scientists, researchers, national-level policymakers, donors, NGO staff and the beneficiaries themselves. CSOs play a crucial role in international development, however, they are having limited impact on policy and practice, and ultimately the lives of poor people. Some of the obstacles that hinder the ability of CSOs to perform their work are the policy processes that exist in some Global South countries. These processes often undermine and block CSO work. In many contexts, however, it is largely about the ways CSOs operate.

This book contributes to and enriches the debate on various civil society developments with new insights and a fresh perspective at the global level by providing concrete examples of civil society responses to the shifting landscape. Natil's chapter (2) introduces shifting landscape challenges facing civil society. It also discusses the definitions of various political, social and financial challenges that have forced civil society organisations to shift or/and accommodate their operations and interventions. Natil's introductory chapter on the debate on the shifting landscape and its implications for the civil society familiarises the reader with the theoretical framework through which the individual chapters are grounded.

Malila's chapter (3) explores the perspectives of CSOs on the way in which the media are changing in their contexts, how they are adapting to changing civic spaces and the potential for social media to overcome restrictive regimes in Malawi, Tanzania, Zambia, South Africa and Mozambique. This chapter establishes an understanding of civic space and the importance of media (both traditional and social) in that space in order to enhance the work of

CSOs in holding governments to account. It also explores how CSOs close civic spaces and bridge the information gap through social media; how they are adapting to changing civic spaces; and the potential for social media to overcome restrictive regimes. Her chapter improves our understanding of how and why CSOs rely on the media in their contexts, how and why they are shifting more to using social media in their accountability work, and whether social media is able to play an effective role in opening civic space. In contexts where public broadcasters have often been unofficial 'state' broadcasters and print journalists are often enticed to report on corruption and accountability only when remunerated, CSOs are harnessing the potential of social media such as WhatsApp, Facebook and Twitter to continue holding public officials to account.

Moheimany and Najafinejad's chapter (4) discusses the changing civil society and hybrid regime in Iran. This chapter discusses the subject of shifts in the status of civil society across two political periods in the Islamic Republic of Iran, namely the reformist (1997–2005) and conservative (2005–2013) periods. The circulation of power between two competing political camps significantly changed the political setting and made two contrary periods within the same political regime and, more interestingly, the same Supreme Leader Ayatollah Khamenei, though with opposite policies and incumbents in the presidency and Parliament. Despite the obstruction of electoral and political processes by Islamic institutions and security forces, in the cases of the two aforementioned periods, the ballot box became the mechanism people used to change the direction of policy: liberal democracy versus Islamic authoritarianism. As a result, not only did the character and behaviour of the state shift towards civil society, the composition and political position of civil society changed too.

El Assal and Marzouk's chapter (5) studies the reinvention of nationalism and the moral panic against foreign aid in Egypt. Financing civil society activities has grown exponentially since the 1990s. Following the third wave of democratisation, several donors, either bilateral or multilateral agencies, have heavily supported and funded the activities of civil society organisations (CSOs) in the Global South. After this transition in the global order, CSOs played a fundamental role to support the spread of liberal norms and neoliberal policies, such as supporting the state by playing an intermediary role in public service provision. This was in addition to its political role in supporting democratisation processes through the expansion of civic education, human rights promotion and advocacy. CSOs, especially organisations that primarily work on advocacy and human rights issues, are often criticised by authoritarian governments for receiving foreign funds. Among several strategies to curtail the activities of these CSOs, banning foreign funds became one way to disempower and undermine the activities of these organisations and stifle the way they operate.

Alkahlout's chapter (6) examines the effectiveness and influence of Qatari humanitarian aid on civil society organisations in the Gaza Strip since the siege in 2007. The research focuses on the challenges facing CSO contributions, current operational practices, and strategies for future development under the continued Israeli blockade, political split of governing bodies and obstruction of democratic life. The overall purpose of this study is to assess the extent to which Qatari aid supports CSOs in the Gaza Strip, and what effect it has on generating the political, economic and social developments that shape daily life in the Strip. The research methods are based on a supportive and integrated combination of a literature review on the existing conflict, and field research. Interviews were conducted with CSO staff in the Gaza Strip, Gazan people and Qatari charity staff in Qatar. The main findings and conclusions suggest that the Qatari humanitarian aid to Gaza in the last decade has had a deterrent effect on the work of the Palestinian CSOs.

Kimura's chapter (7) discusses NGOs' rights-based approach between contextual appropriateness and political transformation in neo-patrimonial Cambodia. It problematises a development NGO's collaborative approach with the government as a rights-based approach (RBA) in Cambodia. The re-politicisation of development practices and studies has been called for by many scholars. For example, there are calls for more "ethnography and political economy" (Bebbington, 2004) and the "return of politics" (Hickey, 2008). However, it is widely held that politically confrontational RBA by NGOs does not work in relation to authoritarian governments as it irritates such governments and makes it impossible for NGOs to operate, hence, non-confrontational approaches are called for. It also discusses whether non-confrontational or collaborative approaches are effective in terms of the political and structural transformation that RBA intends to achieve. It also attempts to analyse NGOs' RBA in a multi-scalar way by employing critical realist theories.

O'Connell's chapter (8) criticises the limits of civil society influence over the left-wing governments in Latin America. The rise to power of left-wing presidents across Latin America during the first decade of the century was preceded by waves of civil society contention that paved the way for those victories. Furthermore, the influence of mobilised civil society did not end upon the election of these leftist leaders, as had often been the case in the past. Instead, members of civil society organisations took up prominent government posts, long-standing demands were adopted as policy, and new constitutions were written with the active participation of social actors. Such levels of civil society influence over government are rare and, therefore, worthy of further study. It also examines two civil society movements – peasant farmers and the environmentalists known as 'Yasunidos' – that sought to influence public policy during the reign of Ecuador's leftist president, Rafael Correa. O'Connell's analysis reveals, however, that the alternative development models that were promised failed to materialise. Instead, the Correa government favoured a model of economic growth based on the continued exploitation of primary commodities, leading to conflict with civil society. In both cases, the movements failed to achieve their key demands. But while the peasant movement was split as much by internal tensions as government co-optation, Correa's attempts to delegitimise and divide the middle-class Yasunidos largely backfired. These cases contain important lessons for understanding the interactions between different kinds of civil society movements and governments.

Yachoulti's chapter (9) investigates the changing face of civil society activism and role in Morocco after the 2011 constitutional reform. The political hegemony of the authoritarian state, the marginality of the middle class and the absence of a culture of democracy have all prevented the development of a truly vibrant and viable Moroccan civil society. This limited influence of civil society activism is despite the aura it has been enjoying nationally and regionally. From a Western civil society perspective, in Chapter 10 Sai offers valuable insights and perspectives about two Irish CSOs, Islamic Relief Ireland (IRI) and Muslim Sisters of Éire (MSOÉ) and their operational practices and contextual influences. Based on interviews with their members based in Ireland, he examines their impact and challenges in Irish society. In recent times, there has also been an increase in the establishment of charity organisations within the Irish Muslim community.

By assessing contexts and engaging policymakers with rigorous empirical research in a systematic way, CSOs can work to overcome both the internal and external challenges they face. The book aims to bring about a heightened awareness of the challenges faced by CSOs, as well as highlight the potential for greater policy engagement for poverty reduction. Most of the contributions included in the edited volume are written by young scholars from various locations. The book, thus, enriches the current debate on the present and, importantly, the future of civil society from a global perspective. It also provides the reader with empirically-based, up-do-date, scientifically-grounded analyses of civil society developments in countries across the globe, that can be appealing not only for an academic audience but also for international agencies, policymakers and practitioners active in the region.

In conclusion, the book distinguishes itself as a new approach to the study of civil society in the global context, by focusing on the shifting landscape of CSOs. This new approach is particularly significant because it is based not only on empirical discussions of individual countries, but also on a clear theoretical framework based on the discussion of and debates on civil society and the socio-political landscape of the global context. In this way, our volume provides a new contribution to theoretical discussions of complexities of shifts politically, socially and financially at a global level. It provides up-to-date analysis on civic engagement and community participation challenges and lessons in Latin America, Africa, MENA and Ireland.

The main contribution of the book is to undertake new research, particularly around informed practice on the ground and present recommendations to policymakers and donors on better ways of providing space for CSO contributions on specific policy issues. This book provides insights and stimulates others to research this growing area of interest. It also introduces lessons learnt by civil society in response to political shifts, social constraints and foreign aid changes, despite the existence of social conservatism, conflict, violence and the absence of democracy and exclusive political systems in a number of countries. It concludes with some implications and offers some direction for future research in the field of CSOs in non-Western and Western contexts.

## References

Aragones, E. and SánchezPagés, S. (2009) 'A theory of participatory democracy based on the real case of Porto Alegre', *European Economic Review*, 53 (1), 56–72.

Baliamoune Lutz, M. (2016) 'The effectiveness of foreign aid to women's equality organisations in the MENA', *Journal of International Development*, 28, 320–341, Online Library (wileyonlinelibrary.com) doi:10.1002/jid.3214.

Bebbington, A. (2004) 'Theorising participation and institutional change: ethnography and political economy'. In Hickey, S. and Mohan, G. (eds.), *Participation: From Tyranny to Transformation*. London: Zed Books.

Busan Global Partnership Forum for Effective Development Cooperation, (2011) Accessed February 25, 2020 https://www.oecd.org/dac/effectiveness/49650173.pdf.

Hanafi, S. and Çuhadar, E. (2010) 'Israel and Palestine: civil societies in despair'. In Paffenholz, T. (ed.), *Civil Society & Peacebuilding: A Critical Assessment*. Boulder, CO: Lynne Rienner.

Hickey, S. (2008) 'The return of politics in development studies I: getting lost within the poverty agenda?', *Progress in Development Studies*, 8 (4), 349–358.

Natil, I. (2019) 'The power of civil society: young leaders' engagement in non-violent actions in Palestine'. In Natil, I., Pieroban, C. and Tauber, L. (eds.), *The Power of Civil Society in the Middle East and North Africa: Peacebuilding, Change and Development*. Oxford and New York: Routledge.

Natil, I. (2014) 'A shifting political landscape: NGOs' civic activism and response in the Gaza Strip, 1967–2014', *Journal of Peacebuilding & Development*, 9 (3), 82–87, doi:10.1080/15423166.2014.983369.

OECD (2011) *How DAC members work with civil society organisations: an overview*. Accessed February 27, 2020. https://www.oecd.org/dac/peer-reviews/Final_How_DAC_members_work_with_CSOs%20ENGLISH.pdf.

Paffenholz, T. and Spurk, C. (2010) 'A comprehensive analytical framework'. In Paffenholz, T. (ed.), *Civil Society & Peacebuilding: A Critical Assessment*. Boulder, CO: Lynne Rienner.

Paffenholz, T. (2010) *Civil Society & Peacebuilding: A Critical Assessment*. Boulder, CO: Lynne Rienner.

UNDP (2013) *Working with civil society in foreign aid*. Accessed February 25, 2020 https://www.undp.org/content/dam/undp/documents/partners/civil_society/publications/2013_UNDP-CH-Working-With-Civil-Society-in-Foreign-Aid_EN.pdf.

Weeden, L. (2015) 'Abandoning "legitimacy": reflections on Syria and Yemen'. In Hudson, M. (ed.), *The Crisis of the Arab State – Study Group Report*. Cambridge, MA: Harvard Kennedy School: Middle East Initiative.

Wildeman, J. (2019) 'Neoliberalism as Aid for the Settler Colonization of the Occupied Palestinian Territories After Oslo'. In Tartir, A. and Seidel T. (eds.), *Palestine and Rule of Power*. Middle East Today. https://doi.org/10.1007/978-3-030-05949-1_7. Cham: Palgrave Macmillan.

# 2 Introducing barriers to effective civil society organisations

*Ibrahim Natil*

## Introduction

Local and global civil society organisations (CSOs) operate and engage in various contexts and cultures. Understanding the different settings where CSOs are embedded is important for different target groups, including scientists, researchers, national-level policymakers, donors, NGO staff and the beneficiaries themselves, as each of these stakeholders has different interests and outlooks. This book will be highly influential as it contains in-depth understanding and evidence of CSO shifts, outlining the problems and challenges that exist which is the first step towards influencing policy by highlighting the social impact of their work. This volume brings together case studies from various countries such as Ireland, Ecuador, Colombia, Egypt, Palestine, Morocco and Iran sharing diverse challenges experienced by CSOs in areas such as civic space, emerging new political shifts and social contexts and funding.

Empirical research will contribute to our understanding of these barriers to effective CSOs and their ability to cope with shifts based on the promotion of active grassroots engagement or what is referred to as 'participatory democracy' as defined by Aragones and SánchezPagés (2009: 56–72). The conceptual framework used in this study comes from the notion of a participatory civil society, researching civic engagement and development despite the challenges of shifts in foreign aid, political and social context. This research considers the main concept of intervention by CSOs, where the core approach is to study the active engagement of activists with emphasis on 'participatory democracy', the promotion of freedom of expression and peaceful change (Paffenholz and Spurk, 2010: 3–29). The participatory democratic approach is reflected by CSOs' abilities to promote societal values of respect for a democratic process and involvement in supporting participatory, transparent and accountable governing institutions during transition periods (Zlatareva, 2008).

Significant work performed by CSOs as well as their credibility across global contexts, earning their right to sit at the policy table, is introduced. Hyaman discusses the question of legitimacy, credibility and effectiveness of

CSOs (Hayman, 2016: 670–680). The legitimacy question has been a crucial issue in whether CSOs are able to mobilise resources and generate local support from the general public, philanthropists and private sector (Wiggers, 2016: 619–628). Legitimacy, credibility and effectiveness have been always questioned by scholars, activists, clients and policymakers as the growth of CSOs has significantly increased over the last two decades, resulting in increased citizen civic engagement and promotion of freedom of expression, owing to social and political shifts (CIVICUS, 2019). The UNDP human development report (1993) defines civic engagement as "a process, not an event that closely involves people in the economic, social, cultural and political processes that affect their lives".

There have been, however, governments in various countries given a very limited civic space for CSOs' operations in the field of human rights and democratic development including limiting access to national and foreign funding (CIVICUS, 2015). Brian Pratt contends that the social implication of shifts in funding may not be the most crucial challenge to CSOs which draws a new challenge to the diverse civil society sector (Pratt, 2016: 527–531). A very narrow space given for civil society to operate freely and effectively as only 4 per cent of the world's population live in countries where fundamental civil society freedoms, association, peaceful assembly and expression are respected (CIVICUS, 2019: 6). These shifts are serious challenges facing different types of CSOs and their functions, responses and sustainability. Their sustainability has been a crucial issue for debate owing to growing challenges as operational, political and financial in nature (CIVICUS, 2015).

Funding CSO activities, however, has grown substantially in certain areas, for example, advocacy for human rights and democracy development with support from major donors, however this is significantly restricted. CSOs are able to generate resources from local contributors, not only from foreign donors and governments, to run their operations (Pratt, 2016: 582). Mawdsley Savage and Kim discuss the paradigm shift in dominant constructions of 'foreign aid' and a substantive shift of power within the architecture of global development governance (2013: 27). The paradigm shift always faces CSOs which hinders their ability to perform their work by influencing policy processes that exist in some of the developing countries owing to the political landscape shifts, such as MENA (see Natil, 2014, 2019, 2020). These processes often undermine and block delivery, engagement and contribution to development and change. CSO intervention, however, is considered where the core approach of active engagement during political shifts can be identified from democracy theory (Paffenholz and Spurk, 2010: 65).

## Political shift

People's active participation and engagement in CSO activity is a form of "participatory democracy" responding to the shifting political landscape in many countries (Natil, 2019, 2020). Aragones and SánchezPagés (2009: 56–72) define 'participatory democracy' as a process of collective decision-making where active citizens have the power to decide on change. Active citizens' participation and engagement in local organisations, student unions, political groups, movements and CSOs is a form of 'participatory democracy' in responding to the lack of democratic process, for instance, in a conflict zone, where the political system may not function (Natil, 2020). Also considered is the existing literature's emphasis on a narrow definition of civil society and citizens' active participation in some countries where conflicts shape the social and political context, for example Thania Paffenholz (2010) discusses civil society in peacebuilding; CSOs intervene in such a context to lead and engage local groups and activists to promote active engagement in responding to shifting social, political and economic circumstances in their own societies. CSO's power of intervention is a participatory process reflected by different mechanisms and processes; for example, through CSOs, universities, public institutions, local councils, political parties and the decision-making process (Paffenholz and Spurk, 2010: 66–76).

CSOs raise the level of activists' awareness about legal and social rights, as well as those relating to the social, economic and political situations; raising their organisational and administrative capacities by empowering their leadership skills and economic initiatives (Tauber et al, 2019: 1–9). New social media tools and older forms of communication are utilised by CSOs to enhance active participation, tolerance, better understanding, balanced reporting and objectivity (Hanafi and Cuhadar, 2010: 207). Civic space is delivered by CSOs to promote active participation, community peacebuilding, tolerance and better understanding, and reporting of human rights violations. Malila's chapter (3) discusses the use of social media by CSOs in their accountability procedures and their effective role in opening civic spaces via bridging the information gap through social media. CSOs introduce a new tool of community empowerment and capacity-building activities to assist clients and their target groups to cope with political shifts. Promotion of networking among CSOs also increases engagement of marginalised groups of citizens, and supporting joint development policies (Paffenholz and Spurk, 2010: 66–76).

The power and impact of networking among civil society groups, and their coordination and cooperation in undertaking effective actions and campaigns in order to make change a reality in terms of politics and aid development, are also considered (Pierobon, 2019: 18–21). Some CSOs seek to empower civic participation by holding the government accountable by reporting discrimination of marginalised groups. As a part of empowering active participation, many organisations aim at promoting freedom of expression through media and advocacy campaigns (Paffenholz and Spurk, 2010: 67). Creating a strong participatory democracy context and a civic space during a political shift is based on CSOs' capacities to intervene and respond to responses to changes in society (Paffenholz and Spurk, 2010: 66–76). In Chapter 4,

Moheimany and Najafinejad discuss changing civil society and the hybrid regime in Iran by exploring the shifts in the status of civil society across two political periods in the country, namely the reformist (1997–2005) and conservative (2005–2013) periods.

CSOs possess the ability to contribute to change which is dependent on a transparent and effective political system whereby citizens can participate and engage freely without any legal or political restrictions (Nugroho, 2011). David Lewis (2013: 337), however, argues CSO activities often serve to "enhance the legitimacy of the state, in terms of a shared international discourse on civil society, and domestically in helping to meet the challenges of rapidly changing societies". This approach is discussed by Kimura, in Chapter 7 to test NGOs' rights-based approach between contextual appropriateness and political transformation in neo-patrimonial contexts such as Cambodia. The re-politicisation of development practices and studies has been highlighted by many scholars. As Bandyopadhyay and Khus argue, civil society context has changed in Cambodia in search of relevant "indigenisation" (2013: 666–668).

However, it is widely held that a politically confrontational rights-based approach (RBA) by NGOs does not work in relation to authoritarian governments in developing countries as it irritates such governments and makes it impossible for CSOs to operate. Lewis (2013) asserts that continuity in the relationship between state and CSOs is at least partially derived from a shared pattern of political, economic and social interactions, and cultural norms (325–340). Kimura argues non-confrontational or collaborative approaches may be contextually appropriate and effective in terms of the political and structural transformation. Bandyopadhyay and Khus (2013) address CSOs' meaningful engagements with government on governance reforms and the importance of autonomy (675).

Continuity in attitudes and modes of interaction between CSOs and the authoritarian government will assist both parties to engage in a cooperative manner (Lewis, 2013: 325–340). Some scholars argue that it becomes crucial to understand how authoritarian and hybrid regimes control and consolidate power over the civil society sphere during transition phases. In Chapter 5, El Assal and Marzouk discuss CSOs as recipients of foreign aid, which has been a crucial issue in Egypt since 2013. The authors argue that the Egyptian media played a significant role in reigniting nationalist discourse by spreading smear campaigns aimed at foreign aid-supporting civil society groups. The shared social and cultural norms, however, have already affected operational policies for CSOs responding to a shifting political landscape (Natil, 2014). This resonates with the situation in the Occupied Palestinian Territories (OPT) after Hamas secured victory in the local and legislative elections. This followed a geographical, social and political division which had already divided the Palestinian Authority (PA) in the West Bank and the Gaza Strip between Hamas and the Palestinian Liberation Organization (PLO) in 2007 (Natil, 2019, 2020).

Some CSOs have already worked with a number of international organisations and foreign donors to implement civil society activities (Wildeman, 2019). The question of foreign aid and Qatari intervention responding to this political shift is addressed by Alkahlout in Chapter 6. However, it is important to mention here the history and scope of CSOs which still draw criticism from local groups in the OPT which claim that the programme ignores Palestinian suffering. CSOs, however, experience socio-political developments including threats to civil society from the state itself, grassroots and/or factional actors (Natil, 2019, 2020). Local CSOs, however, have sought to implement grassroots activities in the West Bank and the Gaza Strip (Hanafi and Cuhadar, 2010: 207). This assists CSOs to remain in active engagement with marginalised and vulnerable groups while acknowledging a list of initial risks including radical groups who might physically threaten the activity's leaders owing to an unprecedented state of poor public freedom and socio-political deadlock (Natil, 2019).

Some activists and leaders from certain CSOs are banned from freedom of expression, freedom of access to the media, the right of association and the right to organise peaceful demonstrations and marches (Natil, 2020). Civil society activists and ordinary citizens also suffer from ineffective, inefficient and insufficient public policies, which have made their lives worse. They still have a limited influence over public policies, owing to these shifts. Hayman argues that CSOs always need multifaceted resources to operate freely, effectively and sustainably, within a proper civic space of a healthier political environment, with a limited reliance on foreign aid (Hayman, 2016: 671).

## Funding shift

Funding shifts have been a serious problem and challenge for CSOs in various countries despite the fact that international cooperation remains a main source of funding. Pousadela and Cruz (2016) discuss the reduction of funding for CSOs owing to a number of factors affecting bilateral donors, economic growth, and operational and financial restrictions stemming from political polarisation and increased government hostility towards CSOs in various countries. Other scholars and practitioners from the field, however, argue that a growing trend of shrinking space for civil society and rapid shifts in the political landscape remain a main challenge for CSOs. El Assal and Marzouk investigate Case 173, 'known as the foreign fund case' in Chapter 5. Funding shifts represent a major barrier to ineffective civil society organisations locally and internationally. CSO operations, for example, have been challenged following the division, and siege on the Gaza Strip and a USA aid cut to UNRWA (Wildeman, 2019).

Foreign aid remains, however, essential for CSO peacebuilding and development programme implementation (Baliamoune Lutz, 2016: 320–341).

UNRWA dealt with the most severe financial crisis since its establishment after the Trump administration withdrew its contributions to UNRWA which amounted to $359.3 million in 2017 (Zanotti, 2018). This included $231.5 million of 2017 bilateral economic assistance that was originally intended for the West Bank and Gaza, including $25 million for East Jerusalem hospitals. USAID also ended its assistance to the Palestinians in the West Bank and Gaza Strip (Zanotti, 2018). Due to unstable social, economic and political circumstances, CSOs still struggle to explore effective, creative and innovative operational techniques in responding to the shifting political landscape (Natil, 2019).

These funding shifts and cuts have had a very serious impact on the local Palestinian CSOs. These circumstances aggravated the work of CSOs, for example OPT, notably their peace and development policies and practices when international funding dropped drastically. This shift of agenda and operations has weakened the intervention of CSOs, owing to decreased foreign aid and unstable political circumstances (Natil, 2016: 78–82). Alkahlout's chapter (6) highlights civil society in the Gaza Strip and Qatari humanitarian aid during this period and investigates the engagement of civil society to ensure that political, social and economic priorities are based on a broad consensus from society (Hanafi and Cuhadar, 2010: 211).

CSOs highlight their reporting of human rights violations to strengthen relationships with international organisations and donors. This relationship, however, does not guarantee grant success or donations without proposing a quality and well-structured project relevant to donors' scope of work, intervention, conditions and values (Murad, 2014). The recipients of the USA government fund, for example, had to sign an 'anti-terrorism waiver', obliging them not to support violence or channel funds to any people who are affiliated with 'terrorist groups' and/or violent activities (Challand, 2009: 104). There were tens of small and newly emerged CSOs established between 2002 and 2005, in response to easily accessed funds from USAID's Tamkeen Civil Society Project, managed by the branch office of Care International in Gaza. Tamkeen aimed to ensure

> increased participation of Palestinian civil society organizations (CSOs) in public discourse to contribute to preserving the critical "space" occupied by Palestinian CSOs, placing them at the heart of the communication nexus between citizens and their public representatives at the local and national levels.
>
> (Chemonics International, 2005)

The recipients of the EU's aid, however, had not required CSOs to fulfil such a requirement until late 2019 when they introduced a new funding condition which created a state of uncertainty among the Palestinian CSOs who rely mainly on EU funding. Many Palestinian activists and scholars such as Dana (2020) argue:

> the pressure created by the systematic cuts to aid funds by international donors will likely and desirably push many organizations to search for alternative resources from within Palestinian society in Palestine and in the diaspora, and to partner with authentic civil society movements and solidarity groups worldwide that would offer international platforms for advocacy activism and possibly financial resources to help rebuild Palestinian civil society along new lines.
>
> (Dana, 2020)

The ability of CSOs to challenge funding shifts is a significant factor in responding to social demands, owing to economic and political shifts; in Chapter 6, Ola Alkahlout discusses the effectiveness and influence of Qatari humanitarian aid on some CSOs in the Gaza Strip and their contribution to responding to social and economic demands since 2007.

## Social shift

The power to understand and interact with social shifts as well as policies imposed by governments has been a serious challenge for CSOs and their operations and responses in different areas around the world (CIVICUS, 2019, 2015). Putnam, Leonardi and Nanetti discuss "facilitating coordinated actions" that can improve the efficiency of the society by active engagement (1993: 167). This also strengthens trust in others, norms, network and the ability to interact, with the result that social cooperation expands to mutual benefit (Putnam, Leonardi and Nanetti, 1993: 167). Maria Zlatareva (2008) also expands on this type of facilitation, and network assistance to strengthen "people's abilities to engage, opening up space for their involvement, facilitating dialogue and consensus building, providing access to information and mobilizing them for collective action". In this volume, O'Connell in Chapter 8 discusses limits of influence upon civil society, particularly on the policies of left-wing governments in Latin America as in the case of Ecuador. O'Connell examines two civil society movements – peasant farmers and the environmentalists known as 'Yasunidos' – that sought to influence public policy during the government of Rafael Correa. Arsel and Angel (2012), however, discuss the changing relationship between state and civil society regarding the role of nature in development.

Correa's government favoured a model of economic growth based on the continued exploitation of primary commodities. This approach led to conflict with civil society (Ortiz, 2015). O'Connell argues that Correa controlled the public sphere by manipulating civil society and the citizen revolution under his authoritarian populist leadership (see Appe, Barragán and Telch, 2019). Decentralisation, however, has been a mechanism to solve a conflict between civil society and the regime in Morocco (Houdret and Harnisch, 2019). The regime's reform strategies have repeatedly articulated participation, fighting poverty and public-service provision in the 2011 constitution. However, spontaneous and sometimes radical positions articulated by members of civil society remain a challenge to Moroccan CSOs' activism and engagement in responding to the shifting landscape in post 2011 Arab spring uprisings, as discussed in Chapter 9.

The constitutional reforms contributed to promoting the role and engagement of CSOs in the process of change while the ability of the regime and a soft opposition to reach a transitional pact greatly matched democratic prospects (Hinnebusch, 2015a). However, structural economic and social reforms did not solve the conflict and increased a sense of disempowerment and helplessness where people could not exercise control over their lives. Morocco's regime, however, increased its techniques of co-optation and exploitation of public wariness with disorder and cultural cleavages to limit democratisation and to delay social mobilisation. Maria Zlatareva (2008) asserts that "citizens organise for collective action and interact with national and local level state institutions but also non-state actors such as CSOs and the private sector, and articulate their interests and exercise control over decisions that affect their lives". The moderation of protestors' demands and lesser mobilisation, reflects the divided social and political landscape engineered by the monarchy over decades (Hinnebusch, 2015b).

These shifts have already created a new social dynamic and context influencing the scope of work and intervention of CSOs in different countries around the world and in modern Ireland in particular (CIVICUS, 2019: 6–7). Eoin O'Mally (2011: 69–86) discusses changing society in a published work, *Contemporary Ireland*. In this changing society, new communities have emerged and new types of civil society organisations, voluntary organisations or 'faith-based charities' led by leaders of the Irish Muslim communities have contributed to positive social interaction. This type of engagement results in better social cohesion (Taylor-Gooby, 2012). Muslim CSOs contribute to a changing society in different ways through their local operational practices and civic engagement with their respective communities. Sai explores different Muslim faith-based CSOs in the Republic of Ireland and their responses to changing society and capacity to navigate social shifts given their operational and financial constraints.

CSOs from the global North, however, come under immense pressure, owing to the question of legitimacy, credibility and transparency (CIVICUS, 2015). The Constitution of Ireland, however, provides a fertile ground for all faiths to engage in Irish civic society by forming associations and engaging in unions for various causes, including charitable purposes. Wiggers (2016) argues that legitimacy and credibility stem from the ability of CSOs to generate resources from their local community and to engage with their entire community, not just those from within (619–628). The use of social networks is to ensure implementation of effective methodologies to interact with participants and to encourage them to share their thoughts and engage in role-play and simulations based on real-life experiences while shifting takes place. The guiding principles for intervention of CSOs working at grassroots level is their reliance on networking, cooperation and coordination as a major method of programme implementation (Paffenholz, 2010).

It is a natural journey of identification of evolving groups, who help in empowering networks and cooperation between CSOs who work for active participation and engagement in civic actions (Tauber et al, 2019: 1–9). Intervention is based on existing social networks or building new coalitions, which include grassroots organisations, both active and working on civic engagement and active community participation. Maria Zlatareva (2008) discusses civic engagement and its role in participation, empowerment and partnership. Each activity is used to facilitate the engagement of participants in a discussion on how they can best apply their engagement in a shifting context. Participants also engage in discussion groups to identify how best to work together to improve the social situation in their locations. CSOs also employ partnerships to promote the local ownership of activities on the ground and to introduce positive change. CSOs sometimes use an integral policy to establish a steering committee of all partners and independents, aimed at creating a process of collective decision-making (Tauber et al., 2019: 1–9).

In the final chapter, Natil concludes by offering implications and recommendations for future research.

## References

Appe, S., Barragán, D. and Telch, F. (2019) *Organized Civil Society Under Authoritarian Populism: Cases from Ecuador*, Non-Profit forum, https://doi.org/10.1515/npf-2019-0039.

Aragones, E. and SánchezPagés, S. (2009) 'A Theory of Participatory Democracy Based on the Real Case of Porto Alegre', *European Economic Review*, 53 (1), 56–72.

Arsel, M. and Angel, N. A. (2012) '"Stating" Nature's Role in Ecuadorian Development: Civil Society and the Yasuní-ITT Initiative', *Journal of Developing Societies*, 28 (2), 203–227, https://doi.org/10.1177/0169796X12448758.

Baliamoune Lutz, M. (2016) 'The Effectiveness of Foreign Aid to women's Equality Organisations in the MENA', *Journal of International Development*, 28, 320–341, Online Library (wileyonlinelibrary.com) doi:10.1002/jid.3214.

Bandyopadhyay, K. and Khus, T. (2013) 'Changing Civil Society in Cambodia: In Search of Relevance', *Development in Practice*, 23, 5–6, 665–677, doi:10.1080/09614524.2013.800835.

Challand. B. (2009) *Palestinian Civil Society: Foreign Donors and the Power to Promote and Exclude*, Oxford: Routledge.

Chemonics International Inc. TAMKEEN Increased Participation by Palestine Civil Society Organizations in Public Decision-Making and Government Oversight, *TAMKEEN Quarterly Progress Report: Fourth Quarter* 2004. Submitted to the U.S. Agency for International Development/Jordan, January 20, 2005.

CIVICUS (2019) 'State of Civil Society Report 2019 – the year in review'. Johannesburg: CIVICUS: World Alliance for Citizen Participation. Accessed February 13, 2020, https://www.civicus.org/documents/reports-and-publications/SOCS/2019/state-of-civil-society-report-2019_executive-summary.pdf.

CIVICUS (2015) 'State of Civil Society Report 2015', Johannesburg: CIVICUS: World Alliance for Citizen Participation. Accessed February 13, 2020, http://civicus.org/images/StateOfCivilSocietyFullReport2015.pdf.

Dana, T. (2020) Criminalising Palestinian Resistance: The EU's new conditions on aid to Palestine. *Shabaka, the Palestinian policy network*. Accessed February 17, 2020, https://al-shabaka.org/commentaries/criminalizing-palestinian-resistance-the-eus-new-conditions-on-aid-to-palestine/.

Hanafi, S. and Çuhadar, E. (2010) 'Israel and Palestine: Civil Societies in Despair'. In Paffenholz, T. (ed.), *Civil Society & Peacebuilding: A Critical Assessment*. Boulder, CO: Lynne Rienner.

Hayman, R. (2016) 'Unpacking Civil Society Sustainability: Looking Back, Broader, Deeper, Forward', *Development in Practice*, 26 (5), 670–680, doi:10.1080/09614524.2016.1191439.

Hinnebusch, R. (2015a) 'Introduction: Understanding the Consequences of the Arab Uprisings – Starting Points and Divergent Trajectories', *Democratization*, 22 (2), 205–217, doi:10.1080/13510347.2015.1010807.

Hinnebusch, R. (2015b) 'Change and Continuity after the Arab Uprising: The Consequences of State Formation in Arab North African States', *British Journal of Middle Eastern Studies*, 42 (1), 12–30, doi:10.1080/13530194.2015.973182.

Houdret, A. and Harnisch, S. (2019) 'Decentralisation in Morocco: A Solution to the "Arab Spring"?' *The Journal of North African Studies*, 24 (6), 935–960, doi:10.1080/13629387.2018.1457958.

Lewis, D. (2013) 'Civil Society and the Authoritarian State: Cooperation, Contestation and Discourse', *Journal of Civil Society*, 9 (3), 325–340, doi:10.1080/17448689.2013.818767.

Mawdsley, E., Savage L. and Kim, S. (2013) 'A "Post-aid World"? Paradigm Shift in Foreign Aid and Development Cooperation at the 2011 Busan High Level Forum', *The Geographical Journal*, 180 (1), March 2014, pp. 27–38, doi:10.1111/j.1475-4959.2012.00490.

Murad, N. L. (2014) Donor Complicity in Israel's Violations of Palestinian Rights, Al-Shabaka Policy Brief: https://al-shab- aka.org/briefs/donor-complicity-in-is-raels-violations-of-palestinian-rights/. Accessed 3 December 2015.

Natil, I. (2020) 'Women's Community Peacebuilding in the Occupied Palestinian Territories (OPT)'. In Richmond, O. and Visoka, G. (eds.), *The Palgrave Encyclopedia of Peace and Conflict Studies*. Cham: Palgrave Macmillan, https://doi.org/10.1007/978-3-030-11795-5_47-1.

Natil, I. (2019) 'The Power of Civil Society: Young Leaders' Engagement in Non-Violent Actions in Palestine'. In Natil, I., Pierobon, C. and Tauber, L. (ed.), *The Power of Civil Society in the Middle East and North Africa: Peacebuilding, Change and Development*. Oxford and New York: Routledge.

Natil, I. (2016) 'The Challenges and Opportunities of Donor-Driven Aid to Youth Refugees in Palestine', *Journal of Peacebuilding & Development*, 11 (2), 78–82, http://dx.doi.org/10.1080/15423166.2016.1197791.

Natil, I. (2014) 'A Shifting Political Landscape: NGOs' Civic Activism and Response in the Gaza Strip, 1967–2014', *Journal of Peacebuilding and Development*, 9 (3), 82–87, https://doi.org/10.1080/15423166.2014.983369.

Nugroho, Y. (2011) 'Opening the Black Box: The Adoption of Innovations in the Voluntary Sector—The Case of Indonesian Civil Society Organisations', *Research Policy* 40 (5), 761–777.

O'Mally, E. (2011) *Contemporary Ireland*. UK: Palgrave Macmillan.

Ortiz, A. (2015) 'Taking Control of the Public Sphere by Manipulating Civil Society: The Citizen Revolution in Ecuador', *European Review of Latin American and Caribbean Studies*/ Revista Europea de Estudios Latinoamericanos y del Caribe, 98 (April), 29–48.

Paffenholz, T. and Spurk, C. (2010) 'A Comprehensive Analytical Framework'. In Paffenholz, T. (ed.), *Civil Society & Peacebuilding: A Critical Assessment*. Boulder, CO: Lynne Rienner.

Paffenholz, T. (2010) *Civil Society & Peacebuilding: A Critical Assessment*. Boulder, CO: Lynne Rienner.

Pierobon, C. (2019) 'Introducing Civil Society'. In Natil, I., Pierobon, C. and Tauber, L. (eds.), *The Power of Civil Society in the Middle East and North Africa: Peacebuilding, Change and Development*. Oxford and New York: Routledge.

Pousadela, I. M. and Cruz, A. (2016) 'The Sustainability of Latin American CSOs: Historical Patterns and New Funding Sources', *Development in Practice*, 26 (5), 606–618, doi:10.1080/09614524.2016.1188884.

Pratt, B. (2016) *Special Issue Overview: Civil Society Sustainability, Development in Practice*, 26 (5), 527–531, doi:10.1080/09614524.2016.1191438.

Putnam, R., Leonardi, R. and Nanetti, R. (1993) *Making Democracy Work*, Princeton, NJ: Princeton University Press.

Tauber L., Natil, I. and Pierobon, C. (2019) 'Introduction' In Natil, I., Pierobon, C. and Tauber, L. (eds.), *The Power of Civil Society in the Middle East and North Africa: Peacebuilding, Change and Development*. Oxford and New York: Routledge.

Taylor-Gooby, P. (2012) 'The Civil Society Route to Social Cohesion', *International Journal of Sociology and Social Policy*, 32 (7/8), 368–385. https://doi.org/10.1108/01443331211249002.

UNDP (1993) *Human Development Report*, Accessed February 18, 2019, http://hdr.undp.org/sites/default/files/reports/222/hdr_1993_en_complete_nostats.pdf.

Wiggers, R. (2016) 'Action for Children: A Model for Stimulating Local Fundraising in Low and Middle-income Countries'. *Development in Practice* 26 (5), 619–628.

Wildeman, J. (2019) 'Neoliberalism as Aid for the Settler Colonization of the Occupied Palestinian Territories After Oslo'. In Tartir A. and Seidel T. (eds.), *Palestine and Rule of Power*, Middle East Today. https://doi.org/10.1007/978-3-030-05949-1_7.

Zanotti, J. (2018) U.S. Foreign Aid to the Palestinians, *Congressional Research Services*, 12 December, available: Accessed February 18, 2019, https://fas.org/sgp/crs/mideast/RS22967.pdf.

Zlatareva, M. (2008) Promoting Civic Engagement in a Post-Totalitarian and EU Accession Context: A Case from Bulgaria. *United Nations Development Programme*, Oslo Governance Centre. Accessed February 19, 2019, https://www.undp.org/content/dam/aplaws/publication/en/publications/democratic-governance/oslo-governance-center/ogc-fellowship-papers/promoting-civic-engagement-in-a-post-totalitarian-a-case-from-bulgaria/PromotingCivicEngagement.pdf.

# 3 Africa CSOs in closing civic spaces

## Bridging the information gap through social media

*Vanessa Malila*

### Introduction

There have been seismic shifts in the manner in which we think about democracy, civil society and the spaces where debate and demands for good governance have been conceptualised in recent years. This is particularly true in Africa, where the euphoria of independence which was heralded in the 1960s has seen an about-turn back to authoritarianism, the rise of the African strongman and the weakening of civil society. Kew & Oshikoya (2014, p. 9) write about the rise of civil society across Africa in the late 1980s and early 1990s resulting in a vibrant and flourishing civil society, that "helped lead the struggle to overthrow repressive regimes and dictators in the march toward democratic governance". However, they also lament the growing restrictions on civil society since the 1990s as a result of the need by political elites to control society. This is what Diamond (2008, p. 36) refers to as "the democratic rollback", which has seen "a more recent creeping authoritarianism that has led to corrupt, ineffective state institutions and bureaucracies" (Kew & Oshikoya, 2014, p. 9).

There can be no doubt that across Africa the space for debate and open communication have been threatened. This paper highlights some of those restrictions and aims to examine the way civil society organisations are using the media and particularly social media as a strategy to work against closing civic spaces. The paper focuses on organisations in the accountability sector, which work to promote accountability in governance rather than work to deliver services that are not provided for by governments. While accountability should lead to better service delivery from governments, the aim of accountability is to promote good governance which fosters the realisation of human rights in particular contexts (Ackerman, 2005). It is these organisations that are often at the forefront of confrontation with repressive and corrupt states as they demand more open, transparent and accountable governance from their political elites.

This chapter aims to understand how civil society organisations use the media and social media to promote accountability and good governance in contexts where governance is significantly compromised. The research views the work of civil society organisations as deeply impacted by the continuing and increasing social, civic and political restrictions that limit the work of accountability across the region. The paper aims to better understand whether social media can be considered a tool for navigating restrictive contexts.

## Civil society, civic space and the media

Comprehensively defining civic space is perhaps an impossible undertaking. However, thinking about civic space as a space which brings together different forms, networks, organisations, institutions and behaviours is not only useful in better understanding how it can be constituted by different stakeholders, but also for two other key reasons. One is that civic space is always changing, "a moving target" (Buyse, 2018, p. 969), where forms and institutions come and go depending on circumstances. If one considers civic space in this way, then it becomes easier to understand how states are able to put pressure on civic space to promote civic action and civic rights. The second important factor is the notion that civic space develops in relation to already existing structures. As Malena argues, civic space

> does not emerge of its own accord. Where it exists, it has been created as a result of persistent and active efforts on the part of state and non-state actors to protect and enable fundamental rights and create the space for citizens and CSOs to contribute to societal goals.
>
> (Malena, 2015, p. 15)

What both of these notions point to is the fact that neither civil society nor civic space are universal concepts, they do not exist in every society and are context dependent. Civil society and the space in which it operates "must be examined with an eye to locally-specific circumstances, embodying a range of different perspectives and world views – rather than considering the concept of civil society in purely theoretical terms" (Pointer et al., 2016, p. 9).

While it has been argued that civic space may not be shrinking or closing but rather changing, what this paper argues is that the space is systematically being closed and restricted because civic space is defined here as a space where human rights and democratic values are promoted and facilitated by the institutions and behaviours one finds within the space. As such, any shifts away from these values is a closing of the space and a restriction on the organisations, individuals and behaviours which promote those values. Undoubtedly, the context in which this happens is different and the power and political dynamics in each circumstance will mean that the manner this happens will vary, but that it is happening is undeniable.

While the definition of civic space may be hard to pin down, it is important to recognise that there are key elements which make up civic space. This allows it to become clear when these are being disregarded and thus impacting negatively on civic space. Civicus argues there are three key pillars to civic space:

1. The first is Freedom of Association. This is the right of any citizen to join a formal or informal group to take collective action and includes the right to form a new group or join an existing group (Civicus, n.d.).
2. The second pillar is Freedom of Expression. This includes the right to access information, critically evaluate and speak out against the policies and actions of state and non-state actors and publicly draw attention to and carry out advocacy actions to promote shared concerns. Here one sees a clear role for the media in terms of providing information to promote free and open civic space and which allows civil society to hold public officials to account (Civicus, n.d.).
3. The third pillar is Freedom of Peaceful Assembly. This is the right of citizens to gather publicly or privately and collectively express, promote, pursue and defend common interests. States not only have an obligation to protect peaceful assemblies, but should also take measures to facilitate them (Civicus, n.d.).

When writing about civic space, the link to freedom of expression, free and independent media, and access to information is regarded as essential. Castells paints this as a delicate balance between the state, civil society and the media and notes that,

> It is the interaction between citizens, civil society, and the state, communicating through the public sphere, that ensures that the balance between stability and social change is maintained in the conduct of public affairs. If citizens, civil society, or the state fail to fulfil the demands of this interaction or if the channels of communication between two or more of the key components of the process are blocked, the whole system of representation and decision making comes to a stalemate.
>
> (Castells, 2008, p. 79)

Voltmer (2004, p. 3) notes that there has been, since the beginning of democratic thought, a central place for debate and free speech. This means the media are at the heart of the arguments put forward for the need to ensure freedom of expression because "the media provide for a free 'marketplace of ideas' where contradicting voices compete for public recognition without the interference of the state". In the African context, the interplay of politics and the market make the ability of the media to play a central role in the public sphere and civil society increasingly complex. White & Mabweazara (2018, p. 55) argue that "efforts towards accurate, honest and critical reporting on the African continent continually clash with personalistic governance which puts itself above the law and seeks to avoid any form of public scrutiny". This partisan press constrains the ability of journalists to fulfil their information and watchdog roles across many African countries. The strong partisan press has been driven by the historical legacy of colonialism across the continent and continues to influence the practice of journalism today. Africa's colonial history drove "the notion that the postcolonial press should serve as a partner of the government" (Ibelema, 2008, p. 13).

The tendency towards patronage by the media ensures that even independent media in many countries are influenced by the ideologies of those in power. The political economic trends affecting the media in Africa also impact on credibility and trust of the media, and their ability to promote accountability in their contexts. Eweka, Omotoso & Olukotun (2017, p, 11) argue that "In Africa, the mass media whether public or privately owned has problem of trust and objectivity, as such, the citizens are frequently reluctant to explore them as an option of political communication, rather, they may choose to explore other means of communication which are usually characterised by hostility".

## The role of social media in African society

Scholars (Mare, 2014; Wasserman, 2011) have argued that social media fulfils an extended role in society by providing an alternative public sphere. This is a space for different voices, marginalised discourse and what Fraser (1992) calls 'counterpublics' to be able to explore ideas outside of the mainstream. This is a space for information sharing and networking "where people are transgressing the hitherto fixed boundaries of what counts as political participation or civic identification" (Wasserman, 2011, p. 146). As such, "social media have provided a communications model that stands as a direct response to the uniformity and perceived conservative neoliberalism of many forms of mass communication" (Rodny-Gumede, 2017, p. 172).

A review of the literature on the use of social media for political and social change illustrates a strong dichotomy between social media's ability to empower and connect diverse people, and social media doing little to affect change or possibly even having a negative effect on change. For example, Rodny-Gumede (2017, p. 177) argues that social media has the potential to broaden debates in context and "debates around social change have benefitted from a strengthened civil society presence on social media". She further notes that social media allows for the voices of the marginalised and those neglected by traditional media to be heard. Others are more critical of the potential for social media to promote new public spheres and provide space for real advocacy. One of the criticisms levelled against social media is the fact that rather than opening up spaces for debate and diversity, it simply brings like-minded people together, further promoting homogeneity and increasing polarisation (Bakshy, Messing & Adamic, 2015; Barberá et al., 2015; Justwan et al., 2018). Furthermore, Fuchs (2014, p. 102) asserts that social media is colonised by powerful corporations and as such "politics is a minority issue on social media". Beyond corporations, there is also the ability of those with vast resources to use social media to promote their own agenda and ensure particular narratives are at the forefront of social media narratives. Fuchs (2014) denounces cyber-utopianism as failing to look beyond the idealised natures of social media and argues that social media fails to promote participation, public debate or diversity.

Regardless of the ideology one adopts, what is clear is the practical uptake of digital and social media in Africa. Internet growth in Africa has been increasing significantly in recent years. Mumbere (2018) reported in 2018 that internet users "are up by more than 20% since January 2017" and that "The number of internet users in Benin, Sierra Leone, Niger, and Mozambique has more than doubled over the past year". Internet World Stats (2019) reports that 37 per cent of the population in Africa have internet access. GlobalStats (2019) reports that of social media usage in Africa, Facebook enjoys 72 per cent of the market share, followed by YouTube (15%), Pinterest (7%) and Twitter (5%). While Africa still falls behind global trends and particularly in relation to Global North statistics, the reality is that social media, smartphones and internet use is growing at a significant rate. The current trends show that "internet and social media use shows no growth in advanced economies but continues to rise in emerging and developing countries" (Poushter, Bishop & Chwe, 2018, p. 3).

## Trends in closing civic spaces across East and Southern Africa

While the turn of the century saw many developed and developing countries enjoying civic freedoms, more recently, the trend is one of restricting and limiting civic space. David Kode argues

> across Africa, major advances in democracy have been affected by restrictions on civic space and on the activities of civil society organisations, the media and individual activists … Overall, civic space in Africa is shrinking and this downward trend is precipitated by laws, policies, physical attacks, threats and demonization of those who stand up for the rights of citizens.
>
> (Kode, 2018)

While Kode notes many of the formal processes used to close and restrict civic space, one should also consider the way in which shrinking civic space additionally refers to closing down and shifting the way people think about civil society and the freedoms inherent in democratic principles, and the struggle to ensure civic norms are maintained in particular contexts. A much more intangible but equally detrimental push against the civic ecosystem. What is undeniable is that globally there has been a shift in freedom in civic space, even if, as Hossain et al. (2018) argue, this affects civil society actors in different ways and at different levels. And, as argued by Buyse (2018, p. 969), this shift has not been incidental, but has become "a structural issue rather than as a range of isolated incidents".

## Formal restrictions: changing and constraining legislation

Legal restrictions draw on both criminal and administrative laws to limit the work of civil society and aim to suppress the work of those in civic space. This could mean actively changing laws to ensure greater barriers for civil society organisations. For example, in Malawi, the NGO Amendment Bill (to amend the NGO Act) has been introduced which the International Center for Not-For-Profit Law says "contains a number of concerning provisions" (2019). They continue, noting,

> From November 2018 to January 2019, the public sphere has continued to be dominated by discussion of the Bill. Moreover, the government appears to have become more determined to stifle civil society despite a massive challenge presented by the median NGOs against the proposed Bill. This is because one of the disturbing new provisions being discussed involved converting the NGO Board into a government statutory corporation [1]. The Bill would also likely lead to the over-regulation of NGOs because it gives the government more powers.
>
> (International Center for Not-For-Profit Law, 2019)

The issue of registration was one that may have been regarded positively at some point because it allowed civil society organisations to claim some legitimacy, however, it is now being used in many African countries to restrict and supress civil society activity and put high financial demands on organisations (Buyse, 2018).

While some of these changes in legislation are directly aimed at civil society organisations and their activities, some work to limit civic space and democratic opportunities more broadly through restrictions on freedom of association, freedom of expression or freedom of assembly. In Tanzania, for example, the Electronic and Postal Communications (Online Content) Regulations 2018 disallows the publishing of content online unless the publisher has the necessary licences. In addition, the Media Services Act 2016 has been strongly criticised by the media and civil society in Tanzania because "it gives sweeping powers to the minister to prevent or put obstacles to the publication of any content that endangers national security or public safety" (Civicus, 2017).

In addition, the Cybercrimes Act of 2015 makes it a criminal offence to publish false information in Tanzania and Kambole argues that "many people have been prosecuted, convicted or sentenced under the new law" (2018, p. 47). In Zimbabwe, it is argued that the Cybercrime and Cybersecurity Bill of 2017 is "viewed as a means, by the government of Zimbabwe, to fast track laws that will stifle freedom of expression, access to information, promote interference of private communications and data, and in severe cases, search and seizure of private devices" (Paradigm Initiative, 2019).

## Indirect challenges to civic space

Equally worrying are reports of indirect challenges to civic space that are often targeted directly at activists, journalists, academics and other individuals. In Mozambique for example, the abduction and beating of a professor and journalist has been reported, as well as the killing of a law professor, Gilles Cistac, and threats to other leaders in civil society organisations which have meant them leaving the country out of fear for their own safety (Mozambiquan Human Rights Defender, 2018, pp. 10–12). The media and activists face similar threats in Tanzania, where one human rights defender writes that not only is freedom of expression being stifled through self-censorship, but where journalists are not self-censoring they are then facing human rights violations, further inhibiting the spaces for public debate and criticism of the state (Tanzanian Human Rights Defender, 2018, p. 74).

Another tactic being employed by repressive African states is the tendency to shut down the internet or mobile communication platforms (such as WhatsApp) when levels of criticism need to be controlled. MISA (2017) reports that although 2017 saw fewer internet shutdowns than 2016, when there were internet shutdowns, they were more frequent or for longer periods which is equally damaging. "Internet shutdowns impede human rights such as freedom of expression and assembly, access to information and political rights" (MISA, 2017, p.10). Additionally, many governments in Africa are taxing social media users in an effort to deter citizens from going online and limiting freedom of expression. In Uganda, for example, the government imposed a tax on over the top (OTT) mobile communication platforms such as Facebook, WhatsApp, Instagram, Twitter and Skype. And in Zambia, a tax has also recently been placed on IP-based calls.

> Taxes like these propagate the misconception that internet access and social media use are luxuries … What citizens have emphasized in protests, and what local researchers have also demonstrated, is that access to a truly open internet is a boon for local economies, education, public health and life in general.
>
> (Internet Health Report, 2019)

Kode (2018) argues that although states often justify internet and social media shutdowns by stating they are required to ensure security, prevent terrorism and ensure territorial integrity, these shutdowns usually take place during periods of heightened political tension such as during elections or in the midst of mass protests. It is clear that these deliberate shutdowns and restrictions of communication spaces such as the internet and social media are aimed at restricting and closing civic space and the freedoms associated with it. They inhibit the ability to organise and thus the freedom of association, the ability to express criticisms and thus freedom of expression, and the ability to mobilise action and thus freedom of assembly.

## Methodology

This study used qualitative and quantitative methods of data collection and analysis in order to better understand the way that civil society organisations regard the potential for social media in promoting accountability in restricted civic spaces. The methodology included a survey with purposively selected civil society organisations which were chosen on the basis of having some focus on accountability of public institutions in their work. In addition to the requirement of carrying out some type of accountability work, the sample was also restricted to organisations or individuals who are based in sub-Saharan Africa. Email invitations to complete the online survey were sent to approximately 250 individuals or organisations whose work falls within the accountability sector. Of these, 39 responses were recorded and used in this study. This is a response rate of 15.6 per cent. The survey included both quantitative and qualitative questions aimed at getting a broad sense of the way civil society organisations regard traditional media, social media and the role of these two institutions in relation to their accountability work and more broadly within their contexts.

In addition to the survey, and in order to gain a deeper understanding of context specific issues, interviews were conducted with 11 individuals who had also completed the survey. Interview participants were selected purposively based on having completed the survey, conducting accountability work and also aimed at gaining perspectives from particular contexts. As such, interviews were conducted with individuals from Zambia (N=2), Tanzania (N=3), Mozambique (N=2), Malawi (N=3) and South Africa (N=1). The purpose of the interviews was to further probe issues raised from the surveys in more detail. Additionally, the individuals selected for the interviews were chosen because their contexts (the countries in which they operate) are facing increasing restrictions on civil society and generally civic space in these contexts has become more restricted (except perhaps South Africa, which still enjoys a relatively open civic space).

## Findings and analysis

### *Traditional media and civil society*

Survey results show that respondents regarded traditional media (print and broadcasting) to play a largely informative role in their contexts. Print media was regarded by all participants as playing an informative role, while broadcasting media was regarded by 87 per cent of participants as playing an information role. Commercial print media are considered to have more freedom generally by participants as compared to either commercial or public broadcasting. For example, commercial broadcasters were considered to have 'little or no' freedom by 36 per cent of participants, but public broadcasting was considered to have 'little or no' freedom by 54 per cent of participants. Commercial print media were considered to have 'complete, a great deal or some' freedom by 67 per cent of participants, but commercial broadcasters only 62 per cent and public broadcasters only 46 per cent of freedom. Interestingly, social media was considered by participants to have significantly more 'complete, a great deal or some' freedom (90%) than either print or broadcast media. Levels of freedom in the media are also related to issues around trust and this again reflects the tension between commercial media, public media and social media. Where commercial media was trusted 'extremely or very' by 49 per cent of participants, only 26 per cent of participants thought the same about public media. On the other hand, Facebook was considered to be 'extremely or very' trusted by 64 per cent of participants, and Twitter by 69 per cent of participants.

What emerges strongly from the survey data is that the media are seen as an information-sharing tool in accountability work and that although civil society organisations cannot do their accountability work without the media, there is no direct accountability function being assigned to the media. Instead, the media are considered to fulfil some accountability role only inasmuch as the information they provide society is used to educate citizens who are then mobilised to act or have a change in their opinion regarding an issue, rather than a direct accountability function.

A further issue raised by the interview participants in relation to the media's role in informing society and its place in the public sphere is that it is only able to fulfil a more monitorial and watchdog function if it works with other actors in the civic space. One participant from Malawi noted:

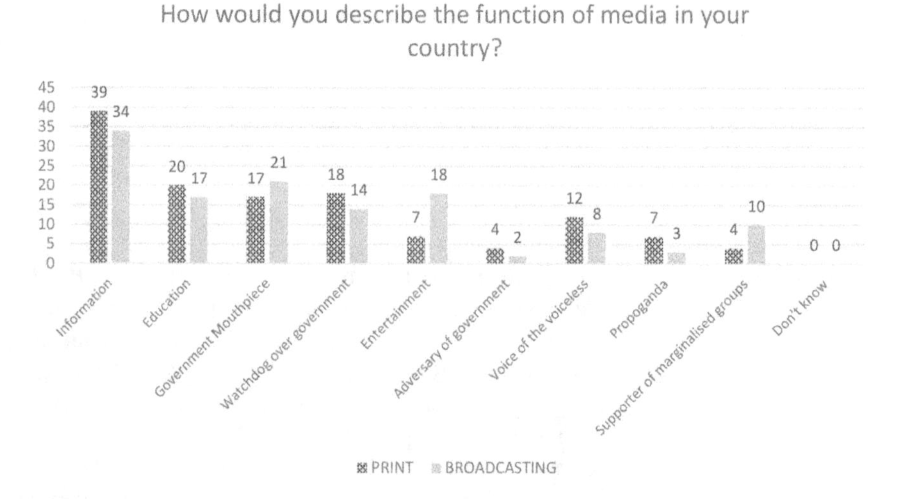


*Figure 3.1* Participants' perceptions about the function of media in their country

> When you say the media is a watchdog, I think we are pushing it a bit too much, we are expecting too much out of one actor. It can't be a watchdog role by yourself, you have to link up a number of actors and … let's not expect to move them out of their area of speciality too much because at the boundary of their action is another actor and we need to find who that actor is and who with them can bring a bit more leverage with each other for change.

The key message here is that civic space is an ecosystem of evolving and interlinked actors and the media are one of these, along with civil society organisations who can work together to promote change within society. This also further highlights the importance of freedom of expression in ensuring open civic space and the ability of CSOs working towards greater accountability to take up an information provision role left vacant by traditional media.

### *Social media and civic space: finding new strategies for navigating the public sphere*

While both the survey and interviews confirmed that traditional media are an important cog in the civil society ecosystem, what is also clear is that as a result of closing civic space, the media are not able to do more than share information that is already in the public domain. This information-sharing role is also further exacerbated by the culture of journalism in Africa, limiting investigative journalism on the continent facilitated by brown envelope journalism (Skjerdal, 2018). Another constraint on the freedom of journalism to practise critical investigative journalism is the tendency towards partisanship by media organisations (Mabweazara, 2018). As a result, civil society organisations doing accountability work have had to turn to social media in an effort to strategically adapt to their current contexts.

Survey results show that WhatsApp, Twitter and Facebook are the most widely used social media by participants. Most participants (74%) use WhatsApp daily, while 59 per cent use Twitter daily and 54 per cent use Facebook daily. When asked to explain their use of social media as depicted in Figure 3.2, participants responded:

> Due to closing of the freedom of traditional media, the organisation has opted to use social media, and with the exception of Facebook, the rest of the platforms are used daily to inform and influence discussion on accountability issues.
>
> Twitter and Facebook help us interact with various stakeholders, including our beneficiaries. It's the fastest way to inform them about our activities and current affairs.
>
> The aforementioned media platforms help us to reach out to a larger audience timely and get instant feedback.

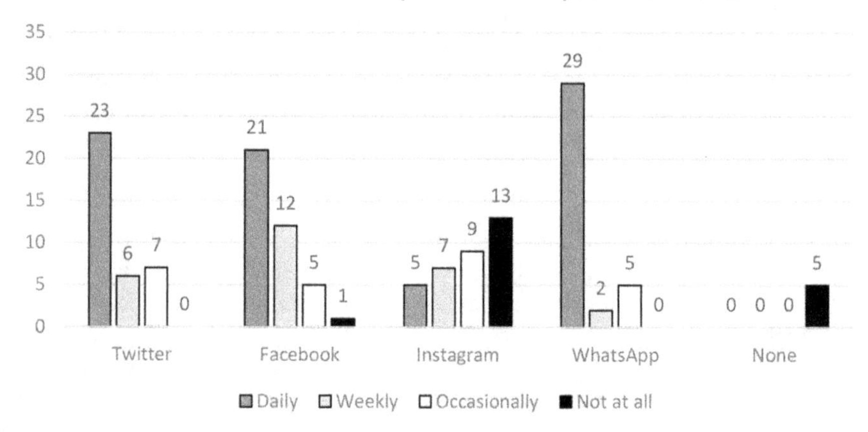


*Figure 3.2* Social media use by civil society organisations

Participants pointed to a number of different advantages for shifting towards a stronger social media strategy as a result of closing civic space in their contexts. One factor, as discussed previously, is that social media is trusted more than traditional media by participants. This is closely related to another advantage pointed out by participants which is the fact that social media use allows civil society organisations direct access to audiences without having to navigate content through media gatekeepers such as journalists and editors. This is particularly important in contexts where journalists and editors are either aligned to particular political parties or are strongly influenced by the threatening pressure on the media to censor their critique of the state. Some of the survey participants noted:

> You control your own content, and social media is somewhat still freer expression online currently in Tanzania than in traditional media.
>
> The message you put across will not be censored in anyway and in fact the risk of your message not coming out is totally removed as in traditional media where editors can decide not to publish a story.
>
> Social media is faster; the message is sent out as it is without being altered.
>
> With social media, I am in complete control at minimum cost with much wider reach.
>
> With traditional media, I have to convince them that my story is news. It can be expensive if there are costs associated with conducting investigative journalism and the story will be published from the perspective of the journalist, not mine.

A key strategy being employed by civil society organisations in using social media in accountability work is to use influential, usually highly visible, independent, non-partisan members of the public such as academics, activist leaders, lawyers, and so on, to support their work. In Tanzania, for example, one participant noted that their communications strategy has consciously moved away from traditional media because of a lack of trust in mainstream media, and are now

> working mostly with social media and we called in what we regard as social media influencers who somehow act as a watchdog in the social media using their Twitter account, their Instagram, Facebook.

This is reiterated by one participant from Zambia who gave examples of prominent civil society actors,

> people who have got huge followings on social media and have almost led from the front in terms of demanding accountability on social media.

These highly influential or prominent individuals work as a strategy on social media in contexts of shrinking civic space because they provide exposure of social issues which are then picked up by other individuals, organisations, mainstream media and political elites. They are hard to ignore, they have some credibility in society because they are regarded as independent of political alignment and are able to use their significant social media following to legitimise their calls for change.

This aspect of visibility and prominence on social media has to, however, be balanced with the negative consequences for those speaking out. In Tanzania, for example, one participant noted in talking about the shift from blogging (as a result of the introduction of the Electronic and Postal Communications (Online Content) Regulations 2017) in that context to the rise of social media:

> If you are famous maybe the people will harass you, they will call you, they will look for you but if you are not that famous sometimes they just ignore you.

This participant continued to explain the dynamics of social media in the context, saying that social media

> is not a tool for accountability because they [the state] just ignore it, it is not taken seriously. But sometimes if all the social media are picking it then they take action.

It is thus a balancing act between drawing too much attention to prominent individuals and thus putting them at risk of being a target by the state and using the voice of ordinary citizens which garners no response from the state and is ignored.

The reaction by the state is taken even further in Mozambique, where the government, according to one participant, has a group of people that are designated to reply to government criticism by prominent voices on social media.

> So all the opinion makers in Mozambique, the strong opinion makers, they [the state] have people on standby to fight back whatever they write and they have allocation of these guys, they call it G40, Group 40, so they have 40 people and they are allocated different major opinion makers in the country to be on their Facebook page, to write back to every time they raise something that is against the government. So they have a machine to fight back social media.

This kind of strategy is one of many used by African governments to further restrict freedom of expression in already closed civic spaces. As previously discussed, there have been a number of instances of internet shutdowns in recent years attesting to the power of social media and the tactics used by restrictive states to oppress the platform.

## Conclusion

The question of whether social media is a tool for accountability remains somewhat unclear, though participants seem to consider it a powerful tool for information sharing and to help them do their accountability work. As the space for traditional media is further restricted due to a number of factors, civil society regard social media as a space where they can better control their own content, have direct access to stakeholders and citizens, and use the power of prominent individuals to draw attention to issues. What comes out strongly from the participants is that social media has given them some agency in their communications and advocacy which was limited with traditional media. This is particularly important in contexts where agency and advocacy are restricted because it allows CSOs to control their messages and perhaps even set the agenda for accountability issues.

However, what is also clear is that a balance has to be maintained between drawing too much attention to an issue or a prominent individual and thus exposing them to threats and negative consequences and using the voice of ordinary citizens to highlight governance and service delivery issues as these are ignored by states. This is perhaps indicative of a lack of strategic planning on the part of civil society about how social media will be used in the current context to achieve their accountability and development goals. When asked whether they had a specific communications strategy for the use of social media, survey participants were almost equally divided between those that did have a strategy and those that did not. It seems that social media is being heralded as a key element of civic space, but civil society is as yet unsure of how to maximise its potential. This potential has to include a strong understanding of the risks of exposing individuals who are too prominent on social media, thus risking repressive retaliation by the state or by interest groups and big business that have the resources to push back in multiple ways, including through social media.

What is further required from civil society beyond their own strategy for using social media in closing civic spaces is to also begin to understand and predict the backlash by states of this emerging platform. It is clear that states across the region are tapped into the potential of social media and have already begun to clamp down on social media use either through legislative restrictions or more crude internet shutdowns and social media taxes. What civil society requires are further strategies for overcoming these restrictions and better use of all media to ensure civic space is able to perform and promote its democratic functions through maintaining critical thinking and debate, accountability and transparency. Many of the CSOs interviewed considered community media as another tool in their work, but separate from traditional and social media. Perhaps what could provide greater opportunities for protecting civic space is a more holistic engagement with all media that takes into account the possibilities of using traditional, community and social media in collaboration with each other rather than as separate spaces for promoting information sharing and advocacy. In doing so, this may ensure that the three pillars of civil society are protected and the behaviours, attitudes and institutions that are critical to civic space find ways of engaging all spheres of society.

## Acknowledgement

This work was supported by the Beit Trust; Hewlett Foundation; OSF-SA; OSISA; and OSF.

## References

Ackerman, J. 2005. *Human Rights and Social Accountability.* (Social Development Papers No. 86). Washington, DC: The World Bank.

Bakshy, E., Messing, S., & Adamic, L.A. 2015. Exposure to ideologically diverse news and opinion on Facebook. *Science*, 348(6239), 1130–1132.

Barberá, P., Jost, J.T., Nagler, J., Tucker, J.A., & Bonneau, R. 2015. Tweeting from left to right: Is online political communication more than an echo chamber? *Psychological Science*, 26(10), 1531–1542.

Buyse, A. 2018. Squeezing civic space: Restrictions on civil society organizations and the linkages with human rights. *The International Journal of Human Rights*, 22(8), 966–988.

Castells, M. 2008. The new public sphere: Global civil society, communication networks, and global governance. *The ANNALS of the American Academy of Political and Social Science*, 616(1), 78–93.

Civicus. n.d. *What is civic space.* [Online]. Retrieved from: https://monitor.civicus.org/whatiscivicspace/.

Civicus. 2017, July 17. *Tanzania: Upsurge in restrictions on fundamental freedoms.* [Press Release]. Retrieved from: https://www.civicus.org/index.php/media-resources/media-releases/2898-tanzania-upsurge-in-restrictions-on-fundamental-freedoms.

Diamond, L. 2008. The democratic rollback: The resurgence of the predatory state. *Foreign Affairs*, 87(2), 36–48.

Eweka, O., Omotoso, S.A., & Olukotun, A. 2017. Introduction. The African policom stew. In Olukotun, A. & Omotoso, S.A. (Eds.), *Political Communication in Africa.* Cham, Switzerland: Springer.

Fraser, N. 1992. Rethinking the public sphere: A contribution to the critique of actually existing democracy. In C. Calhoun (Ed.), *Habermas and the Public Sphere* (pp. 109–142). Cambridge: MIT Press.

Fuchs, C. 2014. *Social Media. A Critical Introduction.* London: Sage.

GlobalStats. 2019. Social media stats Africa. June 2018 – June 2019. Retrieved from: http://gs.statcounter.com/social-media-stats/all/africa.

Hossain, N., Khurana, N., Mohmand, S., Nazneen, S., Oosterom, M., Roberts, T., Santos, R., Shankland, A., & Schröder, P. 2018. *What Does Closing Civic Space Mean for Development? A Literature Review and Proposed Conceptual Framework*, IDS Working Paper 515. Brighton: IDS.

Ibelema, M. 2008. *The African Press, Civic Cynicism, and Democracy.* New York: Palgrave.

International Center for Not-For-Profit Law. 2019, June 14. *Civic freedom monitor: Malawi.* Retrieved from: http://www.icnl.org/research/monitor/malawi.html.

Internet Health Report. 2019. *Taxing social media in Africa.* [Online blog]. Retrieved from: https://internethealthreport.org/2019/taxing-social-media-in-africa/.

Internet World Stats. 2019. *Internet user statistics for Africa.* Retrieved from: https://www.internetworldstats.com/stats1.htm.

Justwan, F., Baumgaertner, B., Carlisle, J., Clark, A., & Clark, M. 2018. Social media echo chambers and satisfaction with democracy among Democrats and Republicans in the aftermath of the 2016 US elections. *Journal of Elections, Public Opinion and Parties*, 28(4), 424–442.

Kambole, J. 2018. Use of criminal laws as barriers to CSO advocacy in Tanzania. In *Southern Africa Litigation Centre. Reflecting on the closing of civic spaces and its impact on marginalised groups in Southern Africa.* (pp. 47–49). Retrieved from: https://www.southernafricalitigationcentre.org/wp-content/uploads/2018/11/SALC-Closing-Civic-Spaces-Report-FINAL-lo-res.pdf.

Kew, D. & Oshikoya, M. 2014. Escape from tyranny: Civil society and democratic struggles in Africa. In E. Obadare (Ed.), *The Handbook of Civil Society in Africa* (pp. 7–24). New York: Springer.

Kode, D. 2018. *Civic space restrictions in Africa. How does civil society respond?* Retrieved from: https://www.accord.org.za/conflict-trends/civic-space-restrictions-in-africa/.

Mabweazara, H. 2018. Reinvigorating 'age-old questions': African journalism cultures and the fallacy of global normative homogeneity. In H. Mabweazara (Ed.), *Newsmaking Cultures in Africa: Normative Trends in the Dynamics of Socio-Political & Economic Struggles* (pp. 1–28). London: Palgrave Macmillan.

Malena, C. 2015. *Improving the measurement of civic space.* [Report]. Retrieved from Transparency & Accountability Initiative website: http://www.transparency-initiative.org/archive/wp-content/uploads/2015/05/TAI-Civic-Space-Study-v13-FINAL.pdf.

Mare, A. 2014. Social media: The new protest drums in Southern Africa. In B. Pătruţ & M. Pătruţ (Eds.), *Social Media in Politics: Case studies on the political power of social media* (Vol. 13) (pp. 315–335). London: Springer.

MISA (Media Institute of Southern Africa). 2017. *So This is Democracy? State of Media Freedom in Southern Africa.* Windhoek, Namibia: Media Institute of Southern Africa.

Mozambiquan Human Rights Defender. 2018. The shrinking space for civil society in Mozambique. In *Southern Africa Litigation Centre. Reflecting on the closing of civic spaces and its impact on marginalised groups in Southern Africa.* (pp. 10–12). Retrieved from: https://www.southernafricalitigationcentre.org/wp-content/uploads/2018/11/SALC-Closing-Civic-Spaces-Report-FINAL-lo-res.pdf.

Mumbere, D. 2018. *Digital in 2018: Africa's internet users increase by 20%.* News report retrieved from Africanews website: https://www.africanews.com/2018/02/06/digital-in-2018-africa-s-internet-users-increase-by-20-percent//.

Paradigm Initiative. 2019. *On Zimbabwe's approval of a Cybercrime and Cybersecurity Bill.* [Online blog]. Retrieved from: http://paradigmhq.org/zimbabwe-cybercrime-bill/.

Pointer, R., Bosch, T., Chuma, W., & Wasserman, H. 2016. *Civil society, political activism and communications in democratisation conflicts. A literature review.* Working Paper. MeCoDEM. ISSN 2057–4002 (Unpublished).

Poushter, J., Bishop, C., & Chwe, H. 2018. Social Media Use Continues to Rise in Developing Countries but Plateaus across Developed Ones. *Pew Research Center*, (22). Retrieved from: https://assets.pewresearch.org/wp-content/uploads/sites/2/2018/06/15135408/Pew-Research-Center_Global-Tech-Social-Media-Use_2018.06.19.pdf.

Rodny-Gumede, Y. 2017. Social media and the re-affirmation of the role of journalism: A cursory discussion of the potential for widening the public sphere in a postcolonial society. *Interactions: Studies in Communication & Culture*, 8(2–3), 169–187.

Skjerdal, T. 2018. Brown envelope journalism: The contradiction between ethical mindset and unethical practice. In H. Mabweazara (Ed.). *Newsmaking Cultures in Africa: Normative Trends in the Dynamics of Socio-Political & Economic Struggles*, (pp. 163–184). London: Palgrave Macmillan.

Tanzanian Human Rights Defender. 2018. Closing civic spaces in Tanzania: The media, sexual and reproductive health, and working on issues of sexual orientation and gender identity. In *Southern Africa Litigation Centre. Reflecting on the closing of civic spaces and its impact on marginalised groups in Southern Africa*. (pp. 74–75).

Voltmer, K. 2004. The mass media and the dynamics of political communication in processes of democratization. In K. Voltmer (Ed.), *Mass Media and Political Communication in New Democracies*, (pp. 1–20). London: Routledge.

Wasserman, H. 2011. Mobile phones, popular media and everyday African democracy: Transmissions and transgressions. *Popular Communication*, 9(2), 146–158.

White, R. & Mabweazara, H. 2018. African journalism cultures: The struggle for free expression. In Mabweazara, H. (Ed.), *Newsmaking Cultures in Africa: Normative Trends in the Dynamics of Socio-Political & Economic Struggles.* London: Springer.

# 4 The changing civil society and the hybrid regime in Iran

*Mohsen Moheimany and Alireza Najafinejad*

## Introduction

Recently, political science has remarked convergence between democratic and authoritarian regimes in relation to their political characteristics and freedoms for civil society (Forrest, 2009). The outcome of this convergence in both has been a growth of NGOs. Cavatorta (2010) notes the motives of this move in liberal democracies. According to him, citizens have been disillusioned and depoliticised due to the concentration of power in a few hands with elites who in practice exclude ordinary people's interest from policies. Kubba (2000) notes the motives in authoritarian regimes: democratic opportunities and the resilience of regimes, although limited, have allowed mobilisation for some political changes. In democratic regimes, people move to NGOs in order to amplify their voice in policymaking, whilst in undemocratic regimes, people view NGOs as a mechanism to assert their suppressed political rights and push back against authoritarian leaders (Cavatorta, 2010; Kubba, 2000). Here, the issue concerns the public scope of NGOs and their representative agency. This is about a duality and convergence between two types of regime.

Historically, after the Cold War, civil society was globally praised as a mechanism of democratisation and also a central element of democracy, especially in the Middle East and North Africa (MENA; Fowler, 1993). Whilst in Iran, elections and spontaneous social movements from below triggered political change and gave rise to civil society organisations in different fields, in other undemocratic countries of the MENA, such as Egypt, Jordan, and Syria, the growth of civil society was their reluctant leaders' decision in response to international pressure (Abootalebi, 1998; Korten, 1990; Hawthrone, 2004). These developments received two kinds of reaction from scholars. A number of scholars, such as Putnam (1993) and Owen (2004), accounted for international variables such as a region's historical trajectory and diplomacy in studying the political setting of authoritarian regimes. A number of other scholars, such as Heydemann (2007), critically questioned such reforms and called them an 'upgrade of authoritarianism', arguing that the real intention of authoritarian leaders was to improve their own reputation and prestige. Regardless of the incentives of leaders or international factors, the scholarship should take into account one important aspect of these reforms which caused certain changes in the institutional and structural setting of the regimes that have implications concerning NGOs. Whilst the political structure of the regimes remained undemocratic in many countries, the limited circulation of power between different political factions and groups took place. In terms of scope and freedoms of NGOs, this circulation has made the policy arena differentiated across different periods within one regime.

Also, the interaction and struggle between states and civil societies have become more complicated (Fawcett & Daugbjerg, 2012). NGOs seek to push back the state offices through their advocacy role, but they have limited freedom and scope. Authoritarian leaders seek to bring the policymaking processes under their ultimate control, but they are constrained by the pressures of non-state actors. From one aspect, instead of a uniform and homogenous state, citizens and NGOs encounter different characters of the state across different political terms.

Here, a question arises about the real scope of freedoms and democratic opportunities in representing people and achieving change by NGOs across different periods. This is especially the case in hybrid regimes, such as Iran, that have combined authoritarianism with democracy, and demonstrated different capacities and contradictory behaviours across time.

## The birth of a mysterious political regime

Ira Lapidus (2000), a historian of the Middle East, used the phrase 'a clerical dictatorship but one of the Middle East's liveliest democracies' to describe the mysterious complexity of the Islamic Republic of Iran (p. 8).

Ayatollah Khomeini, the leader of the 1979 Revolution in Iran, adopted democratic rhetoric and promised to replace the monarchy of Pahlavi with the Islamic Republic that would follow republican democracies across the world (Abdolmohammadi & Cama, 2015). This partially came true concerning the constitution of the regime especially its functional separation of power between three branches and regular elections. However, during the decade of state-building (1979–1989), the conservative Islamists, as the dominant stratum in the establishment, developed the authoritarian character of the regime in favour of Islamic institutions (Abdolmohammadi & Cama, 2015). As a consequence, over the following decades, this political regime evolved into a hybrid system of Islamic autocracy, clerical theocracy, and republican democracy in its architecture, which in terms of ideological legitimacy brings together God's divine and popular sovereignty (Alem, 2002, pp. 105–7; Bashirieh, 2016, pp. 48–51; Alamdari, 2005).

Over the last decades, the interaction between the paradoxical institutions and ideologies within the state, on the one hand, and between two political camps of society, on the other hand, has dynamically shifted the political setting as well as the relationship between state and civil society in opposite directions (Bashirieh, 2016).

The Islamic Republic (hereafter IR) is the radical concept at the core of Iran's political system, which drives all its elements, including leadership, structure, culture, groups, and policies (Huntington, 1996).

## A twofold political ideology

In definition, the state's formal political ideology, as a belief system with a body of consistent notions and thoughts, is seen as the cultural source of discourse and rhetoric of state agencies, as well as communications and policies (Holbrook-Provow & Poe, 1987, p. 399; Charteris-Black, 2018; Savoski, 2018).

The IR ideology in the context of Iran refers to two main notions, including freedom and political Islam, which originated from the words of the slogan of the 1979 Revolution, that is, 'Independence, Freedom, the Islamic Republic' (Mohammadi, 2015; Khajesarvi, 2010). The first word drives the authoritarian and exclusive aspect of the IR ideology, whilst the second supports the democratic aspect of it, and the third represents it as an independent regime with a hybrid architecture. This twofold political ideology is also the origin of the liberal and conservative socio-political streams of society and motivates the competition between their discourses and actions.

While integrating both popular and authoritarian aspects, the IR ideology leans towards political Islam, which as a less democratic concept overrides democratic notions of this ideology. Political Islam, apart from being the formal religion and beyond being a simple Sharia, is an omnipotent ideology that modulates the policymaking and regulates the practices in social and private life in Iran (Karasipahi, 2009; Mir-Hosseini & Tapper, 2006, pp. 73–76; Khajesarvi, 2010; Goudarzi & Najafinejad, 2017). The exercise of Sharia laws in the territory, and across all policy domains, must be the agenda of the government machinery, which has been explicitly stated in the Iranian Constitution. Also, none of the ordinary laws and policies of the state or Parliament should violate Islam, with the Islamic appointive institutions guaranteeing this (Mohammadi, 2015). Nonetheless, contradictorily, IR also places great emphasis on democratic principles. A special section of the Constitution necessitates respect for the rule of people, human rights, citizens' freedoms, and political liberties (Bashirieh, 2016, p. 50). In spite of this respect, as Eslami-Somea (2001) remarks, 'it imparts its own content in conformity with Sharia requirement' due to the strict adherence to Islamic codes (p. 140). This paradox creates an integrative political ideology that is internalised in the formal rules and practices.

As for policymaking, the IR is spelled out by the Supreme Leader, and his subordinate institutions across policy domains, based on jurisprudential interpretation of Sharia. In practice, this discourse not only set the state's strategies but also confined the discourse and actions of the conservative and reformist governments. The general guidelines of the discourse of the current Supreme Leader, Ayatollah Khamenei, have remained remarkably stable over his tenure since 1989 (Holiday, 2011).

Ayatollah Khamenei has often articulated his discourse so that it encompasses both populist democratic and authoritarian Islamic rhetorical elements. As for the authoritarian rhetoric, he has taken advantage of the concept of independence and placed the notion of 'resistance' at the centre of his arguments (Holiday, 2011). He has defined the identity and stance of the IR as an independent political regime with an Islamic nationalism against the hegemonic Western ideologies, especially the one of the US; he uses the alternative term *Mardomsalari* (supremacy of people) to distinguish it from democracy (Holiday, 2011, pp. 80–90).

Concerning the internal politics, he has opposed the liberalist thoughts and secular discourses and undermined their legitimacy (Gheissari & Nasr, 2006, p. 77; Holiday, 2011). Here, the Supreme Leader has always narrated a distinction between self and others (Holiday, 2011). A large number of cultural and educational state organisations and government-sponsored media conceptualise, advocate, and disseminate this distinction in their narratives, practices, outlets, and publications.

In parallel, reviewing the archive of Ayatollah Khamenei's key speeches in relation to the subject 'public participation' shows that he also recognised the freedoms and liberties of people and social groups, as well as their right to choose government rulers and policies. His conversations and verbal orders offer guidelines for active participation in governance (Khajesarvi, 2010). Though, here he has sought to incorporate a localised populist meaning of participation and civil society (Thaler et al., 2010, p. 118). This localisation is an effort to rework democracy in the framework of Sharia, which on an Islamic-nationalistic ground reduces social movements in electoral activism and mass mobilisation, and less in modern civil activism. The example of these mass mobilisations which are often organised by the government is street demonstrations on the anniversary of the Islamic Revolution, 11 February (Bashirieh, 2016, pp. 76–80; Zarifinia, 1998; Holiday, 2011). By promoting this Islamic nationalism, in fact, the conservative streams and institutions have sought to strengthen social cohesion and stability.

In the discourse of IR, the concept of civil society comes with an adjusted meaning too, which is a common phenomenon in Islamic regimes (Cavatorta, 2013; Sajoo, 2004). Ayatollah Khamenei, whilst recommending the inclusion of civil society in policies, has constantly contested the Western concept of civil society and instead replaced it with Islamic concepts, such as *Umma* (the society of Muslims) and *Madinatonabi* (the city of Prophet) under the rule of Islamic leaders and institutions (Feirahi, 1999; Sajoo, 2004). An experienced NGO activist pointed out in his interview that in this Islamic meaning, the function of civil society is defined as facilitating the practice of religious values, such as social cooperation, charity, and devotion more than conducting organised participation or activism. Zarifinia (1998), a former politician, admits this too (pp. 173–180). Also, Ayatollah Khamenei (2016) has tailored civil society to the Islamic Revolution's narratives, saying 'to me, those NGOs that care about the Revolutionary discourse are more privileged than others'. This requires NGOs to be social advocates of the revolutionary establishment.

In the constitutional and ordinary laws, as well as in the strategic policy documents, the role of NGOs has been recognised, albeit limited. The registration and activities of NGOs are subject to the security clearance and official acknowledgement of several Islamic, political, and security authorities (Ajorloo & Poshti, 2016). This brings them under the shadow of government. Nonetheless, NGOs' participatory role in policies has encompassed a wide range from proposing alternatives to appealing the state's decisions.

For the Islamic establishment in Iran, each policy domain of state and society comes with a different degree of ideological significance and a particular profile. Policy domains that directly associate with the fundamentals of the IR ideology—that is, Sharia laws about citizenship and social life—have a higher profile and more significance (Bashirieh, 1995). Since securitisation and patron–client relations are two essential features of the Iranian regime, these also matter in each policy domain (Thaler et al., 2010, p. 38). Association with the function and interests of security, military, or Islamic institutions, increases the political significance of a domain, as well as the interests of individual establishment members, such as conservative clerics and revolutionary figures. Otherwise, technical policy domains are expected to be low profile.

As the literature of political science suggests, political institutions are anticipated to provide fewer access points and present a lower level of tolerance for NGOs and social groups in political domains, whilst, in contrast, they have a higher tolerance and are more receptive in the technical domain (Duyvendak & Giugni, 1995, pp. 96–8). This is evident in Iran too. For instance, the environmental domain is considered a technical domain about which neither the Islamic nor the security–military institutions evince much interest (Aslipur & Sharifzadeh, 2015; Doyle & Simpson, 2006). However, the area of human rights has always been considered high profile, as risky, for the interest of the Islamic and security institutions (Moinifar, 2010; Ertan, 2012).

Therefore, on the one hand, the Islamic and unelected section of the IR ideology systematically confines the opportunities for civil society. On the other hand, its elected section provides potentials for political freedoms and civil rights, thus, social movements (Thaler et al., 2010; Bashirieh, 2016).

## A hybrid regime

Essentially, two significant qualities of a political regime differentiate democracy from authoritarianism, namely electoralism and constitutionalism (Wigell, 2008). In the case of electoralism, four important attributes should feature in electoral processes for choosing institutions of a state, in order for a political regime to be labelled a democracy. These attributes are (i) fairness, (ii) inclusiveness, (iii) competitiveness, and (iv) freeness. In terms of constitutionalism, four fundamental freedoms in the political and governmental processes should be fulfilled for citizens, including freedoms of (i) expression, (ii) organisation, and (iii) information, as well as (iv) freedom from discrimination (Wigell, 2008, p. 237).

Based on the elements presented above, in order to identify the type of a hybrid regime like the IR, a continuum with democracy and authoritarianism at each end can be utilised, in line with Diamond's typology (2002b). It locates the hybrid regime between these two ends, a regime that integrates characteristics of both. It is not a democracy, since it is still far from the full guarantee of freedoms and fully representative government, nor is it authoritarianism, as it is far from full despotism that has no space for liberties and civil rights (Karl, 1995; Diamond, 2002).

For Leader Ayatollah Khomeini and revolutionary clerics, the 1979 Revolution aimed to translate the notion of popular Islamic government into state institutions. The constitution of the IR is thus based on Sharia, jurisprudence, and the supervision of religious scholars and jurists on public affairs. Nonetheless, in the process of establishing the state apparatus from 1979 to 1988, other political groups and thoughts contributed too, for example liberalists, nationalists, and leftists. Therefore, the institutional architecture of the IR also reflected their quest for democracy (Abdolmohammadi & Cama, 2015; Holiday, 2011; Gheissari & Nasr, 2006).

At the core of the IR regime, there is a complicated confluence and interaction between the elected and unelected institutions. The interaction between these sections of the regime that are 'loosely connected and fiercely opposed' runs the process of policymaking, confines political contestations, and determines the distribution of political opportunities for society (Tazmini, 2013, p. 99).

In the republican section, the IR has an elected Parliament and a President who chooses the cabinet of ministers subject to parliamentary approval. On the other side, the unelected institutions with Islamic, security, and military roles, which constitute the core of the establishment, oversee policymaking and legislation, thus in practice overrides the republican section (Tazmini, 2013, p. 99). Since the revolution, the balance between authoritarian and democratic sections has changed as the system has been shifting from a pseudo-democracy towards a semi-democracy with the republican institutions slightly gaining more importance (Bashirieh, 2016, p. 51).

## The unelected section

This section includes: (i) the Supreme Leader, (ii) the Expediency Council, (iii) the Guardian Council, and (iii) the Judiciary, as well as the military, police, and religiopolitical paramilitary forces, notably the Islamic Revolution Guard Corps (IRGC). Whilst the Supreme Leader position at the apex of the state acts as an autocratic religious institution with slight democratic attributes; other institutions maintain the theocracy for conservative streams and clerics as the dominant stratum (Bashirieh, 2016; Thaler et al., 2010).

The majority of institutional power is centralised in the Supreme Leader's hand, and the institutions affiliated with his office (Ganji, 2008). According to the Constitution, he sets the long-term strategies and global agendas of the state (Khajesarvi, 2010). He appoints and dismisses the commanders of the military and security forces, the head of the Judiciary, the Guardian Council members, as well as choosing the head and members of tens of Islamic seminaries, state-sponsored mass media, and cultural organisations across all domains and regions (Tezcur, 2012). He is given the authority to inaugurate or dismiss the elected President, vetoing his agendas and decisions; as well as the decisions and agendas of Parliament (Khajesarvi, 2010).

Notwithstanding its authoritarianism, the appointment of the Supreme Leader is the function of an elected religiopolitical council named as the Assembly of Experts that is legally meant to supervise the performance of the Supreme Leader and the institutions under him. In theory, this is to fulfil popular sovereignty at a high level, but in practice, Ayatollah Khamenei—since his appointment in 1989—has overcome monitoring mechanisms (Kadivar, 2010).

Under his shadow, the Guardian Council and the Expediency Council manage the policymaking and electoral processes. These institutions with Islamic legitimacy restrict both the constitutional and electoral aspects of the regime (Tazmini, 2013). They often have been filled by conservative Mullahs, jurists, and figures and transmuted to authoritarian institutions serving the establishment, with their agendas, meetings, and deliberations mostly inaccessible and unpublished to the public (Thaler et al., 2010, p. 28; Khajesarvi, 2010). They benefit from unlimited powers like vetoing Parliament's decisions, interpreting constitutional and ordinary laws as well as compiling strategic documents and policies. A former Governor-General who served as a politician for more than 20 years said in his interview that, in practice, the public—including NGOs—has little or no access to this level, only the Cabinet and Parliament can intermediate between them. Moreover, the Judiciary safeguards the practice of Islamic codes. It is not independent and has always been under the rule of the conservative Mullahs (Rakel, 2009; Abdolmohammadi & Cama, 2015).

The institutional and ideological influence of the Supreme Leader is extended and sustained across all policy domains and regional divisions with his representatives articulating his discourse across all provinces—the Imam for Friday Prayer Sermon—and, his delegates auditing policies in almost all state institutions—the Islamic Commissars (Tezcur, 2012). These representatives and delegates function as the eyes and ears of the Supreme Leader, which means, in addition to sustaining top-down authority, they can be potential access points for the public to communicate with the highest positions (Thaler et al., 2010).

The unelected institutions also extend into civil society through a body of semi-governmental cultural and economic foundations, as well as religious associations, under the ultimate control of the Office of the Supreme Leader, such as the Organisation for Islamic Propagation, Foundation for Oppressed People, Foundation for Martyrdom and Sacrifice, Assistance Committee, Islamic seminaries, and so on. These are obedient pressure groups, parastatal enterprises, and state-funded agencies which sustain the economic and political interest of the ruling establishment across the lower and middle classes (Tezcur, 2012, p. 123; Rakel, 2009).

In the unelected section, the security and military forces, besides their professional protective missions, also guard the interests and safety of the conservative establishment. In addition to the Police and Military, which have a professionally-defined profile in guaranteeing internal and external safety, the Constitution legitimises the Islamic Revolutionary Guard Corps (IRGC) as a paramilitary institution with a substantial cultural and political authority which answers directly to Ayatollah Khamenei (Tazmini, 2013; Thaler et al., 2010). It is the most potent security–military force that protects the establishment from opposition forces and competing social discourses (Green et al., 2009; Thaler et al., 2010). The IRGC, together with the Police and Judiciary, at times, have used suppressive tools by appealing to the ideological missions assigned to them by the Constitution (Mohammadi, 2013).

The profile and attitudes of the authoritarian institutions practically depend on who controls them (Thaler et al., 2010). Usually, conservatives and fundamentalists run them through patron–client relations and securitisation which enlists the support of the military and paramilitary forces (Thaler et al., 2010). Politicians and clerics with revolutionary and conservative profiles have developed a kinship and political networks. Beyond their political affiliations, however, many of the high-profile political figures from both reformist and conservative camps—mostly from the cleric stratum—have familial connections with one another, and therefore, different levels of leverage in the establishment (Iran Data Portal, 2015). This makes for a vague network of figures with variations in their insider/outsider positions.

In general, political opportunities and participation of civil society in Iran have been limited by the political, ideological, and security approaches of the authoritarian section of the regime, with conservative clerics and factions resisting their rivals' demands and discourse. Nevertheless, the presidential and parliamentary elections have often been competitive and served as forums for questioning national strategies and policies (Abdolmohammadi & Cama, 2015).

## The elected section

The elected president and his cabinet, along with the Parliament, constitute the republican section. The President, according to the Constitution, is the number two political position, after the Supreme Leader. As Thaler et al.

(2010) point out, in high-profile domains, such as domestic security and foreign policy, their authorities compete—depending on the presidency incumbent. In this struggle, executive and budgetary power are in the hands of the President (Gholipur & Ahangar, 2010; Thaler et al., 2010). Whilst the authoritarian institutions restrict political opportunities for the public, the President's position has the potential to open up the structure to public opinion and will. In practice, the President and his appointed cabinet, which also needs the Parliament's approval, are responsible to both authoritarian institutions and Parliament.

After the state-building decade, that is, the 1980s, different presidential terms have been associated with different or sometimes opposite policies and discourses, thus creating distinct political periods (Mosallanejad, 2005). They include (i) 1989–1997: economic reconstruction of Rafsanjani, (ii) 1997–2005: political reforms of Khatami, (iii) 2005–2013: socio-economic justice of Ahmadinejad, and (iv) 2013–2021: rationality and moderation of Rouhani. The second and third periods are the two most different presidencies in the IR history, which indicate the extent of flexibility and capacity of the regime in terms of circulation of power.

Concerning the involvement of people in the executive branch, the chance of NGOs furthering their causes directly through official correspondence is limited. Also, if a proposal is supposed to pass through the lower levels of bureaucracy to the cabinet level, there is a need for political loyalty, personal relationships, or familial links with officeholders or senior officials, because of the clientelistic character of bureaucracy, otherwise the huge bureaucracy and lengthy procedures delay access and impede public demands. A former Director-General in the Ministry of Interior stated that the administration with overlapping rules and complicated codes, instead of facilitating public causes, has been a privilege for policymakers and politicians to repel pressure from social groups and citizens.

Iran's Parliament according to the Constitution has a wide range of authorities, and on paper it has the unlimited freedom of questioning all the elected and unelected institutions. Parliament is supposed to be the most accessible and popular institution. In terms of access for civil society, MPs are legally supposed to frequently allocate some time to meetings with the public, though, there is no minimum and particular method mentioned by laws. In practice, as most political and civil activists complained in their interviews, contacting MPs is hard and, usually, requires personal links or strong political affiliation. Also, as governors and civil activists confirmed in their interviews, the inclusion of social groups in the meetings and decision-making process does not follow a fixed procedure; rather, it depends on the decisions of the Parliament members and the head of commissions.

The powers of the Parliament are limited by the Islamic institutions, as the Guardian Council has rejected many of the Parliament's decisions and bills, particularly the ones aiming at political reforms and democratic changes. Also, the Parliament has been subject to overt and covert pressures from the

Supreme Leader's Office, as well as security forces such as the IRGC, which 'have constrained the agency of MPs and trained their behaviours across different terms', a political activist expressed.

In general, the scope of action and influence of the elected institutions, which are the 'mouthpiece of popular will' and civil society's fledged conduct to policies, is complicatedly confined in their interaction with the Islamic and security institutions (Abdolmohammadi & Cama, 2015, p. 562). Nevertheless, political competition and civil society have had the opportunity to change many policies.

## A hybrid society

Iranian society is hybrid as in terms of composition it encompasses modern and traditional sections. Corresponding with this, instead of a party system, the politics functions based on competition between two major political streams—so-called reformist and conservative (Farhi, 2012). These camps are two significant clusters of individual figures, political parties, mass media, and NGOs with opposing political discourses in relation to domestic policies and international policies, albeit in the framework of the Islamic ideology (Khajesarvi, 2010; Thaler et al., 2010; Holiday, 2011). This factional politics, on the one side, is coordinated with the IR hybrid regime, whilst on the other side with the twofold social cleavages (Thaler et al., 2010).

The traditional cleavage, in terms of social cast, includes people from lower classes in the rural and urban areas, which are led by conservative clerics and members of the religiopolitical foundations and paramilitary institutions such as the IRGC and Foundation for Oppressed People (Kamali, 1998). Regarding the stratum, this cleavage includes the Bazaar guilds and shopkeepers, religious neighbourhoods, Islamic seminaries, farmers, and industrial workers. It is estimated that there should be approximately 52,000 unregistered associations, as well as 4,600 unregistered cultural groups associated with this section of society (Razzaghi, 2010). On the other side, the modern cleavage includes people from the educated middle and upper classes in urban areas that belong to the new strata, including businessmen, bankers, teachers, bureaucrats and technocrats, university students, journalists, intellectuals, human rights activists, scholars, and so on (Bashirieh, 2016; Rakel, 2008). Experts estimate that the number of active NGOs associated with the modern section of society ranges between 5,000 and 8,000 (Beehner, 2007).

The social and political discourse of civil society organisations is identified by their association with social cleavages. The traditional civil society inherited the Islamic conservative discourse from pre-revolution Iran (Karasipahi, 2009). It supports the rule and practice of Sharia laws with a conservative approach to social life and an Islamic interpretation of justice, freedom, and equality, as well as the radical culture articulated by Ayatollah Khamenei and conservative clerics in policymaking (Bashirieh, 1995, 2016). Religious and social leaders of this stream propose incompatibility between modern human rights and political liberties with Islam (Kadivar, 2010). On the other hand, yet within the Islamic framework, the modern section of civil society identifies with: modern human rights, freedoms and liberties in the Western sense, secularism in lifestyle and the abandonment of social controls, prioritising national interests over Islamic rules, rationalism in decision-making, and the rule of law (Thaler, et al., 2010; Bashirieh, 1995; Kadivar, 2010). The NGOs affiliated with this section of society support the reformist camp and take a liberal–secular approach (Bashirieh, 2016; Tazmini, 2013).

## Shifts in the condition and status of civil society

After a decade of economic liberalisations and social advancements in the 1980s, 18 parties from the leftist, liberal, pragmatist, and moderate conservative streams allied with one another and formed an umbrella camp in the middle of the 1990s, which later was labelled as reformist (Rakel, 2008; Tazmini, 2013). Ideologically, reformists were inspired by intellectual modernist clerics, such as Ayatollah Montazeri and Ayatollah Sanei, who believed in upgrading outdated Islamic practices and rules based on global human rights and developments. This camp advocated institutional reforms, arguing that limiting the despotic and authoritarian tendencies of the unelected section of the regime could be curtailed only by modernising social, political, and cultural spheres and reforming the state institutions (Zeidabadi, 2005).

Reformists nominated Muhammad Khatami as their candidate in the 1997 presidential election. Although he was a Mullah affiliated with the establishment and studied theology in Qom—the religious capital of Iran, Khatami was in close contact with democratic theories and Western thoughts due to his career in Germany, that is, President of the Islamic Centre in Hamburg (Alexader & Hoenig, 2008). Accordingly, he entered the electoral campaign with a modern manifesto and liberal discourse based on IR ideology (Feirahi, 1999; Thaler et al., 2010). Mobilised by the youth and women, and along with the middle class, especially the university students, the majority of votes surprisingly were cast in favour of Khatami.

In less than three years, in 2000, the reformist camp, with the same flag and slogan, also gained a solid victory in the election for the sixth term of Parliament and accordingly gained the majority, with 215 seats (Tazmini, 2013, p. 73). As a result, the reformists dominated the elected section in the 1997–2005 period, whilst the conservative camp ruled over the unelected institutions. The reformist camp articulated a set of liberal rhetoric, symbols, and actions which resonated in the state apparatus (Ehteshami & Zweiri, 2009). This was more expressed in their effort to break the predominant dress codes at the high state level, including the President himself. Khatami with a 'smiley face' started to appear with brighter colours of cloaks—light brown; milky; or light grey—which was a symbolic effort to challenge the traditional clergy institution, as dark brown and black were the standard colours. Simultaneously, the government expressed some tolerance for the practice of modern and open dress codes by society, especially for women, as this was becoming a trend in the modern section of society (Tazmini, 2013).

As for his Cabinet, the composition of the ministers and the chief advisors in the President's Office, especially in political and social areas, was made up of men and women who either had the experience of living or studying in European countries and the US or were high-profile academics that had familiarity and association with Western political literature and thoughts. This choice of cabinet members had the intention of promoting rationalisation and modernisation of discourse and practice in the state, consistent with international liberal agendas and models (Ehteshami & Zweiri, 2009, p. 7).

The core reformists' motive was questioning the authoritarianism of the establishment while also criticising the undemocratic tendencies of the Islamic institutions such as the Supreme Leader and Guardian Council (Thaler et al., 2010; Feirahi, 1999). With an emphasis on supporting civil society as a counter force and sphere against the authoritarian establishment, as well as transparency, human rights, and public participation, the formal conversations of the reformist camp encompassed integral notions of 'toleration versus opposition'— including Khatami's iconic slogan of 'long live my opponent' (Namazi, 2000, p. 13; Thaler, et al., 2010, p. 69; Brumberg, 2001, p. 1). In this vein, the reformist Cabinet officially imported and adopted the word NGO, with the same definition as in international documents, into the communications and political vocabulary of the government, and accordingly, the Ministry of Interior used it in official documents. An experienced NGO activist explained in her interview that in a few years this adoption of a Western term became keenly accepted, welcomed, and widely used by the social and political activists.

However, in response to the growing concerns of the establishment about the rise of civil society, Khatami eventually readjusted and softened his narrative about this concept through justifying it with the language and history of Islam, so making it consistent with Ayatollah Khamenei's traditional narrative of Islamic civil society (Feirahi, 1999; Rakel, 2008). This effort, while reducing the establishment's aggressive reactions, resulted in making the term vague in the public sphere (Zeidabadi, 2005).

In practice, the reformist government expanded and enabled civil society in three areas, including (i) political parties, (ii) mass media, and (iii) NGOs. For doing so, reformists amended the legal and administrative procedures and utilised the financial resources and mechanisms of the state. Markedly, the Ministry of Interior under the rule of reformist figures such as Abdullah Noori (1997–1998) and Abdolvahed Mousavi Lari (1998–2005), both from a clerical reformist party, relaxed the procedures in relation to obtaining a licence for political parties, as well as receiving regular governmental grants. As a result, 180 political parties and groups rose and registered during the reformist period. Political activists in their interviews named it the era of the 'blossoming of parties'. In parallel, by relaxing policies of the Ministry of Culture, more opportunities were provided for the emergence of mass media as the number of newspapers and periodicals rose from 274 to 850 at the end of the reformist period (Rakel, 2008, p. 133). Besides print media, public access to the Internet increased towards the end of Khatami's tenure, and users of online media and websites grew by at least 4 million (Omidvar, 2005). However, many of the media and political parties, due to their dependence on governmental funds and physical support, such as offices, were rarely independent or vibrantly active (Kazemi, 2009).

At the centre of political reforms, the reformist government introduced several legal and administrative amendments in order to facilitate the establishment and development of NGOs. With the policies and budget of different state organisations, the experienced social and political activists across the country, especially in the capital, were recommended to establish a formal NGO in their field of activity and organise their activities and human forces into official NGOs. As a result of this, the total number of registered NGOs increased from approximately 75 in 1997 to more than 10,000 in 2005, as reported by the Ministry of Interior (2004). This number was apart from unregistered cultural and social associations that existed from a long time ago. A civil activist who also had the experience of being an adviser to the Governor-General's Office explained that in the initial phases of the rise of NGOs—that is, the first couple of years, mostly the high-profile political and civil activists, the ones affiliated with reformists and state officials, such as family members and friends, succeeded in establishing and registering their NGOs due to their convenient access to offices and their linkage with policymakers. These NGOs and activists spread the state-led enthusiasm from the top down to society so that, over the following few years, thousands of ordinary civil activists and traditional associations across the country joined this movement. As NGO activists explained in their interview, the emerging NGOs were mostly unprofessional organisations. They were friendly, lowly-organised, un-hierarchical, and small groups of interested people that used to have informal networks and activism before. They improved their organisation, registered and reported their activities, and organised the membership, and officialised their interactions with the state until 2004, as the reformist state encouraged them to do.

Most of the emerging NGOs were small (up to ten members) and medium (between ten and 50 members) in size, with a smaller number being large and resourceful, an NGO president said in her interview. The majority of newer NGOs, as some members confirmed in their interviews, had no office and official equipment, rather they either shared their resources and offices or used the spaces and resources lent to them by the government in the event they had close relations with officials and reformists. In many cases, the 'government openly gave some NGOs regular access to office space, stationery, telephone and printing machines, and lent them other resources like state cars in order to help them stand on their own feet over time', a former Governor-General said. Therefore, they were considered as 'governmental NGOs'.

In terms of official registration and agency, NGO founders had to obtain a permit from the relevant state offices in their field of activity, for example from the Office of Youth Affairs in they wanted to work in this area, as well as register with the Ministry of Interior. After establishment, they had to report the list of members, NGO's charter, minutes of meetings, and public performances to the relevant departments in the Ministry of Interior. This meant 'governmental authority and political monitoring' by the state from the first day of establishment, which is contrary to the nature of an NGO. Over the second reformist term, the Ministry of Interior extended its subordinated offices in the area of NGOs, and also included the representatives of security offices and the police in the processes and offices related to monitoring NGOs (Rivetti, 2013). Despite the governmental control, the movement for establishing NGOs became 'a widespread fashion very soon', a local media journalist said in his interview.

In terms of approach and agenda, most of the newer NGOs had no predetermined goal or purpose, nor a designed charter concerning their organisation, regulation, and membership. Thus, the Ministry of Interior designed a typical charter for emerging NGOs and officially delivered it to them, which developed and changed over time regarding the government's political and security agendas, a former local government official said. The government and officials also sought to promote the 'liberal policies and political development' approach between NGOs through formal and informal communications, a former advisor to the local Governor-General Office stated.

In the first reformist term, the government, itself, was unpractised in managing NGO activists, and also the official regulations concerning NGOs and their activities were small and flexible. In the second term, the Ministry of Interior compiled the first official regulations for registered NGOs, named The Executive Regulation for NGOs. This regulation addressed NGOs as formal policy actors, allowed them to act and organise formal activities with the permission of the government, as well as deliver plans, agendas, and alternatives to the government. The regulation stated that NGOs have the institutional right to access documents and information from all organs of the government. Besides this, the reformist-led Parliament specified several articles in the Third (2000) and Fourth (2004) Development Plans so as to allow organs of the government to allocate a tiny part of their financial resources to NGOs—subject to their discretion. By these changes, the reformist State provided for broader public access to centres of policymaking, as well as opening the venues for lobbying policymakers and pressuring them for transparency and accountability (Tazmini, 2013, p. 64). These policies came along with schemes for reducing the size of government machinery, privatising the enterprises, and reducing the dependency on oil revenues (Tazmini, 2013, p. 77). Also, in the public sphere new practices and mechanisms of social activism and participation spread, for example strikes and demonstrations (Tazmini, 2013).

However, the control of the Islamic and security institutions on civil society imposed limits on the scope of NGOs. For example, in the regulations passed by the Ministry of Interior, NGOs were barred from any political activities in the sense of targeting the electoral processes and party activism, which is against their fundamental freedoms. Moreover, the governmental audit boards across the capital and provinces had the authority of revoking NGOs' licences or banning their activities.

In reaction to the reformists' policies on the Parliament and State, the Islamic and authoritarian institutions perceived the reforms as anti-Islamic and retaliated by acting as a parallel government, thus weakening the growing liberal and opposition forces (Gheissari & Nasr, 2006). They also sought to intensify their counter force over different domains of civil activism (Green et al., 2009; Tazmini, 2013, p. 103). Ayatollah Khamenei openly expressed his dissatisfaction over the political and cultural policies of the reformists. He warned that any freedom is meant within the framework of Islamic teachings. He also alleged the critical forces—in this context vocal reformist media and parties—were the agents of enemies and requested the Judiciary and IRGC to confront them (Rakel, 2008). By flashing the green light, the Supreme Leader triggered a series of securitising policies especially during the second term of the reformist period (Ehteshami & Zweiri, 2009). The IRGC employed a specialised Intelligence Unit to expand its political role. For instance, as the records show, the Judiciary closed more than 100 press outlets, 2000 websites, revoked the licences of many vocal NGOs and reformist parties, and detained partisans and journalists under the pressure of the IRGC (Thaler et al., 2010, p. 57; Barzegar, 2005; Rakel, 2008, p. 136). Civil society shrank in size and activism.

Thus, in the reformist period, the two sections of the political regime were divided between two political camps with opposing policy approaches and discourses in relation to governance and civil society. On the one hand, reformists in the elected institutions sought to partially expand freedoms and develop civil society, whilst on the other hand, conservatives in the unelected institutions developed counter forces in order to restrict the scope of action for the emerging civil society. This complicated the distribution of political opportunities in a paradoxical way.

## The conservative period

Amidst a decline in the middle class's hope for political reforms, the conservative camp took the majority in the 2002 local elections due to a low voter turnout in large cities (Amini, 2010). Although this did not undermine the discourse or power of the reformist Parliament and government, it prepared the ground for further victories of the conservatives at higher levels. In 2004, the conservative camp succeeded once again in claiming the majority of seats in the Parliament, thanks to the conservative Guardian Council which disqualified the majority of the reformist candidates across the country—at least 2500 people. Through these two elections, many former security figures and IRGC commanders, hand-in-hand with conservative figures, took back some power in policymaking and legislation (Ehteshami & Zweiri, 2009).

Following these victories, in 2005, a more prepared and united conservative camp entered the presidential election with a populist discourse, which was in line with the revolutionary narratives of Ayatollah Khamenei's discourse. This camp nominated Mahmoud Ahmadinejad, who a few years ago had been the Mayor of Tehran—the capital. In fact, this post granted Ahmadinejad the chance to receive exposure by the mass media and channel his aggressive arguments against the reformist government to the general public. It also granted him access to a large amount of financial and administrative resources in Tehran Municipality, which, as a political activist mentioned in his interview, is considered as a 'launch pad' for the presidency. He was a trustee of the establishment because of his previous career and service, that is, as former Governor-General and an ex-member of the IRGC (Ehteshami & Zweiri, 2009, p. 56). By formulating a radical Islamic narrative originated from the 1979 Revolution and coming from a poor rural family, Ahmadinejad appealed to and echoed the social demands of the lower classes against the reformist camp (Ehteshami & Zweiri, 2009). In addition, he publicly called for a 'combat against economic and political corruption' of the reformist government, especially against state-sponsored 'Oil Mafia'—as he argued—whilst also promising the revival of the legacy of the conservatives during the first decade of the revolution (Rakel, 2009; Thaler et al., 2010, p. 48; Ehteshami & Zweiri, 2009, p. 85). His discourse not only was welcomed by the traditional Islamic seminaries and the IRGC but also received the votes of economically deprived people and conservative clerics (Ehteshami & Zweiri, 2009). Ahmadinejad won the election in 2005, albeit in two rounds.

The manifesto of his conservative government was based on supporting Islamic concepts such as martyrdom and social coordination, and resonating the social conservatism and restrictions (Thaler et al., 2010). Politically, the President did not recognise his opponents and critics as he called them 'dirt and dust', after his second victory in the 2009 presidential election (Sreberny, 2013, p. 5). Consistent with this line, the conservative Cabinet and, notably, the President himself, presented a different set of symbols and actions at the highest political level. Markedly, Ahmadinejad appeared with an informal khaki jacket at most occasions and events, which culturally was associated with the clothing of poor classes in Iran (Ehteshami & Zweiri, 2009). Whilst the educated middle-class people criticised him, the conservative camp asserted that Ahmadinejad's clothing meant he was a 'man of the people' (Kamali, 2013). From one perspective, disseminating this title and clothing style transmitted the signal that the conservative Cabinet would be populist in approaching society, and therefore, less accessible and attentive to the established political and social NGOs.

Ahmadinejad's cabinet members hailed from a conservative background with a similar dress code to the President and the religious women covered with a black veil that resembles a Christian Nun's veil. Their dress code and symbols were associated with fundamentalists in the 1980s, the radical decade of the Revolution (Ehteshami & Zweiri, 2009, p. 54). Furthermore, regarding their background, the ministers and chief advisors were mostly figures previously associated with the IRGC and the Ministry of Intelligence or associated with fundamentalist Islamic seminaries, mostly sporting beards (Ehteshami & Zweiri, 2009). Within the first year of being in power, the government engineered the composition of the administration through replacing most of the reformists and liberals with figures loyal to the conservative camp (Ehteshami & Zweiri, 2009; Rakel, 2008).

The political discourse of the conservatives centred on reducing the gap between rich and poor, as well as glorifying the notion of Islamic justice (Jahangiri & Fatahi, 2010; Rakel, 2008). Consistent with this discourse, the conservative camp advocated an interventionist decision-making style and centralised governance, which did not have any recognition of civil society (Ehteshami & Zweiri, 2009; Jahangiri & Fatahi, 2010). In this vein, Ahmadinejad ended the story by saying 'where there are spontaneous religious associations, there is no need for NGOs' (Radio Zamaneh, 2011). Experienced and critical NGO activists said in their interviews that the conservatives in administration 'perceived NGO as a "Western phenomenon", and in consequence of their cynical views towards the West, defined NGO activists as potential agents and spies of the West plotting in Iran'. Instead of NGOs, the conservative government encouraged mass activism through traditional gatherings across neighbourhoods and mosques. Also, instead of improving the reception of public demands through access points in state apparatus, Ahmadinejad held regular meetings of his cabinet ministers in different provinces. Moreover, with an intention of extending direct access to masses, the state initiated the mechanism of exchanging letters and face-to-face contacts with people during public speeches of the President (Ehteshami & Zweiri, 2009).

Also, by amending the laws and administrative practices, and using financial and security means, the conservative government restricted the scope of critical civil society. As for the political parties, except for conservatives and their allies, the Ministry of Interior over years ceased the previous governmental supports—both political and financial. As a result, two critical political parties, namely the Participation Front and Mujahedin Organisation—associated with and funded by the reformist government— encountered legal bans or became semi-active, while a number of new small-sized conservative parties emerged during the same period. Moreover, some vocal partisans were imprisoned and detained by the security forces, especially by the IRGC's Intelligence Unit (Rakel, 2008). In parallel, the decline in the tolerance of the Ministry of Culture towards opposing and critical ideologies and actors resulted in increased suspicion towards journalists, which led to the closure and banning of many online and print outlets, censorship and official warnings to editors, and detention of tens of journalists (Rakel, 2008, p. 141).

More specifically, the Ministry of Interior, under the command of Mostafa PoorMuhammadi (2005–2008), previously a conservative Judge and Deputy Minister of Intelligence, and Mostafa Najjar (2009–2013), previously an

IRGC commander, focused on NGOs and their activities with the purpose of appropriating them with the Islamic conservative guidelines. At the beginning of Ahmadinejad's time, thousands of NGOs from Khatami's time had been established, settled, and institutionalised in the formal procedures and official documents of state, while on the ground the number of emerging NGOs was still going up too. The said Ministry, in the first step, changed the official title of NGOs to *SAMAN* in the official communications—this word is the abbreviation representing community-based organisations. Through this change, first, the government intended to make a distinction between the self-made notion of Iranian Islamic NGOs and the Western NGO which was on the reformist government's agenda. Second, as an NGO president said in his interview, the conservatives sought to move NGOs from a policy role and advocacy, or political status, to the religious and volunteer activism associated with mass movements in support of Islamic ideology.

In practice, this policy came with different changes. The government set up regular funds/grants for religious and Islamic areas of NGO activism, mostly in cultural and family fields. Also, many of the unregistered religious and traditional associations, seminaries, and groups—affiliated with the IRGC—were informally requested and invited to the Ministry of Interior to register their organisation as an official NGO. The government ceased the access of previously registered NGOs and those critical to the public resources and state offices, critical NGO members stated in their interviews. Moreover, due to the securitising approach of the conservative government, and alongside the growing political leverage of the IRGC, the then Minister of Interior increased the controlling measures on NGOs, for example encouraging governmental audit boards to use their right to revoke the licences of critical NGOs (Ehteshami & Zweiri, 2009).

The government acted with the objective of reducing the role of NGOs to religious activities. For doing so, the cabinet of ministers put an article in the draft of the Fifth Development Plan (2011), with Parliament passing it. Article 3 of that document especially obliged government organisations to support NGOs that are active in the area of the propagation of Islamic values, for example martyrdom and social coordination. As a result, the traditional and religious section of civil society expanded, which was at the expense of the modern section with advocacy functions. The government in fact engineered the composition of civil society in a few years from 2005 to 2009 with the religious, traditional, and conservative NGOs becoming the majority. Many of the new NGOs had closed membership, non-hierarchical structure, unofficial and unreported activities, and an unknown profile in the public.

In order to limit the official and practical agency of NGOs, the Ministry of Interior also removed Article 12 of the Executive Regulations, which deprived NGOs of the right to access all information and documents of governmental organisations. The government also tightened the procedures for issuing permission/security clearance for NGOs. Whilst previously applicants were required to get security clearance only from the Judiciary, Intelligence Service, and Police, the number of required references increased to 13 centres, including the IRGC and in some cases Islamic seminaries.

As a consequence of the conservative government's actions, the general enthusiasm of society in civil activism and establishing NGOs declined over the years. Reformist activists mentioned in their interviews that many NGOs stopped their activities altogether, with many also banned from any activities and audit boards seizing their licences. The independent and critical NGOs had to rely on their own tiny resources and funds, which meant becoming irregular and weak in terms of activity and organisation. They also lost their members over time, and the number of registered members of NGOs did not grow. The official records on NGOs became unavailable, with the official website of the Ministry of Interior not updating its records after 2005. Thus, the available reports on the volume and performance of NGOs relied on the estimation and speculation of civil activists and officials. The Rouhani administration, in 2015, announced that between 2005 and 2013 the volume of NGOs decreased by half, totalling approximately 5,000 (Arman Newspaper, 2014). NGO activists acknowledged this decline in their interviews.

Thus, during 2005–2013, the elected and unelected institutions of the regime went under the uniform discourse and policy of the conservative camp, for the first time since the 1979 Revolution, with greater consistency formed between the conservative clerics and the military wing of the regime (Gheissari & Nasr, 2006; Ehteshami & Zweiri, 2009; Keshmiripour, 2015). This led to a stricter environment which limited the political opportunities for civil society's critical action and discourse.

## Conclusion

As a result of the limited circulation of power between opposing political camps, the political regime of Iran has dramatically changed the status of civil society across different periods. In line with the shifts in the 1997–2013 period, this status in terms of political opportunities shifted from 'open' during the reformist period to 'closed' during the conservative period.

By managing the decision-making process, the composition of civil society, policy preference and strategies, the rigidity of rules, and also changing the distribution of resources amongst loyal and critical civil society actors, the two governments acted quite differently.

During the reformist period, the liberal-oriented government opened up the public sphere and by making the environment more competitive, provided civil society with more opportunities to rise and act. The trends of the reformist government, along with the rise of spontaneous civil society, opened more access points in the state. However, alongside this, the authoritarian institutions under the conservative camp acted as a parallel government and sought to securitise politics and nullify the liberalising reforms.

In contrast, during the rule of the conservative camp, the exclusive strategy of the state towards civil society led to a dramatic decline not just in the volume but also in the vibrancy of civil society organisations. Conservatives also reduced public access and contact with the Executive and the Parliament. The unity of regime institutions made the public sphere climate consistent and strict for civil society.

To summarise, despite the pessimistic literature about undemocratic regimes being monolithic and strict in nature, this chapter showed otherwise; as the hybrid structure of Iran functioned resiliently and dynamically across two periods, so also did civil society.

## References


Abdolmohammadi, P., & Cama, G. (2015). Iran as a Peculiar Hybrid Regime: Structure and Dynamics of the Islamic Republic. *British Journal of Middle Eastern Studies*, 42(4), 558–578.

Abootalebi, A. R. (1998). Civil Society, Democracy, and the Middle East. *The Middle East Review of International Affairs (MERIA) Journal*, 2(3), 45–69.

Ajorloo, E., & Poshti, T. J. (2016). *The Legal System of NGOs in the Islamic Republic of Iran*. Tehran: Parhib.

Alamdari, K. (2005). The Power Structure of the Islamic Republic of Iran: Transition from Populism to Clientelism, and Militarization of the Government. *Third World Quarterly*, 26(8), 1285–1301.

Alem, A. (2002). *The Foundations of Political Science*. Tehran: Nashr-e-Ney.

Alexader, Y., & Hoenig, M. (2008). *The New Iranian Leadership: Ahmadinejad, Terrorism, Nuclear Ambition, and the Middle East*. London: Praeger Security International.

Amini, P. (2010). *The Sociology of the '22nd of Khordad': The 10th Presidential Election*. Tehran: Saghi.

*Arman Newspaper*. (2014, November 11). The Number of NGOs in Iran. http://armandaily.ir/1393/08/20/Files/PDF/13930820-2613-16-4.pdf.

Aslipur, H., & Sharifzadeh, V. (2015). The Environmental Policy Processes in Iran in the Framework of Policy Making Theories. *Iranian Journal of Majlis and Rahbord*, 22(83), 245–271.

Barzegar, J. (2005, June 28). Media During Khatami: The Smiling Face and Crying Eyes. Retrieved March 13, 2018, from *BBC*: http://www.bbc.com/persian/iran/story/2005/07/050728_a_jb_khatami_press.shtml.

Bashirieh, H. (1995). *Political Sociology: The Role of Political Actors in Social Life*. Tehran: Nei Publication.

Bashirieh, H. (2016). *An Introduction to the Political Sociology of Iran: The Age of Islamic Republic*. Tehran: Negah-e-Moaser.

BBC. (2009, June 9). *Guide: How Iran is ruled*. Retrieved October 2019, from http://news.bbc.co.uk/2/hi/middle_east/8051750.stm.

Beehner, L. (2007, July). *Iranian Civil Society and the Role of U.S. Foreign Policy*. Backgrounder.

Brumberg, D. (2001). *Reinventing Khomeini*. Chicago, IL: University of Chicago Press.

Cavatorta, F. (2010). The Convergence of Governance: Upgrading Authoritarianism in the Arab World and Downgrading Democracy Elsewhere? *Middle East Critique*, 19(3), 217–232.

Cavatorta, F. (2013). *Civil Society Activism Under Authoritarian Rule: A Comparative Perspective.* Oxon: Routledge.
Charteris-Black, J. (2018). Competition Metaphors and Ideology: Life as a Race. In R. Wodak, & B. Forchtner (eds.), *The Routledge Handbook of Language and Politics* (pp. 202–2017). London: Routledge.
Diamond, L. (2002a). Elections Without Democracy; Thinking About Hybrid Regimes. *Journal of Democracy,* 13(2), 21–35.
Diamond, L. J. (2002b). Thinking about Hybrid Regimes. *Journal of Democracy,* 13(2), 21–35.
Doyle, T., & Simpson, A. (2006). Traversing More than Speed Bumps: Green Politics under Authoritarian Regimes in Burma and Iran. *Environmental Politics,* 15(5), 750–767.
Duyvendak, J. W., & Giugni, M. G. (1995). Social Movement Types and Policy Domain. In H. Kriesi, R. Koopmans, J. W. Duyvendak, & M. G. Giugni (eds.), *New Social Movements in Western Europe: A Comparative Analysis* (pp. 82–110). Minneapolis: University of Minnesota Press.
Ehteshami, A., & Zweiri, M. (2009). *Iran and the Rise of its Neoconservatives: The Politics of Tehran's Silent Revolution.* London: I.B. Tauris.
Ertan, S. (2012, July). *Gender Equality Policies in Authoritarian Regimes and Electoral Democracies.* Paper presented at the 4th ECPR Graduate Conference. Jacobs University.
Eslami-Somea, R. (2001). *Human Rights in Sharia and Iran Constitutional and Legal System: The Case of Freedom of Expression*, PhD diss., Montreal University.
Farhi, F. (2012, February). Factional Politics and the Islamic Republic. In R. Parsi (ed.), *Iran: A Revolutionary Republic in Transition* (pp. 23–40). Paris: European Union Institute for Security Studies.
Fawcett, P., & Daugbjerg, C. (2012). Explaining Governance Outcomes: Epistemology, Network Governance and Policy Network. *Political Studies Review,* 10, 195–207.
Feirahi, D. (1999). Civil Society: The Dual Origin. In H. Laali (ed.), *What Does Khatami Speak About?* (pp. 72–99). Tehran: Ekhlas.
Forrest, D. (2009). *Abécédaire de la Societé de Surveillance.* Paris: Syllepse.
Fowler, A. (1993). Non-governmental Organizations as Agents of Democratization: An African Perspective. *Journal of International Development*, 5(3), 325–339.
Ganji, A. (2008). The Latter-Day Sultan: Power and Politics in Iran. *Foreign Affairs,* 87(6), 45–62, 64–66.
Gheissari, A., & Nasr, V. (2006). *Democracy in Iran: History and the Quest for Liberty.* Oxford: Oxford University Press.
Gholipur, R., & Ahangar, E. G. (2010). *The Process of Policymaking in Iran.* Tehran: The Research Centre of Iran's Parliament.
Goudarzi, R. M., & Najafinejad, A. (2017). Contemporary Traditionalists and Reformists Iranian Jurists and the Subject of Human Rights. *Muslim World Journal of Human Rights*, 15(1).
Green, J. D., Wehrey, F., & Wolf, C. (2009). *Understanding Iran.* Santa Monica: National Security Research Division.
Hawthrone, A. (2004). *Is Civil Society the Answer?* Middle East Series. Washington, DC: Carnegie Papers.
Heydemann, S. (2007, October). *Upgrading Authoritarianism in the Arab World.* The Saban Centre for Middle East Policy, 13. The Brookings Institution.

Holbrook-Provow, T. M., & Poe, S. C. (1987). Measuring State Political Ideology. *American Politics Quarterly*, 15(3), 399–416.

Holiday, J. S. (2011). *Defining Iran: Politics of Resistance*. Surrey: Ashgate Publishing Limited.

Huntington, S. P. (1996). *Political Order in Changing Societies*. London: Yale University Press.

Iran Data Portal. (2015, November). Family Ties of the Iranian Political Elite. *Tehran: Iran Data Portal*. Retrieved October 2019, from http://irandataportal.syr.edu/family-ties-of-the-iranian-political-elite.

Jahangiri, J., & Fatahi, S. (2010). Analysing Ahmadinejad's Discourse in the Tenth Presidential Election. *Iranian Social Studies*, 15(3), 23–47.

Kadivar, M. (2010, June 18). The Resistance of Supreme Leader Against the 'Assembly of Experts'. Retrieved January 30, 2018, from *BBC*: http://www.bbc.com/persian/iran/2010/07/100718_l39_kadivar_khamenei_khobregan.

Kamali, M. (2013, May 7). Iran's Electoral Elegance: the style Evolution of Mahmoud Ahmadinejad. Retrieved February 2018, from *The Guardian*: https://www.theguardian.com/world/iran-blog/2013/may/07/iran-electoral-mahmoud-ahmadinejad-style.

Kamali, M. (1998). *Revolutionary Iran: Civil Society and State in the Modernisation Process*. Aldershot: Ashgate Publishing Ltd.

Karasipahi, S. (2009). Comparing Islamic Resurgence Movements in Turkey and Iran. *Middle East Journal*, 63(1), 87–107.

Karl, T. L. (1995). The Hybrid Regimes of Central America. *Journal of Democracy*, 6(3), 72–86.

Kazemi, B. A. (2009). *The Reasons of Malfunctioning of Political Parties in Iran: The Islamic Republic Era*. Tehran: The Centre for Islamic Revolution Documents.

Keshmiripour, B. (2015, June 23). The Rise and Decline of Ahmadinejad: The Khamenei's Favourite President. Retrieved February 2018, from *Deutsche Welle*: http://p.dw.com/p/1Fkif.

Khajesarvi, G. (2010). *The Politics and Government in the Islamic Republic of Iran*. Tehran: Imam Sadiq University.

Khamenei, A. (2016, July 2). Organisations in Khamenei's Speech. *The Website of Iran's Supreme Leader*. Retrieved from http://farsi.khamenei.ir/speech-content?id=33694.

Korten, C. (1990). *Getting to the 21st Century: Voluntary Action and the Global Agenda*. Connecticut: Kumarian Press.

Kubba, L. (2000). Arabs and Democracy: The Awakening of Civil Society. *Journal of Democracy*, 11(3), 84–90.

Lapidus, I. (2000, September 25). Review of Elaine Sciolino's Persian Mirrors: The Elusive Face of Iran's. *The New York Times*.

Mir-Hosseini, Z., & Tapper, R. (2006). *Islam and Democracy in Iran: Eshkevari and the Quest for Reform*. London: I.B. Tauris.

Mohammadi, M. (2015). *A Study of the Constitution of the Islamic Republic of Iran*. Tehran: The SD Institute of Law Research and Study.

Moinifar, H. (2010). The Political Participation of Women in the Islamic Republic of Iran. In G. Khajesarvi (ed.), *The Politics and Government in Iran* (pp. 391–436). Tehran: Imam Sadigh Publications.

Mosallanejad, G. A. (2005). *State and Economical Development in Iran*. Tehran: Ghoomes Publication Company Ltd.

Namazi, B. (2000). *Iranian NGOs: Situation Analysis*. Hamyaran Center: Tehran.

Omidvar, K. (2005, October 10). *Internet During the Eight Years of Reformist.* Retrieved March 13, 2018, from BBC: http://www.bbc.com/persian/iran/story/2005/08/050810_pm-ka-internet-khatami.shtml.

Owen, R. (2004). *State Power and Politics in the Making of the Modern Politics.* London: Routledge.

Putnam, R. (1993). *Making Democracy Work.* Princeton, NJ: Princeton University Press.

Radio Zamaneh. (2011, July). *NGOs in the Islamic Republic of Iran.* Retrieved from https://www.radiozamaneh.com/34010.

Rakel, E. P. (2008). *The Iranian Political Elite, State and Society Relations, and Foreign Relations Since the Islamic Revolution.* Amsterdam: Universiteit van Amsterdam.

Rakel, E. P. (2009). The Political Elite in the Islamic Republic of Iran: From Khomeini to Ahmadinejad. *Comparative Studies of South Asia, Africa and the Middle East*, 29(1), 105–125.

Razzaghi, S. (2010). *State of Civil Society in Iran.* Tehran: Asreh Sevom (Third Arena).

Rivetti, P. (2013). Co-Opting Civil Society Activism in Iran. In P. Aarts, & F. Cavatorta (eds.), *Civil Society in Syria and Iran: Activism in Authoritarian Contexts* (pp. 187–203). London: Lynne Rienner Publisher.

Sajoo, A. B. (2004). *Civil Society in the Muslim World: Contemporary Perspectives.* London: I.B. Tauris.

Savoski, K. (2018). Policy-making: Documents and Laws. In R. Wodak, & B. Forchtner (eds.), *The Routledge Handbook of Language and Politics* (pp. 355–366). London: Routledge.

Sreberny, A. (2013). Thirty-plus Years of the Iranian Revolution. In A. Sreberny, & M. Torfeh (eds.), *Cultural Revolution in Iran* (pp. 1–12). New York: I.B Tauris & Co Ltd.

Tazmini, G. (2013). *Khatami's Iran: The Islamic Republic and the Turbulent Path to Reform.* London: I.B. Tauris & Co.

Tezcur, G. M. (2012). Democracy Promotion, Authoritarian Resiliency, and Political Unrest in Iran. *Democratization*, 19(1), 120–140.

Thaler, D. E., Nader, A., Chubin, S., Green, J. D., Lynch, C., & Wehrey, F. (2010). *Mullahs, Guards, and Bonyads: an Exploration of Iranian Leadership Dynamics.* Santa Monica, CA: RAND (National Defence Research Institute).

Wigell, M. (2008). Mapping 'Hybrid Regimes': Regime Types and Concepts in Comparative Politics. *Democratisation*, 15(2), 230–250.

Zarifinia, H. (1998). *Assessing the Political Streams in Iran: From 1980 to 2000.* Tehran: Azadi-e-Andishe.

Zeidabadi, A. (2005, June 31). Khatami and Civil Society: Dead End of Theory and Action. Retrieved March 13, 2018, from *BBC*: http://www.bbc.com/persian/iran/story/2005/07/050731_sm-z-khatami-cs.shtml.

# 5 Reinvention of nationalism and the moral panic against foreign aid in Egypt

*Ahmed El Assal and Amr Marzouk*

## Introduction

Financing civil society activities has grown exponentially since the 1990s. Following the third wave of democratisation, several donors, either bilateral or multilateral agencies, have heavily supported and funded activities of civil society organisations (CSOs) in the Global South. After this transition in the global order, CSOs played a fundamental role to support the spread of liberal norms and neoliberal policies, such as supporting the state through playing an intermediary role in public service provision, in addition to their political role in supporting democratisation processes through the expansion of civic education, human rights promotion and advocacy (Edwards, 2009; Barnett, 2011; Dietrich and Wright, 2015; Dupuy et al., 2016). CSOs, especially organisations that primarily work on advocacy and human rights issues, are often criticised by authoritarian governments for receiving foreign funds. Among several strategies to curtail the activities of these CSOs, banning foreign funds became one way to disempower and undermine the activities of these organisations and stifle the way they operate.

Furthermore, aid effectiveness and monitoring of foreign funds are among the key factors for authoritarian and hybrid regimes to justify their repressive practices and restrictions on foreign aid. Authoritarian governments often claim that funding approval is simply an issue of transparency or of combating "foreign plots" (Ruffner, 2015). As recently observed, governments use both arguments to adopt a more restrictive legal framework on the activities and sources of funding for both local and global CSOs, which are well documented in recent civil society literature (Christensen & Weinstein, 2013; Carothers & Brechenmacher, 2014; Rutzen, 2015; El Assal, 2019).

Amid a growing trend of shrinking space for civil society and rapid shifts in the social, economic and political landscape in the MENA region, it becomes crucial to understand how authoritarian and hybrid regimes control and consolidate power over the civil society sphere during transition phases. Since 2013, Egyptian civil society has been portrayed as an enemy for both the state and the people. After the 25 January 2011 revolution in Egypt, the issue of foreign funds for Egyptian CSOs became the main headline in any policy or public debate regarding civil society legislation in Egypt. In late 2011 the Egyptian security forces broke into the headquarters of many international and national organisations. This sparked what later became known as the foreign fund case.

The main research question that constitutes this chapter is: how did moral panic concerning foreign funds, and the new framing of nationalism, affect the space for civil society organisations to operate in Egypt? In this chapter, the authors examine the reinvention of nationalism discourse after the 2011 uprising and the state of moral panic against foreign aid to civil society organisations. The successive Egyptian governments which came to power after 2011 and 2013 have used nationalist discourses and practices to criticise the provision of foreign aid assistance to civil society organisations. Nevertheless, the Egyptian media significantly played a foundation role in supporting the reinvention of nationalist discourse, since 2013. It played, however, a major role in spreading smear campaigns and widespread foreign aid criticism to civil society groups, particularly after the investigation of Case 173 known as 'the foreign fund case', which constitutes the main case study for this chapter.

This chapter is structured as follows. First, the background to foreign fund Case 173 is presented, which will be followed by a theoretical discussion on the concept of moral panic and how this is related to the Egyptian case study. Afterwards, the authors discuss the reinvention of nationalism in the Egyptian context and trace the origins of the concept and how it has evolved. Moreover, the fate of civil society in Egypt is discussed, building on recent legislation changes and how local organisations adapt under severe restrictions on foreign funding. Finally, results of a thematic analysis of 28 feature articles from two newspapers in Egypt, *Youm Saba* and *Sout el Oma*, is presented. The selected features were written by the newspaper's staff, since articles would represent the opinion of its authors, while features carry more journalistic work from the newspaper. The features which are analysed cover the period between 2016–2018.

## Case 173 in the context of foreign aid policies

Following the 2011 uprising, the allocated foreign aid to civil society organisations in Egypt increased dramatically. As shown in Figure 5.1, the amount of foreign aid channelled to civil society organisations almost tripled from about 51 million USD in 2010 to almost 161 million USD. According to the latest statistics from the Organisation of Economic Cooperation and Development (OECD) – Crediting Report System (CRS), US foreign aid was the highest Official Development Assistance (ODA) given to CSOs between 2010 and 2017. Notably, the received foreign aid amount increased between 2011 and 2013. Yet, the volume decreased gradually after the ousting of former President Morsi in July 2013, with a slight increase in 2015. This influx of foreign funds to civil society organisations after the 2011 uprising, to local

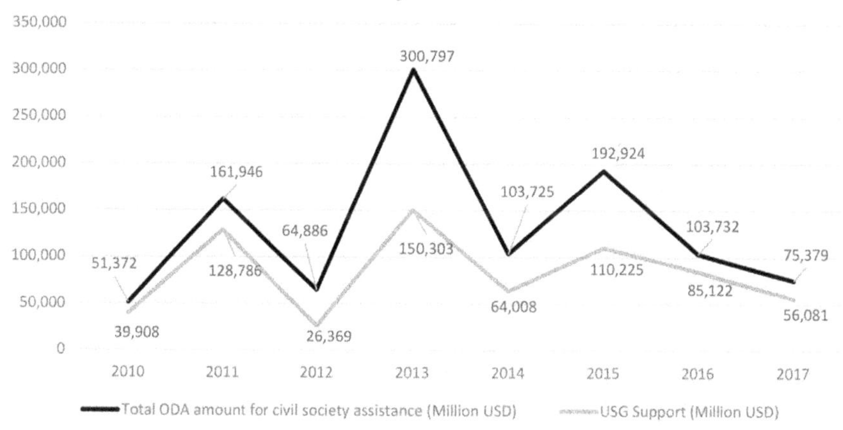


*Figure 5.1* Total amount of ODA support to CSOs between 2010 and 2017
Source: Figures adapted by the author according to the OECD – CRS database.

and international organisations, raised the Egyptian government concerns regarding the type of activities as well as sources of funding for local and international civil society organisations.

Since 2011, foreign aid has become a major policy and public debate concerning civil society activities in Egypt. Only five months after the ousting of former President Mubarak, the Ministry of Justice launched an investigation into foreign funding of local and international civil society organisations' activities in Egypt. Moreover, in December 2011, the Egyptian security apparatus raided the premises of several international civil society organisations, mainly American and German organisations, and arrested about 43 Egyptian and foreign aid workers in a widely controversial legal case known in the media as Case 173.

In June 2013, Case 173 was split into two sections, one concerning international organisations working in Egypt, and another concerning local civil society organisations. The first ruling for the international organisations section of the case was on June 2013, when 32 defendants were given sentences ranging from two to five years in prison, while 11 others were handed a suspended sentence of one year in prison. The Cairo Criminal Court (CCC) charged the organisations' employees with receiving money from foreign sources "with the intention of harming national interests or threatening the state's sovereignty" and running unlicensed organisations (Mada Masr, 2019). However, five years later, in December 2018, all aid workers were acquitted (TIMEP, 2019).

In May 2017, the Egyptian president, el-Sisi, approved a new law that organised the work of civil society organisations, known as law 70 of 2017. The law was primarily drafted by the parliament, in November 2016, and then approved by the president six months later. Notably, the law was drafted and presented to the president without any social dialogue or consultation with independent civil society organisations, despite the fact that many organisations had contributed to previous drafts prepared earlier. As a result, this law had a repressive nature and was widely criticised by local and international civil society organisations, governments and UN agencies. The law put forward harsh sanctions for organisations that receive foreign funding without prior approval from the ministry of social solidarity, whether these funds are from outside Egypt or from foreigners inside Egypt. The punishment of spending from a non-approved grant can lead to severe penalties, that is, imprisonment, fines, or the dissolution of the organisation. The law also brought security agencies to the forefront of the approval processes for any foreign aid grants or operation of international organisations. Any foreign grant would be reviewed and approved by a newly established monitoring mechanism, mainly formulated from different security apparatus.

Several attempts through local organisations and international actors, including the UN, EU and US government, urged the Egyptian government to revisit the newly adopted law – due to its repressive nature. These efforts have forced the parliament to revisit the approved law and prepare an amended law, taking into consideration the main conflicted issues included in law 70. Nevertheless, in August 2019, President el-Sisi ratified a new law No. 149 of 2019 on activities of nongovernmental organisations (NGOs). The new law replaced the controversial law No. 70 of 2017. The law, comprising 97 articles, addresses how the Ministry of Social Solidarity (MoSS) oversees the funding and activities of local and international CSOs in the country and imposes a number of fines against violators. Although some articles in the new law were revised, however, it still didn't address the fundamental flaws that hinder a free and open civil society sector.

In addition to restrictive civil society legislation, Egypt's status of freedom of expression has dramatically fallen a few years after the 2011 revolution, because of stern restrictions by the state which in turn means that self-censorship has become common in the Egyptian media (Mansour, 2015). Since 2011, the majority of the state led Egyptian media have harshly criticised civil society organisations, in general, and human rights organisations, in particular, for receiving foreign funds. This criticism escalated after Case 173, where much of press coverage portrayed civil society organisations as Western mouthpieces aiming to spread chaos or foreign agents seeking to steal foreign funds to become rich.

This discourse has become a predominant narrative to justify restricted legislation aimed at controlling foreign funds channelled to civil society organisations. As described in one of the newspapers, *El Watan* in an investigation report,

> Foreign funding is an accusation that has been following human rights organisations since the 25 January upraising, and even before, as many parliamentarians and politicians described it as easy money "*Elsaboba*". Many human rights activists take advantage of it to become millionaires,

> nevertheless, this in addition to harming national security which has led the parliament to issue a new law to counter that.
>
> (*El Watan*, 2018a)

Another report from the same newspaper, *El Watan* argues that from the parliamentarians' point of view, the new civil work law will "stop the foreign funding faucet" that contributes to "easy money for human rights activists" and is used to "create violence against the state" and it should be controlled (*El Watan*, 2018b).

In the above two examples, explanation of the Cairo Criminal Court and news coverage, human rights defenders and civil society organisation members are framed as a threat to national interest, security and state sovereignty. In the following sections, we argue that this framing is part of a moral panic process started by the state and its media towards human rights organisations in Egypt. In this moral panic framing, the fear for national unity, national values and patriotism is at stake.

## Moral panic: smoke with no fire

'Moral panic' is a criminological term which describes a political discourse (Altheide, 2009 cited in Greer and Reiner, 2014:6). The theory of moral panic highlights the process of how a social problem is brought into the spotlight, yet there is no real interest in exploring the reality of the problem. Instead, it is used to provide a reason for social and legal shift within a criminal justice system (Rohloff and Wright, 2010:404). Moral panic describes the anxiety within society and the official reaction for the rise in reported numbers of certain offences (Cohen, 1972; Young, 1971, Hall et al., 1978 cited in Waddington, 1986:245).

The term 'moral panic' was coined by Young in 1971 in his study of drugs-consuming subcultures (Greer and Reiner, 2014:5). Cohen identified moral panic and its process as

> [a] condition, episode, person, or group of persons emerges to become defined as a threat to societal values and interests; its nature is presented in a stylised and stereotypical fashion by the mass media; the moral barricades are manned by editors, bishops, politicians, and other right-thinking people; socially accredited experts pronounce their diagnoses and solutions; ways of coping are evolved (or more often) resorted to; the condition then disappears, submerges, or deteriorates and becomes more visible.
>
> (Cohen, 1972:9)

In his explanation for the process of 'reaction', Cohen states that it takes place when society perceives a specific subculture or social group as a threat to the wider culture and the values held by society. For Cohen, he perceived the state of this process by the hands of mass media and other social institutions which exaggerate the perceived threat towards society (Cohen, 1972; Hier and Greenberg, 2002, cited in Emmanuel, 2014:2). Cohen states that moral panic can sometimes lead to a long-lasting change within the fabric of society and the policies of the legal system but also it can pass by and be forgotten (Cohen, 1972:9).

In his work, Cohen identified key elements in the process which creates moral panic. He perceived mass media as the main initiator of moral panic through communicating the coded images of deviants and their deviance to construct a certain label in an exaggerated way (Cohen, 1972:31–38, Cree and Clapton, 2016). What comes afterwards is the beginning of the moral panic process. The media will start to predict scenarios to highlight the dangers of allowing this incident to go unanswered, or as Cohen put it "that what had happened was inevitably going to happen again" (Cohen, 1972:38). The main role of the mass media in Cohen's analysis is not only creating labels but as he stated, "symbols and labels eventually acquire their own descriptive and explanatory potential" (Cohen, 1972: 40–41). Another key element seen by Cohen are the moral entrepreneurs; this term was coined by Becker who used it to describe those who create the standards and the rules and the enforcers of these rules, and also what is deemed deviant and what is not (Shulman, 2005:427). The third element is the group of politicians and the practitioners of the criminal justice system, those who represent the social control institutions (Cree and Clapton, 2016; Emmanuel, 2014:4). Finally comes the public which plays a role in believing either the narrative created by the media and politicians or the group under threat.

Hall et al., in their study of the moral panic about mugging in the UK, explored the political motivation behind the moral panic process (Hall et al., 1978). Hall et al. stated that within a capitalist society, there will always be class fractions, and to avoid this class tension the elite will create a moral panic to maintain power, and will use moral panic as a scapegoat (Hall et al., 1978:157). Hall et al. employed the concept of "hegemony" by Antonio Gramsci to understand the disproportionality of the response from institutions and society towards a certain group. In his work, Gramsci argued that the state in a capitalist society will work in favour of the elites to modify civil society to maintain the capitalist hold over it, or in other words, the state will keep reproducing social norms and relations in favour of capitalism (Hall et al., 1978:201). The moral entrepreneurs for Hall et al. were those who create "common sense", who are the elites or as he stated, "(t)he world bounded by 'common sense' is the world of the subordinate classes" (Hall et al, 1978:154).

## Building the nation, creating unity: the Egyptian value of nationalism/patriotism

In moral panic theory, it's important to understand that the main moral entrepreneurs are those who have the exclusive power to define something as a threat to the values of society. But to have this power they need to claim to be the watch guards of these social values, thus if the state in Egypt wants to use moral panic regarding nationalism and patriotism they need to be the only entity to claim total knowledge of these values. It is important to note that in the Arabic language there is no differences between nationalism, 'El Watania' and patriotism, 'El Watania'. In this section, we argue that the Egyptian state as a post-colonial state with a political regime with strong army ties, at least since 1952, can claim this entrepreneur status.

The concept of nationalism was invented in Europe at the beginning of the nineteenth century (Kedourie, 1993:1). Eric Hobsbawm made a connection between the rise of nationalism and the rise of the 'state aspiring national movements' (Hobsbawm, 1994: 78). The term had lots of different definitions, for instance it can be perceived as

> A type of social consciousness or movement, sometimes associated with an ideology but always with ethnic interests, and it should be noted that we do not have interests, but are possessed by them, identified with them, or "constituted out of" them.
>
> (Mead, 1955:386 cited in Drakulic, 2008:222)

Furthermore, Charles Taylor defined it as a collective identity that emerged from ideological relations with others (1994a: 32–6 cited in Drakulic, 2008:223), while Gellner sees it as "primarily a political principle, which holds that the political and the national unit should be congruent" (Gellner, 1983:1).

The definition we are using in this chapter is the consensus among social scientists who perceive nationalism as "appertains to a specific framework for the organisation of social relations and social reproduction" (Anderson, 1983; Gellner, 1983; Balibar, 1996 cited in Gelvin, 1999:74).

If nationalism as a concept focuses on the relation between individuals, the concept of patriotism describes more the relation between individuals and the state or the nation as an entity. Patriotism is the love for and loyalty to one's country (Tan, 2004:137). For Primoratz, it is seen as a "duty of special concern for the well-being of our country and compatriots" (Primoratz, 2009 cited in Sardoc, 2017:45). Robert Audi goes along the same lines when he defines patriotism, perceiving it as

> at least three different kinds of things: a trait of character, as where we speak of a person who is patriotic to the core; an emotion, as where people are described as glowing with patriotism or bursting with pride in their country; and (perhaps by extension from these more basic cases) a position, such as the view that one owes loyalty to one's country.
>
> (Audi, 2009:367)

We can argue that while nationalism is based on a political reality which is translated to a legal fact, patriotism is a value-based emotion. In this chapter we are arguing that post the 2011 revolution in Egypt, the state represented in the Army as the actual ruler of the state between 2011–2012 and then again between 2013 and now has a monopoly over the concept of patriotism and nationalism in Egypt.

There is much work on the origin of Egyptian nationalism as an idea. For instance, Khaled Fahmy argued that Mohamed Aly military conscription and discrimination against Egyptian officers played a role in the emergence of nationalism mainly with the Urabi revolt (Fahmy, 1997, in Geer, 2011:30). On the other hand, Yara Sultan argued that Egyptian intellectuals are the ones who introduced the concept to the Egyptian public (Sultan, 2016:34). Despite the argument of when Egyptian nationalism was conceived it's important to note that the coup of 1952 was an important moment in reconstructing this nationalism and patriotism as well.

The question of nationalism during Nasser is both intriguing and problematic at the same time. According to Sherif Youunis' detailed body of work regarding Nasserism, the free officer movement legitimacy to rule Egypt which required them to make sure that no other ideology could claim to represent the voices of the people (Younis, 2005:95). Which entails that the only ideology the free officers invested in (and Nasser as well) was nationality and patriotism; this was needed to face the other ideologies within society (communists, Muslim brotherhood, liberals). This led the free officers/Nasser to assert this monopoly of nationalism and patriotism on different occasions. For instance, in the philosophy of the revolution, Nasser's own writing and conceptualization for the coup states

> The situation needed a coherent power whose members are brought together within one framework, and who are not involved, to an extent, in individual or class conflicts. This power had to be drawn from the people [al-sha'b], and for its members to be able to trust one another, and for them to have within their capacity the material power which would guarantee a quick and decisive action. These criteria only applied to the army. […] It was rather the development of events which defined for the army its role in the colossal struggle to liberate the nation.
>
> (Nasser, 2005:29 cited in Moustafa, 2017:24)

Here Nasser asserts that the change in Egypt needed a power above individuals and classes, a power that represents all Egyptians which is the army. Then Nasser follows that by saying

> Was it a must that we, the army, had to carry out what we did on 23rd July [1952]? […] The answer is: Yes! There was no escape! Today, I can say: We are living two revolutions, not only one.
>
> (26 cited in Moustafa, 2017:24)

Nasser here shows that the army did not seek power, but due to its nationalistic role it took the role, that it is not there because it wants to, but as Nasser asserts "there was no escape". In her book on the Egyptian army image in popular culture, Dalia Moustafa perceives this as the main foundation to the image of the army as both saviour and hero, an image still dominating the discourse regarding the civil–military relationships in Egypt (Moustafa, 2017:23).

The discourse of Nasser and the history of Egypt also played a role in shaping the idea of nationalism in Egypt. In his work regarding Egypt, Hibbard notes that Egyptian nationalism is not based on a certain ideology as much as a territorial distinction against foreign occupation (Hibbard, 2010:56). However, as Yara Sultan remarked "That is, it appears that the appeal of the Egyptian army itself had initially been more powerful than any specific ideological orientation" (Sultan, 2016:45). This is important to understanding the role of the army in Egypt in political life as an entity with a monopoly over the concept of nationalism as an entity beyond class, religion, race and patriotism as those who sacrifice their lives for the country and always willing to step up to save it.

## National unity as a value threatened by foreign aid

Whether foreign aid is always embraced by low- and middle-income countries is still controversial, due to its political nature. Dupuy et al. argue that authoritarian governments will "forego valuable international assistance and risk their international reputations" when aid to CSOs is seen to challenge their political survival. In addition, they might risk being named and shamed by international organisations, the media and donor governments (2016:300). Given the context of the Egyptian case after the 2011 and 2013 transition, this argument partially explains the formal and informal state discourse and practices against channelling foreign aid to local and international organisations in the country and the adoption of a more restrictive environment for CSOs. The longstanding formal and official links between Egyptian CSOs and bilateral and multilateral donors opened up further debates on the "political nature of foreign funding and reinforced a discourse of distrust of links with global forces" (Abdelrahman, 2011:419).

Abdelrahman (2007) argues that the Egyptian state has always promoted that it upholds the national interests as a major source of legitimacy and for the regime survival. In her argument, Abdelrahman clarifies that the ruling elite, during the twentieth century, restored several symbols and sources to support this claim. This included the promotion of Pan Arab Nationalism and the Arab Unity, as well as the need to counter the threats posed by the Israel State. This manifestation of nationalism, during the Mubarak era, was used to counter criticism by civil society organisations, particularly human rights organisations, of the government. An argument that was heavily used described human rights organisations as the mouthpieces of the West, due to their sources of funding. Abdelrahman (2007:287) sees that in doing so

> The regime has largely discredited the human rights movement which it regards as posing a threat to its hegemony, and has gained a degree of legitimacy in the eyes of the public by representing itself as the protector of national interests.

This nationalisation of the human rights debate, by the establishment of the National Council for Human Rights (NCHR), opened doors for the government to benefit from available foreign funding sources from bilateral and multilateral donors such as the UNDP and the Ford Foundation, as well as from the Netherlands and Denmark (Abdelrahman, 2007). This in return, allowed the government to control, to some extent, the human rights discourse in the country and the messages it sent to the international community.

The crackdown on CSO foreign funding sources can not only be seen from the perspective that governments fear the existence of stronger civil society organisations. Dupuy et al., (2016) confirm this argument and state that authoritarian regimes may impose restrictions on foreign funding to win support among citizens, especially if foreign donors are unpopular due to historical and political reasons. This, of course, can be seen in the context of Egypt specifically, and the Arab world more generally, due to the long-standing Arab-Israeli conflict and US bias towards the Israeli side. Washington's perceived role and influence in the Middle East region has considerably decreased since the Obama era. However, from a historical perspective the key elements of US Middle East policy have not changed significantly (Paragi, 2019). According to GALLUP's survey in February 2012, a large majority of Egyptians, about 85 per cent, said they opposed US money sent to Egyptian civil society groups (Younis and Younis, 2012). Depicting the West as the traditional enemy of the Egyptian nation having directly reflected on the relationship between civil society organisations, who receive foreign aid, and western countries, Prat (2006:13) argues that:

> The foreign funding debate represents Egypt and the West as two diametrically opposed and essentially different entities. The notion of difference and opposition renders the West an enemy that threatens the very existence of the Egyptian nation. This discourse also represents Egyptian civil society as a target for the West in seeking to undermine the Egyptian nation.

While the shrinking of civil society space and the limitation on foreign aid support to civil society organisations intensified after periods of transition in 2011 and 2013, several previous legal measures to restrict the sources of funding to CSOs had been in place during the Mubarak era and even before. During Nasser's era the state established a comprehensive system of state control over civil society to limit the political and social influence of the Muslim Brotherhood, codified in the law of association (law 32 of 1964; Brechenmacher, 2017). The same restrictions on foreign aid existed during the Mubarak era; article 17 of law 84/2002 denies the right of associations to accept contributions from abroad—and in some cases from Egyptian sources—unless specifically authorised by the government. Government approval is often slow or never comes at all.

## The fate of CSOs in Egypt

After almost seven years of judicial dispute, in December 2018, the CCC acquitted defendants in Case 173, known as Egypt's foreign funding case, from charges of receiving unlawfully $60 million in foreign funds to support activities of local and international organisations in Egypt (*Egypt Today*, 2018). The resolution of this phase of the case has been a key sticking point in US–Egyptian relations. The court decision came after a retrial granted by the Court of Cassation in April 2018. From a legal perspective, the court verdict laid the ground for a vital explanation of the foreign funding future in the country. The court reasoning clearly stated that "foreign funding is not a criminal act per the Law", moreover, it clarified that treating such funding as a crime makes it seem "akin to espionage, smuggling, and other sensationalist descriptions intended to agitate public opinion" (TIMEP, 2019).

Nevertheless, Egyptian organisations that were added to the case later in 2016 are still under investigation. Several prominent human rights organisations, such as the Arab Network for Human Rights, Cairo Institute for Human Rights, Egyptian Initiative for Personal Rights, among others, were added to the case by the Egyptian prosecution on the same grounds of accusation of receiving illegal foreign funds. Leaders of these organisations have been exposed to severe measures of assets freeze (Yousef, 2016; Ahram Online; 2017), travel bans (Chick, 2017; Amnesty International, 2018), and closure of their offices (Abaza, 2017; Ruffner, 2015). The court verdict in Case 173 will provide the Egyptian CSOs involved in the same case with a strong argument to challenge the accusations and investigation process. As summarised by the Tahir Institute for Middle East Policy (2018):

> The court's reasoning in Case 173 is narrow, as it does not obligate a constitutional review of any of the relevant penal code and NGO law provisions in question. At the same time however, the court's unequivocal language on both the recognition of NGO registration paperwork and the legality of receiving foreign funding provides a clear basis upon which those who continue to face prosecution under the same case in its second phase can, in a compelling manner and while citing the court's reasoning, legally challenge the freezing of their assets, the listing of their names on the travel ban list, and the bringing of such charges against them.

Most recently, the CCC has postponed a hearing about removing the travel bans imposed on 13 human rights activists affiliated to the organisations under investigation. Although the court ordered the investigating magistrate to present official documentation of the travel ban and the reasoning behind it ahead of the next hearing, the investigating magistrate has failed to present the documentation. In fact, all 13 human rights activists accused in this case and appealing the travel bans have gone to trial, leaving them in a state of "legal limbo" (Mada Masr, 2019).

Responses to restrictions on foreign aid can take several forms, ranging from condemnation of international actors on restrictive measures put in place to threatening to cut other forms of aid channelled to the government. For example, Case 173 raised tensions between both the Egyptian and the US governments. This backlash against local and international organisations "triggered an unprecedented response from the U.S. congress, which delayed and threatened to withhold $1.3 billion in military assistance" (Christensen & Weinstein, 2013:78). During that time, out of the regular annual $1.5 billion US support to Egypt, only $60 million was allocated to support CSO activities. Furthermore, the European Parliament has published several statements and resolutions condemning the restrictions on civil spaces and freedoms in Egypt (Abdel Kouddous, 2018). Other international actors, including the UN, have regularly urged the Egyptian government to adhere to its commitment towards human rights standards and international agreements ratified by the Egyptian government (OHCHR, 2016). The international pressure and criticism of the restrictions against civil society organisations has pushed the Egyptian government to rethink the approved NGO law. In November 2018, President el-Sisi decided to amend the beleaguered NGO law, 18 months after ratifying it and despite having previously refused to do so (Mamdouh, 2018).

## Thematic analysis of selected feature articles (2016–2018)

In order to give more flesh to the claims presented in this article, we conducted a thematic analysis of the 28 feature articles published by two leading newspapers in Egypt: *Youm Saba* (the 7th day) and *Sout el Oma* (voice of the nation) in the period 2016 to 2018 and featuring tags "foreign funding" and "NGO's case". This choice obviously limits the general scope of the research, however, it is dictated by the method applied. Since our primary concern was to identify, analyse and report patterns (themes) within data, in line with Braun & Clarke's take on thematic analysis (Braun & Clarke, 2006:6), we were only interested in journalistic output reflecting opinions of the authors reflected in the overall tone and narrative visible in the pieces. Feature articles offered an excellent opportunity to do this. It needs to be emphasised, however, that the findings based on this method would have been complemented generously by the much broader analysis of the remaining journalistic outputs, also with the use of discourse analysis.

The thus conducted thematic analysis was carried out in the following steps: We started by familiarising ourselves with the data in hand, the different features in the newspapers. Then in the second reading we systematically started to take notes regarding the description of the case and the human rights defenders who were accused. Afterwards we coded the findings, exploring the number of themes generated, which allowed us to identify three main patterns emerging from the approach taken in the feature articles.

We found the following themes clearest in the coverage of foreign funding by the newspapers: international interference, easy money, taking the state down, chaos, terrorism. Clearly, all of the articles contained a negative depiction of the accused human rights defenders (HRDs) and NGOs. The description of their activities varied from accusations of treason to simply calling them illegitimate. The newspapers painted an image of NGOs receiving foreign funding as traitors to the country, conspirators, as if, almost, they amassed their wealth as a result of war. The coverage also painted human rights in general as a way to allow foreigners to interfere in the country's internal affairs, and drew a connection between HRDs in Egypt and international human rights organisations and states such as the US, Qatar, Iran and Turkey.

For instance, *Sout El Oma* published a series of feature articles about the human rights defenders under investigation in Case 173 called "the forbidden funding". The series depicted five activists, two of whom were political activists and the other three human rights defenders. The series of features focused on accusing them of becoming rich from their work, highlighting how many times they travel each month (Abd El Latif, 2017a). In one case, the author spoke of the religion of the wife of one of the HRDs mentioned, highlighting that she is a foreigner and a Muslim, despite the fact that her religion had no substantive implications for the case (Abd El Latif, 2017b). In another article, another HRD was heavily criticised for how he attacked Palestinians on his Facebook page, drawing the conclusion that this is an attempt to be on the good side of Israel, again despite the fact that this has nothing to do with the case (Abd El Latif, 2017c). In another *Sout el Oma* article, the authors referred to the accused HRD's Facebook statuses posted during the Adha feast in Egypt. The feature reports how the alleged "people of evil" participate in the celebrations (Abd El Latif, 2017d).

Another current characteristic of the coverage was the absence of the accused HRD's voice. Only one of 28 feature articles interviewed two of the accused HRDs. The remainder reported only the state voices such as those of the Members of Parliament, or human rights organisations which are not accused of receiving foreign funding. In the second case, all of these organisations' representatives spoke about the danger of foreign funds and the conspiracy towards Egypt. Moreover, there is also a connection painted between HRDs in Egypt and international organisations such as Human Rights Watch and Amnesty International, which are constantly accused of being agents of other countries.

Finally, despite the fact that the case is about foreign funds, the coverage tends to expand the accusations to questions of patriotism, for instance *Sout el Oma* published a list of organisations that did not vote for Amb Mousira Khatab in the UNESCO bid,[1] stating that they are traitors and unpatriotic (Abd El Latif, 2017e). In fact, patriotism or lack of it, is the general theme in branding the human rights organisations, and human rights defenders when it comes to foreign funding.

The above presented results of the thematic analysis of the cases built on accepting foreign funding by NGOs shows the representation of these as entangled with other cases based on rejection of civil society freedoms, political freedoms and the countering of the revolution. Altogether the activities of HRDs and NGOs amount to a threat to Egypt as a symbolic entity to whom patriotic feelings are owed at all times. Each of the arguments used by the authors (and, therefore, approved as an editorial choice by the two newspapers) contribute to the rise of moral panic in Egypt.

## Conclusion

Since the birth of the post-colonial Egyptian state, the reception of foreign funds, in particular by civil society organisations in Egypt has always been presented as an act akin to treason, demonstrating lack of patriotism and a threat to national unity. It is an indisputable fact that the post-1952 regime in Egypt has maintained a monopoly over the concept of national unity and patriotism. This has enabled the state to work as a moral entrepreneur to define what these two concepts entail. This has allowed the state to control public discourse by maintaining moral panic status regarding foreign funds and legitimising the persecution of its recipients.

This reached its highest peak in the aftermath of the 25 January 2011 revolution. Describing civil society organisation members as the mouthpieces of the West and 99accusing the organisations' employees of receiving money from foreign sources have the intention of harming national interests or threatening the state's sovereignty. The state used the case of foreign funding to create an image through the media of human rights defenders as traitors and agents of the West; this led eventually to changes in the penal code and the NGO law of 2017.

In this chapter we tried to highlight the importance of employing criminological theories such as moral panic in non-Western countries. We have attempted to show the validity of the theory to explain the relation between patriotism and nationalism and civil society in Egypt. However, we are aware of the limitation of the analysis, due to the fact that the foreign funding case is entangled with other topics such as civil society freedoms, political freedoms, international relations and the revolution. We recommend a deeper multidisciplinary research employing more quantitative and qualitative tools, across different media to be able to establish a more thorough understanding of the phenomenon of legitimisation of the measures targeting CSO funding.

## Note

1 Amb Mousira Khattab was running for the presidency of UNESCO in 2017; she lost the elections.

## References

Abaza, J. (2017) *Al-Nadeem center for torture victims fights its closure in Cairo* [online]. Available at: https://www.atlanticcouncil.org/blogs/menasource/al-nadeem-center-for-torture-victims-fights-its-closure-in-cairo/ [Accessed: 21 October 2019].

Abd El Latif, A. (2017a) *The Black list of Ngos who refused to support Amb Mousira Khatab* [online]. Available at: bit.ly/2usTfjs [Accessed: 7 February 2020]. [In Arabic].

Abd El Latif, A. (2017b) *How did the people of evil spend their Adha feast* [online]. Available at: bit.ly/2Pqjnmq [Accessed: 7 February 2020]. [In Arabic].

Abd El Latif, A. (2017c) *The stars of the forbidden foreign fund, what they were and what they have become, Gamal Eid* [online]. Available at: bit.ly/37ZpwfN [Accessed: 7 February 2020]. [In Arabic].

Abd El Latif, A. (2017d) *The stars of the forbidden foreign fund, what they were and what they have become, Israa abd el Fattah* [online]. Available at: bit.ly/3950A7S [Accessed: 7 February 2020]. [In Arabic].

Abd El Latif, A. (2017e) *The stars of the forbidden foreign fund, what they were and what they have become, Wael Abbas* [online]. Available at: bit.ly/32qr2GK [Accessed: 7 February 2020]. [In Arabic].

Abdel Kouddous, S. (2018) *European Parliament adopts resolution condemning human rights violations in Egypt* [online]. Available at: https://mada21.appspot.com/madamasr.com/en/2018/12/13/news/u/european-parliament-adopts-resolution-condemning-human-rights-violations-in-egypt/ [Accessed: 25 October 2019].

Abdelrahman, M. (2007) 'The nationalisation of the human rights debate in Egypt'. *Nations and Nationalism*, 13(2), 285–300.

Abdelrahman, M. (2011) 'The transnational and the local: egyptian activists and transnational protest networks'. *British Journal of Middle Eastern Studies*, 38(3), 407–424.

*Ahram Online* (2017) *Continued asset freeze for two Egyptian rights activists shows 'worrying trend': EU* [online]. Available at: http://english.ahram.org.eg/NewsContent/1/0/254952/Egypt/0/Continued-asset-freeze-for-two-Egyptian-rights-act.aspx [Accessed: 21 October 2019].

Amnesty International (2018) *Egypt: Repeal draconian NGO law following President's calls for review* [online]. Available at: https://www.amnesty.org/en/latest/news/2018/11/egypt-repeal-draconian-ngo-law-following-presidents-calls-for-review/ [Accessed: 21 October 2019].

Anderson, B. (1983) *Imagined communities: Reflections on the origins and spread of nationalism* (Revised edition). London; New York: Verso.

Audi, R. (2009) 'Nationalism, patriotism, and cosmopolitanism in an age of globalization'. *The Journal of Ethics*, 13(4), 365–381.

Barnett, M. (2011) *Empire of Humanity: A History of Humanitarianism*. Ithaca, NY: Cornell University Press.

Braun, V. and Clarke, V. (2006) 'Using thematic analysis in psychology'. *Qualitative Research in Psychology*, 3(2), 77–101.

Brechenmacher, S. (2017) *Civil Society Under Assault: Repression and Responses in Russia, Egypt, and Ethiopia*. Washington, DC: Carnegie Endowment for International Peace.

Carothers, T. and Brechenmacher, S. (2014) *Closing Space: Democracy and Human Rights Support Under Fire*. Washington, DC: Carnegie Endowment for International Peace.

Chick, K. (2017) *Egypt's civil society is on life support* [online]. Available at: https://foreignpolicy.com/2017/12/13/egypts-civil-society-is-on-life-support/ [Accessed: 20 October 2019].

Christensen, D. and Weinstein, J.M. (2013) 'Defunding dissent: Restrictions on aid to NGOs'. *Journal of Democracy*, 24(2), 77–91.

Cohen, S. (2002 [1972]) *Folk Devils and Moral Panics: The Creation of the Mods and Rockers*, 3rd edn. London: Routledge.

Cree, V. and Clapton, G. (2016) *Revisiting Moral Panics.* Bristol: Policy Press.

Dietrich, S. and Wright, J. (2015) 'Foreign aid allocation tactics and democratic change in Africa'. *Journal of Politics*, 77(1), 216–234.

Drakulic, S. (2008) 'Whence nationalism?'. *Nations and Nationalism*, 14(1), 221–239.

Dupuy, K. et al. (2016) 'Hands off my regime! Governments' restrictions on foreign aid to non-governmental organisations in poor and middle-income countries'. *World Development*, 88(1), 299–311.

Edwards, M. (2009) *Civil society.* Cambridge: Polity Press.

*Egypt Today* (2018) Unlicensed NGOs' foreign funds' defendants acquitted of charges [online]. Available at: https://www.egypttoday.com/Article/1/62291/Unlicensed-NGOs-foreign-funds-defendants-acquitted-of-charges. [Accessed: 20 October 2019].

El Assal, A. (2019) 'Human Rights Organizations and Navigating the Political Configuration of Power in Post-2011 Egypt'. In Natil, I., Pieroban, C. and Tauber, L. (eds.), *The Power of Civil Society in the Middle East and North Africa: Peace-building, Change, and Development.* London: Routledge.

*El Watan* (2018a) Foreign aid … easy money to collect millions … evil arms to spread chaos [online]. Available at: https://www.elwatannews.com/news/details/3567500. [Accessed: 7 February 2020]. [In Arabic].

*El Watan* (2018b) NGOs Law, the state arm to shut down the suspicious foreign fund tap [online]. Available at: https://www.elwatannews.com/news/details/3656830. [Accessed: 7 February 2020]. [In Arabic].

Emmanuel, D.B. (2014) 'Globalization: Cohen's theory and the moral panic'. *Afro Asian Journal of Social Sciences*, 3(III), 2229–5313.

Geer, B. (2011) *The Priesthood of Nationalism in Egypt: Duty, Authority, Autonomy.* PhD thesis, SOAS (School of Oriental and African Studies).

Gellner, E. (1983) *Nations and Nationalism.* Ithaca, NY: Cornell University Press.

Gelvin, J. (1999) 'Modernity and its discontents: On the durability of nationalism in the Arab Middle East'. *Nations and Nationalism*, 5(1), 71–89.

Greer, C. and Reiner, R. (2014) 'Labelling, deviance, and media'. *Encyclopaedia of Criminology and Criminal Justice*, 1(1), 2814–2823.

Hall, S., Critcher, C., Jefferson, T., Clarke, J. and Roberts, B. (1978) *Policing the Crisis.* London: Palgrave Macmillan.

Hibbard, S. (2010) *Religious Politics and Secular States: Egypt, India, and the United States.* Baltimore, MD: Johns Hopkins University Press.

Hobsbawm, E.J. (1994) *Nations and Nationalism Since 1780: Programme, Myth, Reality*, 2nd edn. Cambridge: Cambridge University Press.

Kedourie, E. (1993) *Nationalism*, 4th, expanded edn. Oxford: Blackwell.

*Mada Masr* (2019) Civil society leaders fight travel bans as 9-year NGO foreign funding case drags on [online]. Available at: https://madamasr.com/en/2019/09/15/feature/politics/civil-society-leaders-fight-travel-bans-as-9-year-ngo-foreign-funding-case-drags-on/ [Accessed: 25 October 2019].

Mamdouh, R. (2018) *Amending the NGO law: Why did Sisi choose to revise it now and will the changes be meaningful?* [online]. Available at: https://mada21.appspot.com/madamasr.com/en/2018/12/05/feature/politics/amending-the-ngo-law-why-did-sisi-choose-to-revise-it-now-and-will-the-changes-be-meaningful/ [Accessed: 25 October 2019].

Mansour, S. (2015) Stifling the Public Sphere: Media and Civil Society in Egypt. In *Media and Civil Society in Egypt, Russia, and Vietnam*. Washington D.C.: National Endowment for Democracy and International Forum for Democratic Studies.

Moustafa, D. (2017) *The Egyptian Military in Popular Culture*. London: Palgrave Macmillan UK.

Office of the High Commissioner for Human Rights (2016) *Zeid urges Egypt to halt repression of NGOs* [online]. Available at: https://www.ohchr.org/en/NewsEvents/Pages/DisplayNews.aspx?NewsID=18521 [Accessed: 20 October 2019].

Paragi, B. (2019) *Foreign Aid in the Middle East: In Search of Peace and Democracy*. London: I.B.Tauris.

Prat, N. (2006) 'Human Rights NGOs and the "Foreign Funding Debate" in Egypt'. In Chase, A., and Hamzawy, A. (eds.), *Human Rights in the Arab World: Independent Voices*. Pennsylvania: University of Pennsylvania Press.

Rohloff, A. and Wright, S. (2010) 'Moral panic and social theory'. *Current Sociology*, 58(3), 403–419.

Ruffner, T. (2015) *Under Threat: Egypt's Systematic Campaign Against NGOs*. Washington, DC: Project on Middle East and Democracy.

Rutzen, D. (2015) 'Civil society under assault'. *Journal of Democracy*, 26(4), 28–39.

Sardoc, M. (2017) 'The anatomy of patriotism'. *Anthropological Notebooks*, 1, 43–55.

Shulman, D. (2005) 'Labeling Theory'. In G. Ritzer (ed.), *Encyclopedia of Social Theory* (Vol. 1, pp. 427–428). Thousand Oaks, CA: SAGE Publications.

Sultan, Y. (2016) *Between Egyptian Nationalism and Religion: Imagining the Nation from Below*. MA thesis, American University in Cairo.

Tan, K.-C. (2004) *Justice Without Borders: Cosmopolitanism, Nationalism, and Patriotism*. New York: Cambridge University Press.

TIMEP (2019) *TIMEP brief: Case 173: Egypt's foreign funding case* [online]. Available at: https://timep.org/reports-briefings/timep-brief-case-173-egypts-foreign-funding-case/. [Accessed: 7 February 2020].

Waddington, P.A. (1986) 'Mugging as a moral panic: A question of proportion'. *British Journal of Sociology*, 37(2), 245–259.

Young, J. (1971) The Role of the Police as Amplifiers of Deviancy, Negotiators of Reality and Translators of Fantasy. In Cohen, S. (ed.), *Images of Deviance*. Harmondsworth: Penguin Books.

Younis, M. and Younis, A. (2012) *Egyptian opposition to U.S. and other foreign aid increases* [online]. Available at: https://news.gallup.com/poll/153512/Egyptian-Opposition-Foreign-Aid-Increases.aspx [Accessed: 15 October 2019].

Younis, S. (2005) *The Sacred March*. Cairo: Meret.

Yousef, N. (2016) *Egypt freezes assets of several human rights advocates* [online]. Available at: https://www.nytimes.com/2016/09/18/world/middleeast/egypt-freezes-assets-of-several-human-rights-advocates.html [Accessed: 20 October 2019].

# 6 Civil society in the Gaza Strip

## Qatari humanitarian aid

*Ola Alkahlout*

### Introduction

Armed conflicts leave people facing poverty, displacement, unemployment, loss of life, lack of education, destruction of state infrastructure, absence of safety and security, and so on. Governments are slow to respond compared to the international community, donors, UN agencies, international organisations, and national civil society organisations (CSOs). These entities play a major role in responding to humanitarian crises, in the aftermath of life-changing incidents (Roy 2013). The Gaza Strip (GS) has been suffering the consequences of decades of occupation, wars, the continuing blockade imposed by Israel and Egypt, and an internal division between major political parties (United Nations 2017). The persistent destruction of the infrastructure, livelihood, schools, hospitals, shelters, agricultural land, factories, and so on, has left a heavy toll on the Gazan people. The Israeli military operations against the Gaza Strip in 2014 alone, for example, caused '2,131 Palestinians being killed, 110,000 internally displaced, 18,000 housing units destroyed or severely damaged, and 108,000 people left homeless' (Human Rights Watch 2014). The typical international support was not apparent on the scene due to donor fatigue, Arab Spring's humanitarian crisis, and changes in international politics. Two actors, however, were involved in meeting the needs of Gazans: the Qatari government and the Palestinian CSO. It is worth mentioning that, without the work of the Palestinian civil society, such as *Ard El-Insān* Palestinian Association, life under occupation would have been close to impossible (Costantini, Salameh, and Issa 2015; Roy 2013; and UNHCR 2013).

This chapter studies the impact of Qatar humanitarian aid in supporting Palestinian civil society organisations (CSOs) in 2019. It further discusses how it contributes to shape the political, economic, and social developments in the Strip. The chapter builds on: (i) a literature review; (ii) data collected from in-depth interviews conducted with the Gazan people and representatives of civil society staff in Gaza; and (iii) the author's interviews with charity staff in Qatar, in 2019.

## Background

The Gaza Strip is a part of the de jure State of Palestine which borders Egypt on the southwest for 11 kilometres, and the state of Israel on the east and north along a 51-km stretch (UNRWA 2019). The Gaza Strip is a small seaside enclave of 362 square kilometres on the eastern coast of the Mediterranean Sea. It is considered to be the third most densely populated area in the world. It is often referred to as overcrowded, especially as the extensive Israeli buffer zone within the Strip renders much land off-limits to Gaza's Palestinians (Suisman et al. 2007; Brauch et al. 2011; and Copeland 2011). The territory is inhabited by up to two million Palestinians with Sunni Muslims making up the predominant part; there are also around 1,300 Christians in Gaza (Gledhill 2014; PCBS 2015). The Gaza Strip is semi-arid, with sand dunes along the coastline, and has a generally hot, dry climate (30 degrees Celsius and higher) in summer. The winters are warm, during which practically all the annual rainfall occurs (Tippman and Baroni 2017).

The deprived Strip suffers from severe environmental problems, including desertification, salination of fresh water, lack of sewerage treatment, waterborne diseases, soil degradation, and depletion and contamination of underground water resources; furthermore, Gaza is dependent on Israel for its water, electricity, telecommunications, and supply of other utilities (Hamdan et al. 2007; The World Bank 2018). The land area is small for a high-density population such as that of Gaza. This does not only make daily life for Palestinians problematic, but it also affects their health, safety, and security, amongst other issues. Palestine has faced many conflicts in its history such as the wars with Israel in 2008 and 2012, and the struggle between its political parties, Hamas in Gaza, and Fatah in the West Bank. These conflicts continually aggravate the situation in Gaza (Eguiguren and Saadeh 2014).

## Gaza conflict history

Palestinians have been living under one of the most protracted conflicts in modern history. The conflict has never stopped since the First World War. Following the Arab-Israeli war in 1948, Gaza was administrated by Egypt until the Israeli army occupied GS during the 1967 Six Day War. The Oslo Agreement of the 4th of May 1994 ratified the Gaza-Jericho Agreement between the Palestinian Liberation Organisation (PLO) and Israel: Israel's governance over the GS would be transferred to the new Palestinian self-rule authority PNA (Fisher and Wicker 2010; and UNRWA 2014).

Hamas, the Islamist Movement in Gaza and the West Bank secured a decisive victory in the 2006 elections (Roy 2013; Dunning 2016). Israel consequently denounced Hamas as a 'terrorist' organisation, and imposed a siege on the area (Hroub 2006; Milton-Edwards and Farrell 2010; and Al-Jazeera 2017). Israel now controls six of Gaza's seven land crossings, its maritime borders and airspace, and the movement of goods and persons in and out of the territory, on one side, while Egypt controls one of Gaza's land crossings on the other (Schmitt, Arimatsu, and McCormack 2010). The authors add that, the Israeli government subsequently reduced the supply of fuel and electricity to the GS resulting in further destruction of the already exhausted economy and distortion of basic services, including health and sanitary amenities. Israel has declared a no-go buffer zone that stretches deep into Gaza: if Gazans enter this zone they are shot on sight (Schmitt, Arimatsu, and McCormack 2010).

Gaza has therefore become an 'open air prison' for the past 12 years. Israel has adopted a military escalation strategy over the Strip since 2007, and the siege became more intense. Twelve years have been underpinned by continual air raids and assassinations by Israel in the Gaza Strip (United Nations 2015). The United Nations, international human rights organisations, and the majority of governments and legal commentators consider the territory to be still occupied by Israel, supported by additional restrictions placed on Gaza by Egypt. The system of control imposed on Gaza by Israel is described as an 'indirect occupation' (Schmitt, Arimatsu, and McCormack 2010).

## The impact of the conflict on Gazans

The Israeli military relationship with Gaza began to take on a more brutal form since 2006: escalation of the military strategy adopted saw the siege on Gaza intensify (Elkahlout 2018). OCHA (2019c) states that, the Gazan fatalities from 2008–2019 total 4,979, compared to Israeli fatalities from 2008–2019 of 233 (Atalla 2016); Almusaddar (2018) and OCHA (2019c) say the main Israeli military wars with the Gaza Strip were:

1. 2008/2009 – Cast Lead operation – with 812 + 1,037 = 1,849 Gazan fatalities;
2. 2012 – Pillar of Cloud operation – with 252 Gazan fatalities;
3. 2014 – Protective Edge operation – with 2,270 Gazan fatalities;
4. 2018 – Great March of Return – with 260 Gazan fatalities.

These continued conflicts have caused immense suffering in Gaza over the years. They have left hundreds of thousands of Gazans facing hardship in every aspect of their daily lives. The siege further harmed the health system, which was struggling even before these events; signs of humanitarian crises are clearly obvious. The already insecure, impoverished, and imprisoned Gazans have continued to live under dire conditions; moreover, the Israeli government has stopped virtually all goods and services from entering GS (except occasionally allowing some basic foodstuff and medicines), as well as restricting almost all citizens from entering and leaving the Strip (United Nations 2015). UNDP (2016) and Elkahlout (2018) explain the wars have caused 'vast damage to public and private infrastructure including schools, hospitals, water and power plants, industrial infrastructure and agricultural land'. The interviews also confirmed that, there is an absence of what is 'good' for human life. Mohammed, one of the interviewees aged between 35 and 40, unemployed and supporting a family of five, said 'I cannot afford the minimum food for my kids, and there is no job. The life in the Gaza Strip has become unbearable'.

Hassan, one of the interviewees aged between 30 and 35, who works as a civil servant in the Ministry of Economy for the Government of Gaza, supporting a family of five, also added 'There is no spot in the Gaza Strip [in which] you feel safe. Everyone is threatened with death at any time'.

Casualties were not only caused by the Israeli military incursions into Gaza: the battle of Gaza in 2007 between Hamas and Fateh also resulted in 118 Palestinians being killed, and over 550 wounded (ICRC 2007). The party-political affiliation and patronage system are consequently not absent from the scene in Gaza. The internal Palestinian political divide, and the prolonged closure of the Rafah Border Crossing with Egypt, continue to hamper economic and social development (UNDP 2016). Poverty and child labour, for example, have drastically increased. MEMO (2019) declares that, the poverty rate in Gaza exceeds 80 per cent; OCHA (2019b) confirms that, 2019 witnessed an increase in poverty and child labour in Gaza. OCHA (2019b) also adds: about 68 per cent of households in Gaza experience moderate or severe levels of food insecurity, and the unemployment rate increased from 44 per cent in 2017 to 52 per cent in 2018.

The resilience of families is increasingly being eroded in a continued destabilised economy and weakened social fabric. The vulnerability of certain groups, particularly children, is exacerbated. Child labour, including children engaged in hazardous occupations such as mechanical workshops, has become a common mechanism to alleviate poverty on a daily basis (PCBS 2017). OCHA (2019a) states that, this deterioration is taking place in the context of a worsening financial crisis for the Palestinian Authority (PA). The PA refused to receive the partial tax remittances collected on its behalf by Israel, since February. The reason given is, as long as Israel continues to deduct the amount it deems the PA is paying to families of 'martyrs' and prisoners, it cannot accept the taxes. Israel calls these 'stipends' a 'pay for slay' policy, and encourage violence. Palestinians consider the families of these dead or imprisoned people as heroes in their struggle for an independent Palestine, and deserve support. According to a Reuters report of 4 October, 2019, the cash-strapped PA will, once again, accept tax revenues collected by Israel (Reuters 2019). Zureik (2017) explains, from its economy side, Israel is benefiting from the siege on Gaza, as 80 per cent of the aid goes to the Israeli companies to finance Gaza. The siege is not only a political issue, but also economic in favour of Israel. It is important to note that, both in terms of Israeli political or economic levels, the biggest losers are the Gazans, as international and local organisations have stated.

Gazans, on the socio-economic level, are deprived of being able to access the goods necessary for daily needs such as food, basic medicines, electricity, and so on (Asharq Al-Awsat 2019). Humanitarian aid from governmental and non-governmental organisations meets the basic needs of Gazans, but is not sufficient to meet the daily needs. The blockade does not only affect Gazans, but also the charitable organisations. These organisations, including civil society, are hampered by the blockade by not being allowed to bring in essential goods due to Israel's almost total control of imports and aid passing into the Gaza Strip (Alarab 2016).

The Qatari government's role has been prominent in this intervention more than once. It has mediated between the Israeli government and Gaza to allow electricity to be supplied to the Gaza Strip (Tanani 2019). This deprivation has caused serious problems not only for households, but also for hospitals and clinics. Patients who need immediate operations have been left to suffer or even die due to the lack of electricity (Abu Ramadan 2015).

## Civil society organisations in Gaza

According to the World Bank: 'Civil society … refers to a wide array of organizations: community groups, non-governmental organizations [NGOs], labour unions, indigenous groups, charitable organizations, faith-based organizations, professional associations, and foundations' (Baldwin and Teater 2012; Jezard 2018). The World Health Organization (WHO 2019) defines civil society as 'the space for collective action around shared interests, purposes and values, generally distinct from government and commercial for-profit actors', which includes 'women's organisations, faith-based organisations, professional associations, trade unions', and so on. Civil society is not homogeneous, according to WHO: the boundaries are often indistinct between civil society and government or commercial entities. Local representation and legitimacy are key factors in these civil society relationships, as there is no single or unique type of civil society. Civil society groups are essential in helping to solve community problems. They provide a collective voice for the community's needs regarding schools, hospitals, and government support for these projects.

Palestinian civil society organisations in the Occupied Palestinian Territories (OPT) have played an important role in supporting the Palestinians' steadfastness and resilience. CSOs cover a large sector of organisations, associations, and frameworks that form the civil society, including clubs, unions, co-operatives, professional groups, the press, and different kinds of associations with their various interests (Costantini, Salameh, and Issa 2015). Constantini et al. (2015) state: the CSO in Palestine can be seen as encompassing three levels of organisations: (i) large, internationally-based NGOs, often with local staff but with leadership and funding from outside the country; (ii) domestic NGOs with professional staff, and occasionally with foreign funding; and (iii) an array of highly localised community-based organisations, sustained by modest funds, volunteer efforts, or, at most, with small professional staff, sometimes receiving international assistance.

There are approximately 1,005 CSOs in Gaza out of 2,793 in the State of Palestine (Costantini, Salameh, and Issa 2015). CSOs provide services in a variety of areas including health, education, and rehabilitation services, services for the disabled, housing, agriculture, environment, social welfare support, and economic development (USAID 2013). Eguiguren and Saadeh (2014) explain that, CSOs in Gaza now lead immediate relief to humanitarian and other urgent needs, rather than planning and designing community services or long-term objectives. The CSOs have had decades of experience in supporting the Palestinians, due to the lack of adequate public services provided by either the Israeli occupation authorities or later, by the PA. CSOs have a greater capacity to design products and implement services in certain areas such as agriculture, the environment, and research and development which will benefit a wide range of beneficiaries.

CSOs have the expertise to raise awareness such as first aid to minimise damage in the affected areas through publications, community workshops, and analysis of these areas. This international approach has not resonated with most Gazans interviewed. The majority of interviewees agreed that, some of the aid arrived in Gaza, but its distribution and the implementation of projects, is questionable. Mahmoud, an unemployed man in the 55–60 age group, supporting a family of nine, said 'We think they [CSOs] are delivering support to those who deserve it, despite some of it [probably] also going to relatives and friends'.

The question whether aid such as the monthly payment of US$100 has reached the needy in Gaza, Mohammed, an unemployed man in the 35 to 40 age group, supporting a family of five, said:

> I don't think so. Why [did] they cut it off from me after five months, and take [pay] someone else for six months? Also, they cut off the payment after four months, and the others were taken for only two months.

This may be understandable in an unstable area with renewed old conflicts and a challenging atmosphere, but the sufferers are always the same – the Gazans. According to the Analytical Survey of Civil Society Organizations in Palestine (PCBS 2015), CSO operations have faced many complications, limitations, successes, and failures. The complications are undoubtedly caused by the current status – represented by the continuation of the Israeli blockade, political split and obstruction of democratic life, the unstable political situation of Arab countries, donor fatigue, and so on. These complications present great challenges, which may be new in their nature to CSOs, but have also resulted in setting the role and status of these organisations.

One of these challenges, for example, was the political split in 2007. Civil society has generally been affected in ways that make conditions more restricted and difficult. Abu Ramadan says Hamas's *de facto* authority in Gaza has issued about 45 laws concerning CSOs. It has, furthermore, taken forceful action against CSOs affiliated to Fatah, or those led by pro-Fatah individuals. Hamas shut down some CSOs, and flooded the membership rolls of others in order to make it possible to elect pro-Hamas boards, as was the case in the Patients' Friends Society (Abu Ramadan 2015). The Ministry of Interior in Gaza also carried out strict and non-benign control over competing civil institutions which were not part of the political vision of Hamas. The motive was to search for administrative or technical gaps in order to control the specific society. The PNA in the West Bank passed about 70 resolutions on similar lines (Abu Ramadan 2015). The split between Fatah and Hamas is not only on the leaders' level, it is also present amongst the Gazans themselves. The relationship between Gazans and political parties is based on party affiliation rather than addressing the main problems: return of their rights and land, and finding a solution with Israel.

AWARD (2017) says: A recent obstacle to CSOs in Gaza was the Central Bank (PNA) freezing accounts of CSOs. NGOs in the Gaza Strip complained about their Palestinian accounts being frozen – highlighting that this not only threatened the services they provided to beneficiaries, but also endangered their relationships with (foreign and local) financiers and suppliers. It is reported that, banks operating in the Gaza Strip have also refused to open bank accounts for newly registered NGOs, even if they had obtained the required certificates from the Ministry of Interior in Ramallah. The Gaza banking system continues to function, with Hamas reluctantly accepting that, any effort to exert control over Gaza banks, or interfere with the Gaza operations of the Ramallah-based Palestinian Monetary Authority, would make the Gaza financial system collapse. International sanctions stemming from anti-Hamas terrorism measures in many countries would quickly be applied. Owing to the Palestinian political split, some Fatah-affiliated organisations were harassed or closed after 2007 (UNHCR 2013).

The influx of donor funds has dramatically shrunk due to the anti-Hamas 'terrorism' measures, the Gulf Crisis, and the military coup in Egypt. Qatar's response to the very high needs in Gaza clearly became the main active donor in Palestine on a sustained basis (Zureik 2017). The following section sheds some light on the Qatari government's aid practices, followed by a presentation of the author's study of the role Qatari aid has played in supporting Gaza CSOs in its response to the humanitarian crisis in the Gaza Strip.

## Qatari's support to Gaza Strip

Qatar is a wealthy country owing to having one of the world's highest per capita GDP, and the third largest reserves of natural gas in the world (Tok, Alkhater, and Pal 2016). The GDP per capita in Qatar was last recorded at 63,222.10 US dollars in 2018 (Trading Economics 2019). The tiny Gulf state has become known all over the world for relief programmes and helping the needy, 'healing wounds', spreading education, developing resources, building mosques, digging water wells, and building health centres (Gharaibeh 2013). The government of Qatar has been consistent amongst the largest bilateral donors working in Gaza for the past decade (Elkahlout 2019). Elkahlout adds: the Qatari Committee for the Reconstruction of Gaza was established in 2012, to carry out relief and reconstruction work in the Gaza Strip. It succeeded in providing jobs, hospitals, and housing on a neighbourhood scale, infrastructure projects, and roads.

The majority of interviewees confirmed that, Qatar is clearly the main active donor in Gaza on a sustained basis, especially during the siege of Gaza. The pro-Qataris attribute this interest to Arab nationalism, the Islamic *ummah*, and human motivation, despite having observed Qatari aid to Gaza is motivated by religiously rooted principles of charitable giving (Zureik 2017; Researcher's interviews). Commentators signal three main motives driving the Gulf States' humanitarian aid policies: (i) diplomacy and stability; (ii) solidarity with the Palestinian cause; and (iii) humanitarian concerns (Barakat and Zyck 2010). There is no doubt that, solidarity with the Palestinians at the public and official level is substantial and genuine, as long as there is regional stability, and Qatar's state interests are served. This, together with humanitarian concerns, accounts for the generous aid policies towards the Palestinians. Qatar is consequently not the only Gulf state to support Gaza: Saudi Arabia provided assistance to the Palestinians which exceeded its disbursements by US$350 million out of US$500 million, distributed on the implementation of reconstruction projects or support to the PA. This accounted for 33 per cent of the total Gulf support (El-Safadi 2016). Supporting Gaza is not the only interest in the Qatari agendum; soft power,[1] preserving its sovereignty, and seeking international public support for Qatar's interventions. Qatar's financial interventions were evident in the Arab uprisings through its provision and support of governments and popular revolutions. Qatar supported former President Mohamed Morsi's Muslim Brotherhood government in Egypt, and was instrumental in removing the Libyan leader Ghaddafi from power, and providing aid to the revolution in Syria (Rivlin 2013). Qatar also donated US $500 million to Tunisia to bolster its foreign currency reserves (Baabood 2014). Qatar also supported the Tunisian economy with $1.25 billion dollars in 2017 (Qatar Day 2017). Qatar has recently supported the Turkish economy with US$15 billion in economic investments between the two countries (The Guardian 2018).

Qatar has consistently supported Gaza since 2007 – from when Hamas seized control of the territory and the subsequent imposition of the Israeli blockade (Zureik 2017). Barakat and Zyck (2010) say: Qatari humanitarian aid flows bilaterally from government-to-government or from donors to specific groups within the affected states such as NGOs, educational institutions, health care providers, municipalities and others; most of the funding is allocated to Gaza rather than to the West Bank. There are two main reasons for this. First, Qatar has forged a closer relationship with Hamas in Gaza, and in this sense, it has perpetuated its close relationship with the Moslem Brotherhood of Egypt with whom Hamas has an affinity. Second, and more importantly, the Gaza Strip has come under punishing Israeli attacks that have resulted in extensive destruction of Gaza. It was therefore logical to divert Qatari funding to rebuilding Gaza.

Table 6.1 explains Qatar's support for Gaza from 2012 to 2019 (adapted from Zureik 2017; Gaza Reconstruction Committee 2019; and Tanani 2019).

Qatar donated US$407 million in October 2012 to Gaza after the Second Israeli War, for the reconstruction of the Gaza Strip. The donation was provided for the implementation of 'vital' projects, including the construction of a residential city named Sheikh Hamad Bin Khalifa Al-Thani, with about 2,500 apartments. There was a subsequent, harsh climatic phenomenon – the Alexa Depression – which hit the Gaza Strip for several days, resulting in floods in the Gaza Valley and low-lying areas. The State of Qatar directed a US$5 million grant to 'save' the situation in Gaza. The Qatari Committee for the Reconstruction of Gaza provided urgent support after the 2014 war on the Gaza Strip, with a grant of US$30 million to the health sector and hospitals, and to shelters and the owners of destroyed houses.

The war grant was followed by another US$50 million in 2015, in which the State of Qatar rebuilt 1,000 housing units that were completely demolished during the war. Qatar provided a US$34 million grant in 2016, which included a financial reward for Gaza employees. Qatar announced a donation of US$12 million in 2017, to fuel the power plant in the Gaza Strip for three months. There were several more grants from the State of Qatar. The first grant was US$9 million humanitarian aid divided as follows: US$2.6 million for food parcels, blankets, and cooking gas; US$500,000 for hospital fuel and the Ministry of Health; US$2 million for medicines and medical supplies; US $1 million to repair the homes of poor people; US$1 million to pay for the fees of university students; and US$2 million for humanitarian and sickness aid. The second grant was US$13.7 million in humanitarian aid and service

*Table 6.1* Qatar aid and grants for the Gaza Strip 2012–2019

| *Year* | *Type of grant* | *Value (US $ million)* |
|---|---|---|
| 2012 | Reconstruction grant | 407 |
| 2013 | Low depression grant | 5 |
| 2014 | War grant | 30 |
| 2015 | Reconstruction grant | 50 |
| 2016 | The Gaza Staff Grant | 34 |
| 2017 | Gaza Electricity Support | 12 |
| 2018 | Humanitarian Relief Grant | 9 |
| | Service and humanitarian grants | 13.7 |
| 2019 | Support electricity, Gaza staff, and humanitarian assistance | 150 |
| | Grant of the Emir of the State of Qatar to the Palestinian people | 480 |

support. Qatar provided a US$150 million grant at the end of the year, earmarking US$60 million to run the power plant for six months. US$10 million was allocated to the salaries of Gaza employees per month, and disbursements of emergency cash assistance to poor families worth US$100 each, distributed in three instalments. A US$480 million Prince Sheikh Tamim bin Hamad Al-Thani grant was given in 2019 to the Gaza Strip and the Palestinian Authority.

## Qatar and Gazan CSOs

Qatari methods of aid delivery included working directly with United Nations agencies and other local and international charity organisations. Islamic Relief World Organisation (IRW), The Qatar Red Crescent, Qatar Charity, and the Qatari Committee for Reconstruction have been heavily involved in supporting CSO projects and initiatives. Building the capacity of CSOs, for instance, through income generation and livelihood projects. Jamal, who works as a civil engineer on engineering projects supervised by IRW staff, said 'There is a partnership between Islamic Relief and Qatar Charity that supports it in its projects. Some of these projects fund orphans to ensure their care, full care, psychological and health support, education support and recreational development'.

A previous interview with Mahliya Almulad, the Middle East and Partner Relations Coordinator, highlights the latest official statistics by the Ministry of Social Affairs. They show the number of orphans in the Gaza Strip exceeds 22,776. The total number of sponsored orphans in Gaza is 6,933 (Almulad 2017). IRW (2019) reported that, the objectives of the orphans' programme are achieved through conducting activities such as providing livelihood support, encouraging education, providing food security, promoting community action, and making time to play. Mohammed, Project Engineer who worked as supervisor to Nasser Medical Complex, said 'Through Qatar Red Crescent the heart section in the hospital has been fully restored'.

Qatar Red Crescent approves a package of health projects to be implemented in the Gaza Strip to help build the capacity of the Palestinian Ministry of Health. These projects are initiated through the medical education programme, and the support and development of health institutions there, as part of the Health Sector Promotion Plan for 2016–2017 (Al-Jazeera 2017). Diab, adviser, Relief and International Development Division, QRCS, confirmed that, all the projects that have been implemented by the Qatari Red Crescent have enhanced the capacities of the Palestinian CSOs such as Palestinian Health Ministries working with WHO to develop a strategy for the health sector to guide donors' work in Gaza.

QRC was also involved in offering young Palestinian medical doctors the opportunity to receive four-year scholarships to be trained in Doha. Every doctor selected signed an agreement to return back to Gaza after finishing his or her training. The capacity developed in this project is great support to the fragile Palestinian medical sector in Gaza. This aid does not solve the problem of the Palestinian political split or the Palestinian-Israeli conflict from its roots; however, there is no doubt that, these aid projects have had a positive effect in Gaza society, as confirmed by most of those interviewed.

## People satisfaction with Qatari aid delivery in Gaza

Qatari aid was well received in the Gaza Strip, where the majority of interviews were conducted for this research. The respondents confirmed that, they had received Qatari aid. They also said that, they had been positively affected by this aid through the establishment of Hamad Town and Hamad Town Hospital for Prosthetics, and Support for Gaza Electricity and Operation of Generating Stations. This aid also provided support for the construction of the Asda'a Prison, and financial support for the provision of diesel to the electricity station. Interviewees showed their appreciation of the work conducted by the Qatari funding in Gaza in supporting the poor. Omar, from the 30 to 35 age group, a civil engineer working for the Gaza government on projects of the Ministry of Health, supporting a family of seven, said 'Although I am not included in the programme's beneficiaries, I appreciate the work the Qataris are doing to alleviate the suffering in Gaza'.

Ahmed, another Palestinian met in Gaza, in the 25 to 30 age group, was a volunteer nurse who worked in many hospitals. He worked on an ambitious graduate employment programme, but was now unemployed and supporting a family of two, and said: 'Without the Qatari aid, I would never have dreamt of having a flat for me and my small family'. Ahmed has benefited from the housing programme Qatar has built in Southern Gaza. He added:

> We were lucky to be selected after we had been scrutinised to meet the conditions of the Qatari Committee. The only difficulty we are facing is to meet the monthly payment while we do not have stable salaries on a monthly basis. The Qatari representative in Gaza, Mr Ammadi, has kindly listened to our appeal and decided to postpone all 2019 payments.

To show his gratitude, Ahmed has named his newborn son Mohammed Ammadi.

Regarding the point mentioned in the above section 'Civil society organisations in Gaza', and the integrity of CSOs working in Gaza, the interviewees had reservations about the implementation of the aid that came from Qatar. Areej, a female in the 40–45 age group, an engineer for the Government of Gaza at the Ministry of Communications and Information Technology, said 'Yes, I was the recipient of the Qatari grant because I am a Hamas employee! – But they deceived us! They misled us! They told us it is a grant, but they deducted repayment from us retroactively'.

It was agreed among some of the interviewees that, Qatari aid is typically given to beneficiaries based on their political affiliation. This cannot be avoided in Gaza as there politics mixes with humanitarian work.

The Qatari grant of US$100 per month is not enough, according to some interviewees. Mohammed, in the 35–40 age group, worked as a taxi driver, and is now unemployed, supporting a family of five, said 'It had a good effect, thank God, but it goes lightning fast, as head of a family and I have three children, barely enough to run my affairs for half a month, if we forget the debt!'

One can conclude that, the assistance Qatar gives to Gaza CSOs to improve living conditions is very effective, despite the interference of political affiliations and the integrity of the work of CSOs on one hand, and the Qatari challenges that face it in the conflict, on the other. Barakat and Zyck (2010) mention that, Qatar was forced at times to turn to Israel to ensure the delivery of aid. There are some commentators who believe Qatar's aid to Gaza has been mainly motivated by a willingness of the country to keep a foot in the Palestinian portfolio; without Qatari support, the Hamas government and CSOs in Gaza would not have been able to survive the unjust sanctions. It is argued that, this support has widened the rift among the Palestinian factions.

Qatar is accused of implementing an Israeli agendum by pro-Fatah supporters in order to have a continuous Palestinian division. The Qatari delegate to Gaza, Mr. Ammadi was compelled to defend his country's stand in a recent incident: Qatar was accused of giving 'money for calmness'. Mr Ammadi explained that, his government's support for Gaza is merely based on humanitarian motivation, and it will continue to support the Palestinian people. These strenuous efforts found their translation in the Gazan streets, but have not solved the root problem: to end this suffering that has resulted from the political split and the conflict. The Emir and senior officials in the Qatari government assert, 'Qatar has an active role in building and preserving peace' (Permanent Mission 2017). The Qatari UN's representative, Sheikha Alia, gave a speech in which she illustrated Qatar's approach to peacebuilding by working 'to achieve sustainable development and solve the root causes of extremism, violence and human trafficking, in addition to promoting and strengthening education, global security, and human rights' promising a sustainable funding commitment (Gulf-Times 2017). Qatar has demonstrated serious efforts to mediate peace deals in Darfur, Yemen, Gaza, and so on, over the last decade (Barakat 2014). Qatar's attempts to resolve the conflict in the Palestinian political split between Fatah and Hamas (AIJAC 2012), for example, was unsuccessful. There were also several attempts at reconciliation between Hamas and Fatah in 2017 (Majed 2017), but it also seems that the political atmosphere is not suitable for Qatar's peace-making efforts. This can be attributed to the ongoing Gulf crisis and the hostility between Qatar and Saudi Arabia and Egypt. Egypt and Saudi Arabia and the United Arab Emirates will not allow any role to be played by Qatar in reaching a reconciliation agreement between Hamas and Fatah.

The generosity of Qatari humanitarian aid and the efforts of CSOs have undoubtedly helped in some way to generate the political, economic, and social developments that shaped daily life in the Gaza Strip in 2019; however, today, the Gazans have become interested in the food basket rather than pay attention to the main problems affecting their lives. This could possibly be the reason for Israel's continued control of Palestine.

## Conclusion

This chapter has discussed and analysed the extent to which Qatari humanitarian aid has had an impact through its support of civil society organizations (CSO) in the Gaza Strip in 2019. It has helped to generate the political, economic, and social developments that shape daily life in the Gaza Strip. The problems faced by Gaza are not only political or economic, but also the damage to its natural resources such as desertification, salination of fresh water, and lack of sewerage treatment. The impact of the Arab countries' blockade on Gaza has affected its basic needs such as the supply of electricity and water, and Qatar's dependence on Israel for the passage of goods. The history of conflict has played a major part in Gaza's current situation: Gaza's part of the Palestinian conflict with Israel and the surrounding Arab states on one hand, and Gaza's conflict within itself, on the other. The political split in 2007 between Fatah and Hamas, and the expressed dissatisfaction with Israel's conduct towards the Palestinians as a whole, and Gaza in particular. Israel consequently imposed the siege on the Gaza Strip. These conflicts have had a continuous impact on Gazans, such as preventing adequate support for health, education, food, shelter, and so on. During the last 12 years, Israeli military attacks killed 4,979 Gazans (OCHA 2019c), and the losses were not limited to lives: the poverty rate in Gaza exceeds 80 per cent (MEMO 2019).

This was clear from some of the interviewees' points of view – 'life in the Gaza Strip has become unbearable'. This environment has made it a fertile ground for the work of CSOs, but their work has been hindered by the conflicts. The civil society organisations work in Gaza has been well received by international public opinion regarding their provision of services in health, education, housing, agriculture, environment, social welfare support, and so on. This work is not going smoothly, however, in part due to party-political affiliations, and in part to relatives and friends' affiliations. There is bias in the aid distributions, according to some of the interviewees. Qatari support for the Gaza CSOs comes directly from the Qatari government or through Qatari charities such as Qatar Red Crescent and Qatar Charity. Qatari humanitarian aid was well received on the Gaza street but with reservations shown regarding the impartiality of CSO work. The political situation challenges Qatari aid efforts. Israel's control of goods and services provided by Qatar's aid programmes entering Gaza has hampered the Gazans' relief from the continued suffering it endures.

The Qatari government's defence for this 'failure' is explained as being 'money for calmness'. The accusation from Fatah groups affiliated to the Government of Qatar claim Qatar is providing support to the Hamas government to strengthen the Palestinian divide, and thereby proving it to be stronger than the PA. The Qatari government defends this by saying the main purpose for Qatari humanitarian aid is for all Palestinians. Qatar and Qatari advocates claim that its aid to the Palestinians stemmed from its pro-Palestinian stance.

## Note

1 Soft power is 'the ability to affect others to obtain the outcomes one wants through attraction rather than coercion or payment. A country's soft power rests on its resources of culture, values, and policies' (NYE JR 2008: 94).

## References

Abu Ramadan, M. (2015). 'Is there a Possible Environment for Civil Society in Palestine?' Accessed October 31, 2019 [online] available at http://lnnk.in/q4D.

AIJAC (2012). 'The Latest Fatah-Hamas Agreement in Doha'. Accessed October 31, 2019 [online] available at http://lnnk.in/r5w.

Alarab (2016). 'Occupation Impedes the Work of Civil Society Organizations in Gaza'. Accessed October 31, 2019 [online] available at http://lnnk.in/rkD [Arabic].

Al-Jazeera (2017). 'Milestones of Qatar's Support to the Besieged Gaza Strip'. Accessed November 01, 2019 [online] available at http://bit.ly/34wcvt1.

Almulad, M. (2017). 'Middle East & Partner Relations Coordinator (PFPD – IPD Division)' [interview by the author]. *Islamic Relief Worldwide*, 6/07/2017.

Almusaddar, D. (2018). 'The Great March of Return and the Palestinian Nakba'. Accessed February 16, 2020 [online] available at http://bit.ly/3208UmX.

Asharq Al-Awsat. (2019). 'Poverty Rate in Gaza Strip Highest Worldwide'. Accessed October 31, 2019 [online] available at http://lnnk.in/rxz.

Atalla, O. (2016). '3 Israeli Wars on Gaza' (*Infographic*). Accessed February 16, 2020 [online] available at http://bit.ly/3bKo4kr.

AWARD (2017). 'West Bank/Gaza'. Accessed November 01, 2019 [online] available at http://bit.ly/2WFZLgE.

Baabood, A. (2014). 'Gulf Countries and Arab Transitions: Role, Support and Effects'. Accessed February 16, 2020 [online] available at https://bit.ly/2K5YB8A.

Baldwin, M. and Teater, B. (2012). *Social Work in the Community: Making a Difference.* United Kingdom: Bristol University Press.

Barakat, S. (2014). 'Qatari Mediation: Between Ambition and Achievement'. Accessed January 17, 2019 [online] available at https://goo.gl/cKrbjw.

Barakat, S. and Zyck, A. S. (2010). 'Gulf State Assistance to Conflict-Affected Environments'. Accessed October 31, 2019 [online] available at http://bit.ly/2WwKTRs.

Brauch, H., Spring, Ú., Mesjasz, C., Grin, J., Kameri-Mbote P., Chourou, B., Dunay, P., and Birkmann, J. (2011). 'Coping with Global Environmental Change, Disasters and Security: Threats, Challenges, Vulnerabilities and Risks'. Accessed October 31, 2019 [online] available at http://bit.ly/2C11d3p.

Copeland E. T. (2011). 'Drawing a Line in the Sea: The Gaza Flotilla Incident and the Israeli-Palestinian Conflict'. Accessed October 31, 2019 [online] available at http://lnnk.in/r0A.

Costantini, G., Salameh, E., and Issa, M. (2015). 'Analytical Survey of Civil Society Organizations in Palestine'. Accessed October 31, 2019 [online] available at http://lnnk.in/q6D.

Dunning, T. (2016). 'Hamas, Jihad and Popular Legitimacy: Reinterpreting Resistance in Palestine'. Accessed November 01, 2019 [online] available at http://bit.ly/2Wxdru4.

Eguiguren, R. and Saadeh, L. (2014). 'Protection in the Occupied Palestinian Territories'. Accessed October 31, 2019 [online] available at http://lnnk.in/raD.

El Safadi, N. (2016). 'Gulf Support for Gaza in Numbers. Good Hands Ease the Siege and Longevity'. Accessed October 31, 2019 [online] available at http://lnnk.in/sqz.

Elkahlout, G. (2019). 'Post-Conflict Housing Reconstruction in the Gaza Strip'. Accessed November 01, 2019 [online] available at http://bit.ly/2oH1DJs.

Elkahlout, G. (2018). 'Reviewing the Interactions between Conflict and Demographic Trends in the Occupied Palestinian Territories: The Case of the Gaza Strip'. Accessed November 01, 2019 [online] available at http://bit.ly/2WxqcVC.

Fisher, D. and Wicker, B. (eds.) (2010). *Just War on Terror?: A Christian and Muslim Response.* New York: Ashgate.

Gaza Reconstruction Committee (2019). 'Projects of the Gaza Reconstruction Committee'. Accessed November 01, 2019 [online] available from http://bit.ly/339d2Au.

Gharaibeh, A. (2013). 'Qatari Relief Aid Reaches Distressed People all Over the World'. Accessed January 10, 2018 [online] available at https://goo.gl/GLf1aV.

Gledhill, R. (2014). 'Gaza's Tiny Christian Community Under Siege'. Accessed October 31, 2019 [online] available at http://lnnk.in/seA.

Guardian, The. (2018). 'Turkish Lira Rallies as Qatar Invests $15bn, but Markets Slide – as it Happened'. Accessed January 10, 2018 [online] available at https://goo.gl/jKoGzu.

Gulf-Times (2017). 'Qatar Reaffirms its Active Role in Building Peace and Tolerance'. Accessed January 17, 2019 [online] available at https://goo.gl/CmbiiD.

Hamdan, L., Zarei-Chaleshtori, M., Chianelli, R., and Gardner, E. (2007). 'Sustainable Water and Energy in Gaza Strip'. Accessed November 01, 2019 [online] available at http://bit.ly/2N4aA8S.

Hroub, K. (2006). *Hamas.* London: Pluto Press.

Human Rights Watch (2014). 'World Report 2015: Israel/Palestine. Events of 2014'. Accessed October 31, 2019 [online] available at http://lnnk.in/rHz.

ICRC (2007). 'Gaza-Westbank – ICRC Bulletin no. 22 / 2007'. Accessed October 31, 2019 [online] available at http://lnnk.in/soz.

IRW (2019). 'Orphans and Children'. Accessed October 31, 2019 [online] available at http://lnnk.in/skz.

Jezard, A. (2018). 'Who and what is "Civil Society"?' Accessed October 31, 2019 [online] available at http://lnnk.in/rzz.

Majed, M. (2017). 'Does "Qatar" Initiative Succeed in Ending the Palestinian Division?' Accessed November 01, 2019 [online] available at http://lnnk.in/tQx.

MEMO (2019). 'Poverty Rate in Gaza Exceeds 80%'. Accessed October 31, 2019 [online] available at http://lnnk.in/rrz.

Milton-Edwards, B. and Farrell, S. (2010). *Hamas: The Islamic Resistance Movement.* Cambridge, United Kingdom: Polity.

Nye Jr, S. J. (2008). 'Public Diplomacy and Soft Power'. Accessed January 17, 2019 [online] available at https://goo.gl/oPEQwK.

OCHA (2019a). 'Overview'. Accessed October 31, 2019 [online] available at http://lnnk.in/smz.

OCHA (2019b). 'Child Labour Increasing in Gaza'. Accessed October 31, 2019 [online] available at http://lnnk.in/rnz.

OCHA (2019c). 'Data on Casualties'. Accessed November 01, 2019 [online] available at http://bit.ly/2Ht047F.

PCBS (2017). 'PCBS: On the Eve of the International Children's Day, 20/11/2017'. Accessed October 31, 2019 [online] available at http://bit.ly/39EY2xj.

PCBS (2015). 'Palestinians at the End of 2015'. Accessed October 31, 2019 [online] available from http://bit.ly/2Hvo9e5.

Permanent Mission (2017). 'Qatar Confirms its Active Role in Building Peace and Tolerance'. Accessed January 17, 2019 [online] available at https://goo.gl/UxyGzo.

Qatar Day (2017). 'Qatar Emir Pledges $1.25 Billion to Support Tunisian Economy'. Accessed November 04, 2017 [online] available at https://goo.gl/t1EAnZ.

Reuters (2019). 'Palestinians to Resume Taking Israeli Collected Tax Money'. Accessed November 01, 2019 [online] available at http://lnnk.in/rNz.

Rivlin, P. (2013). 'Qatar: The Economics and the Politics'. *Middle East Economy* 3 (4), pp. 1–104.

Roy, S. (2013). 'Hamas and Civil Society in Gaza: Engaging the Islamist Social Sector'. Accessed October 31, 2019 [online] available at http://lnnk.in/rgD.

Schmitt, M. N., Arimatsu, L., and McCormack, T. (2010). 'Yearbook of International Humanitarian Law – 2010' Accessed October 31, 2019 [online] available at http://lnnk.in/q5B.

Suisman, D., Simon, S., Glenn, R., Anthony, C. R., and Schoenbaum, M. (2007). 'The Arc: A Formal Structure for a Palestinian State'. Accessed October 31, 2019 [online] available at http://lnnk.in/rfA.

Tanani, R. (2019). 'Gaza between Relief and Sustainability … Case Study is Qatari Aid' Accessed November 01, 2019 [online] available from http://bit.ly/2N4Ssfc.

The World Bank (2018). 'Economic Monitoring Report to the Ad Hoc Liaison Committee' Accessed October 31, 2019 [online] available at http://lnnk.in/rJz.

Tippmann, R. and Baroni, L. (2017). 'The Economics of Climate Change in Palestine' Accessed October 31, 2019 [online] available from http://lnnk.in/rjz.

Tok, E. M., Alkhater, R. M. L., and Pal, A. L. (2016). *Policy-Making in a Transformative State: The Case of Qatar*. London: Palgrave Macmillan.

Trading Economics (2019). 'Qatar GDP Per Capita'. Accessed November 01, 2019 [online] available at http://bit.ly/2u6qCZm.

UNDP (2016). 'Introduction and Context – Challenges to Development in Gaza'. Accessed November 01, 2019 [online] available at http://bit.ly/2WIJWpz.

UNEM (2009). 'Environmental Assessment of the Gaza Strip'. Accessed October 31, 2019 [online] available at http://lnnk.in/q1B.

UNHCR (2013). 'Freedom in the World 2013 – Gaza Strip'. Accessed October 31, 2019 [online] available at http://lnnk.in/r3w.

United Nations (2017). 'Gaza Ten Years Later'. Accessed October 31, 2019 [online] available at http://lnnk.in/sEA.

United Nations (2015). 'Report on UNCTAD Assistance to the Palestinian People'. Accessed October 31, 2019 [online] available at http://lnnk.in/rhz.

UNRWA (2019). 'Working in the Gaza Strip'. Accessed November 01, 2019 [online] available at http://bit.ly/39Bhg6X.

UNRWA (2014). '2014 oPt Emergency Appeal Annual Report (Including the 2014 Gaza Flash Appeal Report)'. Amman, Jordan: United Nations Relief and Works Agency for Palestine Refugees in the Near East 2015.

USAID (2013). 'CSO Sustainability Report 2013 for the Middle East and North Africa'. Accessed October 31, 2019 [online] available at http://lnnk.in/q8D.

World Health Organization (2019). 'Civil Society'. Accessed October 31, 2019 [online] available at http://lnnk.in/ssz.

Zureik, E. (2017). 'In Gaza Blockade, Humanitarian Organizations can No Longer be Neutral'. Accessed October 31, 2019 [online] available at http://lnnk.in/rcD.

# 7 An NGO's rights-based approach between contextual appropriateness and political transformation in neo-patrimonial Cambodia

## A critical realist analysis

*Rikio Kimura*

## Introduction

This chapter will problematise a development NGO's collaborative approach with the government as a rights-based approach (RBA) in Cambodia. The repoliticisation of development practices and studies has been called for by many scholars, for example, 'ethnography and political economy' (Bebbington, 2004) and the 'return of politics' (Hickey, 2008). However, it is widely held that politically confrontational RBA by NGOs does not work in relation to authoritarian governments in developing countries as it irritates such governments and makes it impossible for NGOs to operate, hence non-confrontational approaches are called for (Macpherson, 2009; Plipat, 2005; Patel and Mitlin, 2009). However, whilst non-confrontational or collaborative approaches may be contextually appropriate, are they effective in terms of the political and structural transformation that RBA intends to bring about? To answer this question, based on the critical realist ontology and epistemology (Bhaskar, 2008; Sayer, 2000), this chapter attempts to analyse the NGO's RBA in a multi-scalar way by employing critical realist theories (Jessop, 2005; Hay, 2006) and methodology (Oliver, 2012).

RBA has emerged from a deeper understanding, in which poverty is caused by structural and political problems such as inequality and exclusion; hence, its root cause is the deprivation of human rights, which is associated with those injustices (Kawamura, 2008). Thus, the shift to RBA means a shift from the service-delivery approach, which tends only to address the symptoms of poverty, to the approach that aims at the fulfilment of rights (Cornwall and Nyamu-Musembi, 2004), through which the structural causes of poverty are addressed (Uvin, 2007). RBA was conceptualised in the West (Cornwall and Nyamu-Musembi, 2004) and it is thus based on the universal concept of human rights (Nelson and Dorsey, 2008). However, the explicit claim for rights assumed in Western democracy tends to be unacceptable to authoritarian governments in developing countries, which have allowed little political space for such practices, hence non-confrontational approaches are called for (Macpherson, 2009; Plipat, 2005; Patel and Mitlin, 2009).

Life with Dignity (LWD), a local rights-based development NGO, is the case in the study. The Cambodian office of the Lutheran World Federation (LWF), an international NGO, which operated in Cambodia for more than three decades, became a local NGO, and was renamed LWD in 2011. LWF took the service-delivery and community development approaches. Encouraged by its international headquarters, it tried out RBA from 2006. As it began implementing RBA, LWF encountered a major clash with the government:

> The crisis that erupted this year [2006] was over land rights. In the area of IRDEP Oral [one of LWF's programme sites], several villagers were arrested. LWF Cambodia was blamed for inciting people to oppose the local authorities. Work and collegial relationships between LWF Cambodia and local government staff were strained. Intervention by the staff of the Phnom Penh office with the local authorities, aided by Mr. Yash Ghai, the UN Secretary General's Special Representative for Human Rights in Cambodia, highlighted the plight of those arrested.
>
> (Busch, 2008, p. 99, comments in brackets added)

By attempting RBA, including this incident, LWD adapted it to Cambodia's authoritarian political context, reflected in its collaborative approach with the government. It has been working in a context where there have been decentralisation reforms and land grabbing for more than a decade.

Although LWD began operating in Cambodia after the fall of the Khmer Rouge back in 1979, its operation needed to be 'depoliticised' in the volatile political environment of the socialist regime throughout the 1980s. Even in the early 1990s, as a development NGO, it jumped on the bandwagon, in terms of its depoliticised stance, with the influx of international development NGOs around the time of the United Nations Transitional Authority in Cambodia (UNTAC). By then, international development NGOs had generally focused on service delivery and thus were depoliticised in the context of the neoliberal Washington Consensus where the service-delivery role of government shrank and NGOs were expected to fill that gap. Thus, those development NGOs that started operating in the early 1990s were never politicised until the RBA discourse arrived in Cambodia in the 2000s. LWD, which pioneered RBA in the mid-2000s, became the leading rights-based development NGO in Cambodia.

## Context[1]

In this section, I will highlight the four dimensions of the Cambodian context, which are pertinent to this study: namely, decentralisation, neo-patrimonialism, land grabbing and social land concessions. These dimensions have influenced LWD's RBA both strategy-wise and outcome-wise.

### *Decentralisation*

Since the late 1990s, the donor community had pushed the Cambodian government to adopt decentralisation reforms, as they saw that these would bring about democratic local governance and efficient service delivery (Blunt and Turner, 2005; Craig and Porter, 2006; Pak, 2011). Therefore, it was devolution, which entailed political and democratic decentralisation with the substantial transfer of decision-making, and financial and administrative control to the local government (Blunt and Turner, 2005; Craig and Porter, 2006; Pak, 2011). In particular, the success of a pilot decentralisation programme at the commune[2] level, financed by donors in the late 1990s and early 2000s, convinced policymakers to implement decentralisation as a priority policy (Heng, Kim and So, 2011), and part of the government's strategic thinking was to gain more funding from donors by implementing decentralisation (Blunt and Turner, 2005).

Another strategic thinking of the Cambodian People's Party (CPP), the ruling party, to implement decentralisation, was to enhance its credibility and legitimacy (Blunt and Turner, 2005; Pak, 2011; Plummer and Tritt, 2012). Since the Khmer Rouge rule in the 1970s, local authorities had been involved in violence and intimidation for purposes ranging from sending people into military service to winning votes, thereby making them unpopular (Plummer and Tritt, 2012; Pak, 2011). Decentralisation has included the elections of commune councillors, resulting in more effective, people-friendly candidates (Pak, 2011). Furthermore, in all four elections held since 2002 until my fieldwork in 2012, the CPP prevailed, thereby establishing its legitimacy. During the fieldwork, the CPP was still able to control commune councils, as these were ultimately accountable to the party (Pak, 2011).

In spite of the CPP's self-interested motives, decentralisation resulted in more democratic space (Öjendal and Sedara, 2011). People started seeing their electoral power made a difference. Consequently, to be re-elected, councillors were compelled to be effective in fulfilling citizens' demands whilst in office (Thede, 2009).

In addition, the commune councils' new role in development also contributed to the opening up of democratic spaces. Their primary role is to select and implement local development projects by using the Commune Sangkat[3] Fund. From the rights-based framework, the role of villages in relation to the fund is considered as demanding their rights to development (in the forms of, for example, roads and small bridges) from a council by submitting a proposal. Öjendal and Sedara (2011) found an increasingly conducive environment where people felt freer to demand such rights. Therefore, decentralisation has granted an enabling context for RBA.

### *Neo-patrimonialism*

Cambodian society has historically been patronage-based (Pak et al., 2007; Hughes, 2003; Öjendal and Sedara, 2006). At government level, neo-patrimonialism has emerged, in which government institutions, or more precisely their heads, tend to prioritise their resource allocations and devise or bend their policies according to personal patronage networks (Pak et al., 2007; Öjendal and Sedara, 2006). Rather than reforming ineffective or corrupt government policies, derived from neo-patrimonialism, the political elites tend to use in-kind charity (in the forms of, for instance, clothing and food) for citizens to gain votes and political legitimacy (Craig and Pak, 2011; Pak et al., 2007; Interview, an LWD facilitator, 3 September 2012). Whilst central elites, including government officials, military and businessmen, seek rent from the state and business activities involving the state, they are obliged to finance such charity (Craig and Pak, 2011; Milne, 2015; Un and So, 2011). Land grabbing, a major rent-seeking activity by such central elites, significantly contributes to such charity (Milne, 2015; Un and So, 2011).

### *Land grabbing*

The root of land grabbing can be traced back to the insecure land tenure caused by the abolition of private land ownership during the socialist Khmer Rouge regime (Un and So, 2011). Many rural citizens' lands have officially remained state property since then, although in practice they have occupied lands on a customary basis (Un and So, 2011). State land is categorised into state public land, which should be preserved, and state private land, which can be put to use for various types of concessions. The 2001 Land Law, enacted partly as a result of pressure from the World Bank with its neoliberal policies, formalised economic land concessions (Neef, Touch and Chiengthong, 2013), which are 'a mechanism to grant private state land through a specific economic land concession contract to a concessionaire to use for agricultural and industrial-agricultural exploitation' (Council for the Development of Cambodia, 2011a, Article 2). However, without oversight mechanisms, these have encountered a political problem where state public lands, including people's lands by possession, have been transformed into state private lands through rent-seeking complicity between central political elites and domestic and foreign investors (Un and So, 2011). As discussed, informal revenue from such neo-patrimonial practice is used for strengthening CPP's political legitimacy through charity (Milne, 2015; Un and So, 2011). Consequently, economic land concessions have opened up the vast space for people's land by possession to be grabbed legally by the politically and economically powerful and thus granted an unconducive environment for people's right to land to be fulfilled.

### *Social land concessions*

Social land concessions are 'a legal mechanism to transfer private state land for social purposes to the poor who lack land for residential and/or family farming purposes' (Council for the Development of Cambodia, 2011b, Article 2) and were enacted, together with economic land concessions, under the 2001

Land Law. The World Bank has been the key counterpart to the government in this initiative and financed and provided technical support for its pilot project (Neef, Touch and Chiengthong, 2013). The overall picture is one where because of lack of political will, land distributed under social land concessions is considerably smaller (around 17,000 hectares) than land granted to investors through economic land concessions (approximately 2,200,000 hectares), and is of poor quality for farming (LICADHO, 2015; Open Development Cambodia, 2017; 2018). Moreover, Neef, Touch and Chiengthong (2013) found that social land concessions were used not necessarily for pro-poor development but for maintaining the Cambodian government's patronage power through superficially benevolent land distribution and for diverting attention from land grabbing.

## Theoretical framework

The ontological and epistemological framework that I employed for this study is that of critical realism (Bhaskar, 2008; Sayer, 2000). According to Bhaskar (2008), the 'empirical' is the domain where we can observe and experience events; the 'actual' is the domain of events whether they are experienced or not; and the 'real' are structures and their causal powers to generate events, whether they have actually generated events or not (See Table 7.1). A structure exerts its causal power because of its predated nature that embodies a particular historical distribution of resources and vested interests (Lewis, 2002) and hence is considered as a generative mechanism. Critical realists consider a generative mechanism as an emergent property brought by the conjunction of multiple elements of the society (Sayer, 2000). This study attempted to dig beneath the empirical and actual levels in order to illuminate the domain of the real, the level of generative mechanisms that were brought about by the conjunction of multiple forces converging in the research sites and caused events (the actual) and then experiences (the empirical) to occur.

With regard to the view of agency, critical realism sees that people draw on structures in order to act, and in turn, such actions of people reproduce or transform those structures (Lewis, 2002). Hence, it considers that people are knowledgeable and reflexive about structures over them (Jessop, 2001). However, as mentioned, structures exert their causal powers because of their

*Table 7.1* Domains of real, actual and empirical

| | *Domain of real* | *Domain of actual* | *Domain of empirical* |
|---|---|---|---|
| ***Mechanisms*** | X | | |
| ***Events*** | X | X | |
| ***Experiences*** | X | X | X |

(Source: Bhaskar, 2008, p. 2).

predated nature and in turn, people are susceptible to the influences of such powers.

In line with this critical realist ontology, Jessop's (2001; 2005) strategic-relational approach considers agency as structurally constrained and context-sensitive and thus tries to identify ways in which actors strategically examine the contexts for selecting their actions. On the other hand, it treats structure as strategically selective, thereby privileging some actors and policies over others (Jessop, 2001; 2005). More elaborately, 'some practices and strategies are privileged and others made more difficult to realise according to how they "match" the temporal and spatial patterns inscribed in the relevant structures' (Jessop, 2005, p. 51). Hence, it tries to find 'the relations between structurally-inscribed strategic selectivities [structures] and (differentially reflexive) structurally-oriented strategic calculation [agency]' (Jessop, 2005, p. 48, comments in brackets added). For instance, the Cambodian decentralisation is a kind of structurally-inscribed strategic selectivity that favours citizens, and the structurally-oriented strategic calculation by citizens has been to make use of such a favourable policy for their own benefit.

I employed Gramscian thought as a deeper-level political analytical approach or to penetrate the domains of the empirical, the actual and the real, because of its affinity with critical realism. There is 'a [critical] realist construction of some of Gramsci's ideas and concepts' (Joseph, 2002, p. 28, comments in brackets added) and, particularly, Gramsci extends the Marxist notion of hegemony based on economic dominance to 'political leadership more generally and to society as a whole' (Joseph, 2002, p. 28), implying various generative mechanisms in a society that exercise the powers of constraint over people. Furthermore, 'hegemony remains tied to the question of how different political groups operate, but assumes that these groups operate on a diverse terrain of structures, practices and generative mechanisms' (Joseph, 2002, p. 29), suggesting that social and political forces are emergent properties deriving from the conjunctions of various elements in society.

More specifically, Gramsci invented the notion of 'consensual domination' based on his observation of 'the failure of a revolutionary mass workers' movement and the rise of a reactionary fascism supported by much of the working class' in Italy in the 1920s (Carnoy, 1984, p. 65). Based on his extended notion of hegemony, Gramsci shows that to maintain their vested interests, the powerful in the society 'must succeed in presenting its own moral, political and cultural values as societal norms' (Hay, 2006, p. 69), known as 'common sense' (Ledwith, 2011). In particular, they may employ the 'passive revolution,' the acceptance of certain demands by citizens to prevent their hegemony from being challenged (Ledwith, 2011) in the domain of the actual. To counter such subtle tactics designed to manipulate citizens' mindset (in the domain of the empirical if experienced), citizens need to engage in a 'war of position,' a battle at the level of consciousness and perception (Carnoy, 1984; Hay, 2006).

## Methodology

This study is an ethnographic case study with a grounded theory approach (Charmaz and Mitchell, 2001). In line with the critical realist ontology and epistemology, I used a fresh approach, that of the critical realist grounded theory (Oliver, 2012). Sayer (2000) states that 'an explanation of social practice will involve a … regress from actions through reasons to rules and thence to structure' (pp. 75–76). Hence, the critical realist grounded theory emphasises individual or collective meaning in the domains of the empirical and the actual, taking this as a point of departure in this regress towards understanding causal relations in a multi-scalar manner and thus generative mechanisms (Oliver, 2012). Therefore, whilst overall I have tried to present the viewpoints of social actors in the field, later on in data analysis I re-cast their meaning-making within the extant theoretical frameworks and knowledge—namely, the literature and specialists' view—to situate the empirical and actual in relation to the real.

I chose two rural provinces out of the four in which LWD was working, to triangulate by multiple geographical locations. I selected four sample villages, two from each site. On the first research site, for several years now, people have encountered land grabbing in the name of economic land concessions for plantation.

In total, I spent five months in Cambodia doing fieldwork between 2011 and 2012. I spent four weeks on participant observation, and then conducted four focus group interviews with beneficiaries and four with LWD facilitators. After that, I conducted 45 individual interviews with beneficiaries, non-beneficiary villagers, village leaders, commune chiefs, district governors, and LWD facilitators and senior staff. In addition, the data analysed included LWD's organisational documents and the district government's development plan. One of the implications of the re-casting process of the critical realist grounded theory is that one has to go back and forth between the field and the literature to verify the connections between what is happening and experienced in the field (namely, the empirical and actual) and what in the domain of the real has caused that. Hence, I did follow-up email interviews in 2013 and follow-up in-person interviews in 2014 and 2015 with a few senior staff and a few experts on Cambodia's land issues.

## Findings

### *Decentralisation*

#### *Collaborative approach with Government*

Building on the democratic spaces allowed by decentralisation as a structurally-inscribed strategic selectivity that favours citizens, LWD's RBA has been reinforcing interactions between citizens and the local government to enhance participation by the former as well as accountability by the latter, specifically commune councils. In particular, rather than taking a confrontational approach towards the local government, LWD takes a collaborative stance through gentle prompting and developing their capacities. For instance, I observed that LWD encouraged commune councillors to attend village-level meetings so they could understand people's problems and be accountable to them. In addition, through RBA training, commune councils have recognised their duties and started fulfilling them (Cossar, 2011).

*Confidence and capacity building*

As mentioned, LWD had been implementing service delivery and community development before adopting RBA. LWD has harnessed such traditions as a springboard for enhancing its beneficiaries' capacities and confidence in rights-claiming.

Even after adopting RBA, LWD has used the service-delivery approach. Staff at both research sites mentioned that a certain level of material–economic development was essential prior to people's rights-claiming where their immediate needs existed, partly owing to the vast lack of social services even with decentralisation. One facilitator stated:

> We want community-based organisations to be strong and sustainable … it is done through establishing savings groups or bank groups for them to have a better life. When they have a better life, their rights-claiming starts working as well. In other words, if their life is not better, they are not interested in claiming their rights because they have to meet their immediate needs.
>
> (Interview, 16 July 2012)

LWD's continuous service-delivery approach plays a key role in this regard. Beneficiaries, at both research sites, who were part of the community-based organisations (CBOs) and staff from every organisational level, pointed out that beneficiaries' participation in CBOs helped develop their confidence and capacity to claim rights. In particular, their roles in CBOs have prompted them to speak in front of others. One Farmer Field School leader stated:

> Before, I was illiterate and didn't really dare to speak to other groups … After taking part in the Farmer Field School … I was frequently invited to join the meetings. I now have some guts to speak … after they asked me, I dared to answer and spoke better than before.
>
> (Interview, 12 September 2012)

> Increasing confidence in speaking in CBOs is the first step towards claiming rights (Focus group, a facilitator, 6 July 2012). LWD fosters this kind of confidence so that beneficiaries could eventually speak out, for example, in village development planning meetings.
>
> (Interview, senior staff member, 18 September 2012)

Furthermore, beneficiaries at both research sites, who were part of CBOs, as well as staff from every organisational level, mentioned that beneficiaries' roles in CBOs (particularly village development committees) encouraged them to engage with commune councils and district offices. One village development committee member stated:

> Before, I had not worked as a village development committee member. At that time, I did not dare to communicate or talk with the commune council. After working as a committee member, I dared to speak and communicate with them because it's relevant to my work.
>
> (Interview, 23 March 2012)

Whilst their discussion items with the local government might be purely administrative and routine, another village development committee member mentioned that the conversation went beyond such tasks to include an informal yet genuine rights-based conversation:

> The commune council called me to join meetings ... When I went there, they allowed us to ask questions ... and to ask questions about laws ... So I started asking like, when laws were made and announced, how the laws were used .... I just asked questions and they answered.
>
> (Interview, 11 September 2012)

The practice of addressing those in higher social positions is still foreign in hierarchical Cambodia. LWD created intentional and interactional spaces between the local government and people, which were necessary for RBA.

*Increased rights understanding*

In rights training, instead of didactically teaching abstract rights notions, LWD has helped beneficiaries connect their rights with their realities, thereby incrementally increasing their understanding of rights. In the training on climate change and RBA, a facilitator asked beneficiaries how climate change was related to rights. Some of their answers were as follows:

- Climate change affects people through floods, which relates to human rights [rights to life and security]
- Climate change causes illness and so is related to health [rights to health]
- Climate change causes lack of water [rights to water, rights to life and security, and rights to subsistence]. There will be no water for cows [rights to food and rights to subsistence].

(Field notes, 13 September 2012, comments in brackets added)

Even though they could not express the technical rights terms listed in my brackets, they understood that climate change affects their various rights.

LWD conducts rights-based training dialogically. On many occasions, I observed facilitators posing questions to create dialogues with beneficiaries during training. Weimer (2012) highlights the power of questioning: 'questioning can be learner-centred and transformative when … the questions offer learners the chance to figure things out for themselves' (p. 447).

Many beneficiaries and staff from every organisational level stated that with increased understanding of rights, beneficiaries enhanced their confidence. The following Farmer Field School member indicated that whilst she was still afraid of the local government, she hung on to rights to overcome such fear:

RESEARCH ASSISTANT: If you, aunties or sisters, have to approach the commune council and the district office, like the example we just gave, what do you think?

RESPONDENT: I am afraid to approach them, but if there is any really urgent matter, I will go and ask them for help and they will solve it.

RESEARCH ASSISTANT: Why are you afraid of them?

RESPONDENT: Because we are poor, that's why we're afraid.

RESEARCH ASSISTANT: Because you think that you are poor?

RESPONDENT: Yes, but no matter how poor we are, there are still the laws and they will solve it for us.

(Focus group, 3 April 2012)

## ***Land grabbing***

### *Confidence and capacity building*

LWD has been enhancing beneficiaries' confidence and their capacity to deal with land grabbing. Similar to the findings in the previous section, beneficiaries' understanding of their rights contributed to their confidence in dealing with the land concessionaires, according to two beneficiaries, one facilitator and one senior staff member. In land rights awareness activities, LWD reminds beneficiaries that if they hold land for five years, they can claim their right to it, supported by local authorities as witnesses, and community land maps (Email interview, senior staff, 17 October 2013). LWD also tells them to be firm in their claims (Email interview, senior staff, 17 October 2013). Newell (2006) points out that citizens should not only be aware of their land rights but should also be able to efficaciously use them to counter land grabbing.

In addition to the general confidence- and capacity-building efforts mentioned above, LWD gave beneficiaries practical methods to help them claim land rights. Such methods included forming groups and networks, and holding demonstrations. The formation of groups and networks was to forge 'power with' in dealing with issues through the local government or dealing with concessionaires directly. CBOs are the basis for such actions, whilst in some of its programme sites, LWD helps beneficiaries form advocacy networks starting from village-level advocacy focus people to commune- and provincial-level networks. A facilitator explained this:

> I used to see one region in which all the people in the commune, comprising three villages, cooperated well and dared to claim their rights … the company went into the villages for construction at night. The people also went to sleep there at night, waiting for the company. They called all the networks that supported their rights-claiming and, consequently, their struggle ended successfully.
>
> (Focus group, 16 July 2012)

If beneficiaries deal with issues through commune councils and these do not respond, LWD encourages beneficiaries to consider demonstrating, to solicit interventions from district and provincial governments.

This, together with democratic spaces grown through LWD's collaborative approach with the government, has better positioned beneficiaries in their struggles with land grabbing. Two beneficiaries and some staff from different organisational levels indicated beneficiaries had increased their confidence in dealing with land grabbing. One village development committee member lost part of her land and was compensated with US$100 per hectare by the concessionaire, but now asserted as follows:

RESEARCH ASSISTANT: Last time, because you had no experience in communicating with the village leader or the commune council, you received only $100 per hectare. If land grabbing happened again, what would you do?

RESPONDENT: I would ask for the full price of $250 or $200, like other people. Now I can contact the commune chief by phone or go to his house directly. Before, I had little knowledge and didn't know what to do. If it happened now, I wouldn't allow my land to be taken away like last time.

(Interview, 6 April 2012)

*Land grabbing as manifestation of powerful generative mechanism*

As mentioned, economic land concessions have allowed land to be grabbed legally by the politically and economically powerful. In other words, the neo-patrimonial Cambodian government and the interests of neoliberal actors, including the World Bank and domestic and international investors, have converged, which has become a powerful generative mechanism (the real) for pervasive land grabbing (the actual and empirical). In particular, decisions on land concessions deals have been made at central government level, leaving the local government unable to have a say in them (Blunt and Turner, 2005; Heng, Kim and So, 2011; Plummer and Tritt, 2012). When asked how the commune council helped to solve the land grabbing of the research site, the commune chief's voice became quieter and he started looking nervous, saying:

COMMUNE CHIEF: The commune has already been trying its best, as I have just told you. The commune will just do what it can, based on the commune's ability. If it is related to the big companies, and the commune cannot solve it, the commune will report to the higher level [the district office] in order to let them solve it.

RESEARCHER: Okay, will the district handle the issue? Is the district able to solve the issue?

COMMUNE CHIEF: [They] solve those problems, as I have just said, it is possible. [But] if we talk about the villagers who accepted those [solutions], they are not satisfied, they accepted [those] with regret. If they do not take those, they will get nothing.

(Interview, 10 July 2012, comments in brackets added)

The most salient official argument for economic land concessions is congruent with neoliberalisation. The testimony of the same commune chief clearly shows such an orientation:

> I would like to clarify that investment has always had adverse effects … But in the light of the benefits from the company which is investing, although it really brings about adverse effects, the majority of the villagers have received wages from the company, which are sufficient. Some of those villagers have jobs, and they can live on those wages. Every day, thousands of [US] dollars are coming into my commune.
>
> (Interview, 10 July 2012, comments in brackets added)

This falls within the official discursive justification of land concession deals by the government, in that they are for 'job creation' and 'economic development' (Neef, Touch and Chiengthong, 2013; Schneider, 2011). Similarly, in the district development plan, whilst the reduction of land conflicts and the provision of land rights course are mentioned, there is an antithetical mention of attracting business investments and allocating some zones for those. Jessop (2001) argues, in relation to his strategic-relational approach, that 'discursive paradigms privilege … some discursive identities/positioning, some discursive strategies and tactics, and some discursive statements over others' (p. 1225). These official discursive justifications indicate economic land concessions as a structurally-inscribed strategic selectivity that disfavours citizens, since land grabbing as the empirical and actual has emerged through the powerful generative mechanism (the real) where the vested interests of the politically and economically powerful converged.

### *Unintended complicity through social land concessions*

Whilst LWD has enabled citizens to deal with land grabbing, it has been involved in social land concessions on the same research site without problematising it. In addition to meeting the needs of the landless poor, LWD's justification for working on social land concessions is to influence the government with good model cases of social land concessions funded by the World Bank so that the government may implement these through the proper procedures as well as on a larger scale (Interview, senior staff, 8 February 2015), in line with LWD's service-delivery orientation and principle of working with the government.

However, and as mentioned earlier, Neef, Touch and Chiengthong (2013) found that social land concessions were not necessarily used for pro-poor development but for maintaining the Cambodian government's patronage power through superficially benevolent land distribution and for diverting attention from land grabbing. In this study too, when asked about the economic land concessions, the district governor oddly started doodling in his notebook and his face became serious, perhaps indicating his nervousness. Then he said:

> There has been no problem with the people's land. They do not work on their private land. This is because they live on state land. If people live on state land, they can still be granted that land. But if companies want to buy that land, then the government prepares other land for people and transfers them to such land … The government facilitates the transfer of lands to them. Four hundred families who do not have land are in the process of obtaining social land concessions. LWD provides materials and information for people in this social land concession project.
>
> (Interview, 9 September 2012)

This can be considered as a passive revolution bringing about the consensual domination of its citizens in the domains of the actual and empirical, although the government has no premediated plans for social land concessions to be use this way (Interview, NGO staff member specialised in Cambodia's land issue, 18 February 2015). LWD has implemented the social land concessions financed by the World Bank, and hence, as an unintended consequence, LWD, together with the bank, has contributed to the Cambodian government's efforts to maintain its neo-patrimonialism.

Furthermore, in 2014, LWD received the rather controversial second phase of funding for social land concessions from the World Bank. The bank had suspended the release of further new loans from its own funding since 2011, due to the unresolved issue of urban land grabbing in Phnom Penh, in which some of those evicted had not been properly compensated. This second phase of funding was controversial because although the urban land grabbing had still not been resolved, the bank released the funding. The media and the NGO community, including two major NGO networks in Cambodia, harshly criticised this move by the bank. LWD's justification for receiving this funding was that it met the dire needs of people who had settled in the existing social land concessions, which LWD had been assisting (Interview, senior staff, 8 February 2015), in line with their service-delivery orientation.

From its operational point of view, LWD has a hybrid structure as a rights-based and service-delivery organisation because of its historical evolution. However, there is a trade-off relationship between these approaches which LWD's acceptance of the second phase of funding for social land concessions illuminates. On the one hand, LWD should have been part of the united front of the anti-land grabbing movement, together with major NGO networks, in order to counter consensual domination and not to send the wrong signal to the government or other NGOs as the leading rights-based development NGO. On the other hand, it is understandable that it did not want to abandon the landless poor looking to LWD for assistance because of its service-delivery roots.

As seen, LWD has attempted to empower its beneficiaries to claim their rights in the context of land grabbing. However, it has worked with the social land concessions, which are, in effect, used to maintain neo-patrimonialism by parsimoniously distributing government land to the landless and thereby diverting people's attention from land grabbing (Neef, Touch and Chiengthong, 2013). Hence, it seems meaningless to empower its beneficiaries to contest land grabbing whilst simultaneously through the social land concessions, LWD and the Cambodian government have, in effect, become complicit in pacifying Cambodians' frustration with land grabbing.

### *Complicity with neoliberalism*

For a more comprehensive analysis, the other strand of the generative mechanisms for land grabbing, namely the neoliberal structure associated with neo-patrimonialism, needs to be traced. Springer (2011) argues that Cambodia's political elites and their patronage networks have been using neoliberalism for their own benefits: 'the patronage system has allowed local elites to co-opt, transform, and (re)articulate neoliberal reforms through a framework which asset strips public resources, thereby increasing people's exposure to corruption, coercion, and violence' (p. 2554). The neo-patrimonial Cambodian government and the neoliberal structure, including the World Bank's neoliberal policies and the interests of domestic and international investors, have converged, thereby becoming an emergent property in the domain of the real. This has caused the privatisation of state public land and consequently engendered pervasive land grabbing in the domains of the actual and empirical. In fact, this phenomenon is symptomatic of the larger neoliberalisation process in Cambodia. The Cambodian government has employed the discursive justification of 'order,' 'stability' and 'security' over citizens' rights in order to facilitate neoliberal reforms and to fulfil the interests of elites (Springer, 2010). Such consensual domination has been utilised to justify the government's authoritarianism in the form of violence from above as in the case of land grabbing (Springer, 2010). This consensual domination needs to be countered through the war of position, a battle at the level of perception by LWD, the leading rights-based development NGO. However,

LWD's depoliticised roots seem to have hampered this and ironically made it complimentarily facilitate neoliberalisation on the ground (Choudry and Kapoor, 2013; Petras, 1999), as indicated by its involvement in social land concessions.

## Conclusion

This study has examined the effectiveness of a non-confrontational RBA by LWD, which is reflected in its principle of working with the government. Through capacitating and sensitising both citizens and the local government, this approach has gradually brought about positive shifts in the relationship between citizens and local government. However, the principle of working with the government is a double-edged sword that has made LWD blind to the imperativeness of RBA to penetrate deep-seated injustices embedded in land grabbing, namely neo-patrimonialism with a neoliberal twist. Such a stance is the product of their position within the community of depoliticised development NGOs in Cambodia as well as in relation to the oppressive government, which has made it difficult for them to think and act differently.

## Notes

1 This section, and the section on Methodology, in particular, share similar content to those in Kimura (2019) as both it and this chapter are based on my doctoral thesis.
2 There is a five-tier administration system in Cambodia: national, provincial, district, commune and village.
3 *Sangkat* is equivalent to a commune in towns and cities.

## References

Bebbington, A. 2004. Theorising participation and institutional change: ethnography and political economy. In: Hickey, S. and Mohan, G. (eds.) *Participation: from tyranny to transformation*, London: Zed Books.

Bhaskar, R. 2008. *A realist theory of science*, New York: Routledge.

Blunt, P. and Turner, M. 2005. Decentralisation, democracy and development in a post-conflict society: commune councils in Cambodia. *Public Administration and Development*, 25 (1), 75–87.

Busch, M. 2008. *Angkor L: a short history of LWF Cambodia 1997 to 2007*, Phnom Penh: Lutheran World Federation Cambodia.

Carnoy, M. 1984. *The state and political theory*, Princeton, NJ: Princeton University Press.

Charmaz, K. and Mitchell, R. G. 2001. Grounded theory in ethnography. In: Atkinson, P., Coffey, A., Delamount, S., Lofland, J. and Lofland, L. (eds.) *The Sage handbook of ethnography*, Thousand Oaks: Sage.

Choudry, A. and Kapoor, D. 2013. Introduction: NGOization: complicity, contradictions and prospects. In: Choudry, A. and Kapoor, D. (eds.) *NGOization: complicity, contradictions and prospects*, London: Zed Books.

Cornwall, A. and Nyamu-Musembi, C. 2004. Putting the 'rights-based approach' to development into perspective. *Third World Quarterly*, 25 (8), 1415–1437.

Cossar, J. 2011. LWD Cambodia is meeting the needs of the people it serves: report of mid term evaluation of LWD country strategy 2009–2014. Unpublished Internal Document, Life with Dignity.

Council for the Development of Cambodia. 2011a. Sub-decree on economic land concessions [Online]. Available: http://www.cambodiainvestment.gov.kh/sub-decree-146-on-economic-land-concessions_051227.html [Accessed 16 February 2020].

Council for the Development of Cambodia. 2011b. Sub-decree on social land concessions [Online]. Available: http://www.cambodiainvestment.gov.kh/ja/sub-decree-19-on-social-land-concessions_030319.html [Accessed 16 February 2020].

Craig, D. and Pak, K. 2011. Party financing of local investment projects: elite and mass patronage. In: Hughes, C. and Un, K. (eds.) *Cambodia's economic transformation*, Copenhagen: NIAS.

Craig, D. and Porter, D. 2006. *Development beyond neoliberalism?: governance, poverty reduction, and political economy*, Abingdon: Routledge.

Hay, C. 2006. (What's Marxist about) Marxist state theory? In: Hay, C., Lister, M. and Marsh, D. (eds.) *The state: theories and issues*, Basingstoke: Palgrave Macmillan.

Heng, S., Kim, S. and So, S. 2011. Decentralised governance in a hybrid polity: localisation of decentralisation reform in Cambodia. Cambodia Development Resource Institute Working Paper 63 [Online]. Available: https://cdri.org.kh/publication/decentralized-governance-in-a-hybrid-polity-localization-of-decentralization-reform-in-cambodia-by-heng-seiha-kim-sedara-and-so-sukbunthoeun-working-paper-63-november-2011/ [Accessed 16 February 2020].

Hickey, S. 2008. The return of politics in development studies I: getting lost within the poverty agenda? *Progress in Development Studies*, 8 (4), 349–358.

Hughes, C. 2003. *The political economy of Cambodia's transition, 1991–2001*, London: RoutledgeCurzon.

Jessop, B. 2001. Institutional re(turns) and the strategic-relational approach. *Environment and Planning A*, 33 (7), 1213–1235.

Jessop, B. 2005. Critical realism and the strategic-relational approach. *New Formations*, 56, 40–53.

Joseph, J. 2002. *Hegemony: a realist analysis*, Abingdon: Routledge.

Kawamura, A. 2008. Scopes of the human rights-based approaches to development: analysing, transforming, raising self-awareness, and sharing visions for development. In: Asia Pacific Human Rights Information Centre (ed.) *Asia-Pacific human rights review 2008: new paradigm for development: scope of human rights-based approaches to development [Japanese]*. Tokyo: Gendai-jinbun-sha.

Kimura, R. 2019. Transformative learning through an NGO's rights-based approach in Cambodia: a multi-scalar analysis. *Compare: A Journal of Comparative and International Education* [Published online].

Ledwith, M. 2011. *Community development: a critical approach*, Bristol: The Policy Press.

Lewis, P. A. 2002. Agency, structure and causality in political science: a comment on Sibeon. *Politics*, 22 (1), 17–23.

Licadho. 2015. On stony ground: a look into social land concessions. A Brief Paper Issue [Online]. Available: http://www.licadho-cambodia.org/reports/files/208LICADHOReport-LASEDSocialLandConcessions2015-English.pdf [Accessed 16 February 2020].

Macpherson, I. 2009. The rights-based approach to adult education: implications for NGO-government partnerships in Southern Tanzania. *Compare: A Journal of Comparative and International Education*, 39 (2), 263–279.

Milne, S. 2015. Cambodia's unofficial regime of extraction: illicit logging in the shadow of transnational governance and investment. *Critical Asian Studies*, 47 (2), 200–228.

Neef, A., Touch, S. and Chiengthong, J. 2013. The politics and ethics of land concessions in Rural Cambodia. *Journal of Agricultural and Environmental Ethics*, 26 (6), 1085–1103.

Nelson, P. J. and Dorsey, E. 2008. *New rights advocacy: changing strategies of development and human rights NGOs*, Washington, D.C.: Georgetown University Press.

Newell, P. 2006. Corporate accountability and citizen action: cases from India. In: Newell, P. and Wheeler, J. (eds.) *Rights, resources and the politics of accountability*, London: Zed Books.

Öjendal, J. and Sedara, K. 2006. Korob, Kaud, Klach: in search of agency in rural Cambodia. *Journal of Southeast Asian Studies*, 37 (3), 507–526.

Öjendal, J. and Sedara, K. 2011. Real democratisation in Cambodia?: an empirical review of the potential of a decentralisation reform. Swedish International Centre for Local Democracy Working Paper No. 9 [Online]. Available: http://www.globalstudies.gu.se/digitalAssets/1341/1341375_icld_wp9_printerfriendly.pdf [Accessed 16 February 2020].

Oliver, C. 2012. Critical realist grounded theory: a new approach for social work research. *British Journal of Social Work*, 42 (2), 371–387.

Open Development Cambodia. 2017. Allocated land for social land concession [Online]. Available: https://opendevelopmentcambodia.net/dataset/?id=allocated-land-for-social-land-concession [Accessed 16 February 2020].

Open Development Cambodia. 2018. Economic land concessions (ELCs) [Online]. Available: https://opendevelopmentcambodia.net/dataset/?id=economiclandconcessions [Accessed 16 February 2020].

Pak, K. 2011. *A dominant party in a weak state: how the ruling party in Cambodia has managed to stay dominant*. PhD Thesis, Australian National University.

Pak, K., Horng, V., Eng, N., Ann, S., Kim, S., Knowles, J. and Craig, D. 2007. *Accountability and neo-patrimonialism in Cambodia: a critical literature review.* Cambodia Development Resource Institute Working Paper 34 [Online]. Available: https://cdri.org.kh/publication/wp-34-accountability-and-neo-patrimonialism-in-cambodia-a-critical-literature-review/ [Accessed 16 February 2020].

Patel, S. and Mitlin, D. 2009. Reinterpreting the rights-based approach: a grassroots perspective on rights and development. In: Hickey, S. and Mitlin, D. (eds.) *Rights-based approaches to development: exploring the potential and pitfalls*, Sterling: Kumarian Press.

Petras, J. 1999. NGOs: in the service of imperialism. *Journal of Contemporary Asia*, 29 (4), 429–440.

Plipat, S. 2005. *Developmentising human rights: how development NGOs interpret and implement a human rights-based approach to development policy.* PhD Thesis, University of Pittsburgh.

Plummer, J. and Tritt, G. 2012. Voice, choice and decision: a study of local governance processes in Cambodia. *Cambodia: Governance Partnership Facility—The Commune Series* [Online]. Available: http://asiafoundation.org/resources/pdfs/voicechoicedecisionlocalgovCB.pdf [Accessed 16 February 2020].

Sayer, A. 2000. *Realism and social science*, Thousand Oaks: Sage.

Schneider, A. E. 2011. *What shall we do without our land?: land grabs and resistance in rural Cambodia*. International Conference on Global Land Grabbing, 6–8 April 2011, University of Sussex.

Springer, S. 2010. *Cambodia's neoliberal order: violence, authoritarianism, and the contestation of public space*, Abingdon: Routledge.

Springer, S. 2011. Articulated neoliberalism: the specificity of patronage, kleptocracy, and violence in Cambodia's neoliberalisation. *Environment and Planning A*, 43 (11), 2554–2570.

Thede, N. 2009. Decentralisation, democracy and human rights: a human rights-based analysis of the impact of local democratic reforms on development. *Journal of Human Development and Capabilities*, 10 (1), 103–123.

Un, K. and So, S. 2011. Land rights in Cambodia: how neopatrimonial politics restricts land policy reform. *Pacific Affairs*, 84 (2), 289–308.

Uvin, P. 2007. From the right to development to the rights-based approach: how 'human rights' entered development. *Development in Practice*, 17 (4–5), 597–606.

Weimer, M. 2012. Learner-centred teaching and transformative learning. In: Taylor, E. W., Cranton, P. and Associates (eds.) *The Handbook of transformative learning: theory, research, and practice[Kindle iPad Version]*. San Francisco: Jossey-Bass.

# 8 Civil society and left-wing governments in Latin America

## The limits of influence

*Chris O'Connell*

## Introduction

The first decade of the 21st century witnessed a series of electoral wins by leftist presidents across Latin America. This unprecedented political phenomenon generated a large body of scholarship, with much of that attention coming to focus on the influence of civil society on bringing these leaders to power. Social mobilisation in opposition to neoliberal economic measures created waves of contention and brought down governments. A wide array of social actors came together not only to challenge neoliberalism, but to articulate innovative policy alternatives. Furthermore, the influence of mobilised civil society did not end with the election of these leftist leaders, as in the past. Instead, members of civil society organisations took up prominent government posts, long-standing demands were adopted as policy and new constitutions were written with the active participation of social actors. Such levels of civil society influence over government are rare and therefore worthy of further study.

This chapter analyses the political influence of civil society in the context of one Latin American country – Ecuador – where civil society sought to influence the policies of left-wing president Rafael Correa. Ecuador was previously renowned for the strength of its social movements, which contributed to ousting three presidents. Correa was elected as a political outsider, without the support of an organised political party but with the tacit backing of civil society. This chapter considers the impact of two important social actors during the Correa presidency: rural social movements seeking the reform of the agricultural sector along the lines of food sovereignty; and the urban Yasunidos movement that organised to resist oil exploitation in Ecuador's Amazon rainforest. These cases reveal the importance of a relational approach to the study of civil society influence on politics, but also point to the importance of creating suitable institutions to allow for deeper and sustained social engagement.

## Theorising civil society influence in Latin America

While scholarship relating to the political influence of civil society is a relatively recent phenomenon in some regions of the world (Amenta, 2014), this issue has been studied for many years in Latin America (Escobar & Álvarez, 1992; Foweraker, 1995). During the last 30 years, trade unions in the region have been replaced as the leaders of civil society by 'new' social movements (Ibid). These movements – including indigenous and peasant movements, neighbourhood associations, environmental collectives, issue-specific organisations, NGOs and citizen groups – are heterogenous and fragmented (Escobar & Álvarez, 1992). Early analysis tended to focus on the internal dynamics of movements, highlighting elements such as mobilisational structures and issue framing (McAdam, McCarthy & Zald, 1996).

With regard to wider influence, the literature focussed on political opportunities, which tended to relate to the national contexts of movements. Nevertheless, this literature came to be seen as overly movement-centric (McAdam & Tarrow, 2010: 259), and focus shifted to the interaction of movements with institutional democracy. For some, movements represented the possibility of a new form of 'deepened' democracy (Roberts, 1998). Others viewed social movements as inherently anti-democratic, with indigenous movements said to 'feed off the politics of rage, race, and revenge' (Naim, 2004: 104). Van Cott, however, argued that indigenous movements both strengthen democracy and challenge democratic institutions (2007: 127). While some viewed social movements as 'the new protagonists of profound social change' (Wolff, 2007: 19), others considered this a 'romantic interpretation' (Foweraker, 2001: 844).

Studies of the influence of social movement in the region came to centre on approaches to state power. Petras and Veltmeyer (2005: 165) considered attempts by social movements to seek power via representative politics a 'dead end' and a betrayal of their true ethos. Other scholars, however, saw this as the 'inevitable institutionalism' of social movements, as they were forced to engage with the state in order to satisfy demands (Foweraker, 2001: 846). Zamosc (2007: 4) expanded this idea by classifying movements by whether they sought influence or power, while conceding that the line separating the two was fluid. Petras and Veltmeyer (2005: 3) concurred that all social movements in Latin America, in one way or the other, were 'engaged in a struggle for state power'. Expanding on this, Silva (2009: 10) argued that the literature had overstated the extent to which movements were concerned with identity politics over material demands.

The political influence of social movements in Latin America has been studied in a variety of ways. One example is Smulovitz and Peruzzotti's (2000) concept of 'societal accountability': a non-electoral form of civil society influence that hinged on protests 'triggering' democratic institutions, such as legislatures, judiciaries, ombudsmen and the media (Ibid: 151–3). Other scholars identified a separate, non-institutional path to influence via 'street politics' (Machado, Scartascini & Tommasi, 2011). This path, the authors contended, was more likely to succeed where political institutions were weak (Ibid), as has been argued is the case in Latin America (Weyland, 2004).

One example of that influence is captured by the literature on presidential ousters. Scholars differed as to whether the series of ousters across the region since the return to democracy in the 1980s were examples of institutional (Pérez-Liñán, 2007) or non-institutional forms of control (Hochstetler, 2006), or a combination of the two (Marsteintredet & Berntzen, 2008). What was clearer, however, was that sustained social mobilisation was central to the fall of these presidents. Furthermore, scholars contended that the threat of ousters served to condition the behaviour of presidents. Hochstetler (2006: 410) noted that mobilisation could restrain presidents' behaviour, while Pérez-Liñán (2007: 11) asserted that presidents learned and 'adapted their strategies accordingly'. As a result, mobilised civil society was said to be the new 'moderating power' in Latin American politics (Philip & Panizza, 2011: 41).

But how and in what circumstances did this power act to modify politics in the region? In this context, it is necessary to consider other factors that combine to determine the impact of mobilisations on political outcomes (Escobar & Álvarez, 1992). As Amenta notes, there are 'no magic bullets' when it comes to explaining when and why movements matter (2014: 18). Instead, he proposes a political mediation model that is 'contingent on specific circumstances' (Ibid). One element is the ability to sustain mobilisations, which is considered 'crucial' to impacting political decisions (Philip & Panizza, 2011: 49). Achieving this, however, is not straightforward, as collective action of this kind is costly to maintain in terms of time, resources and security.

For this reason, Silva (2009) proposes a relational approach to the study of civil society influence. In order to affect political outcomes, social movements require not only organisation and suitable framing, but highly articulated horizontal linkages with other social actors and the wider citizenry. This level of unity is crucial as the power of civil society is collective in nature (Ibid: 33). In other words, the broader the articulation the greater the mobilisation's influence, with those achieving coordination between movements and the middle classes said to reach a 'higher plane' of collective power (Ibid: 38). Such levels of unity and sustained mobilisation are challenging for 'new' social movements, as they tend to be 'more cyclical and ephemeral' than labour movements (Roberts, 2008: 342).

Along with the ability of civil society organisations to articulate bonds and frame shared demands, their relations with other power players also matter. In the context of contemporary Latin America, another group that competes for political influence are local elites, either organised via business associations or autonomously. Scholarship has demonstrated that the power of business elites grew significantly during the 1990s and early 2000s, when neoliberal hegemony in the region led to widespread privatisations and deregulation of the economy (Weyland, 2004). Furthermore, wealthy elites can often choose from a range of additional levers for influencing policymakers, including personal connections, campaign contributions and privileged access. It is a huge challenge for social actors to trump the influence of local elites, whose preferences are typically opposed to those of civil society (Hunt, 2016).

Furthermore, the influence of civil society must also be considered relative to the power of political actors. According to Luders (2010), an important context for determining the level of influence of social mobilisation is the vulnerability of their 'target'. In the context of contemporary Latin America, 'outsider' presidents presented such vulnerable targets. While over time some of these leftist leaders came to be viewed as strong and uncompromising, they often took office in precarious circumstances, lacking the support of a well-institutionalised political party. Additionally, upon taking power these presidents faced the 'vehement opposition' of well-resourced elites (Hunt, 2016: 8). In those circumstances, social mobilisation presented a real and credible threat to presidential survival, but also a key potential source of support.

This chapter examines the issue of the political influence of civil society in the context of the so-called 'Shift to the Left' in Latin America. Many of the broadly leftist presidents elected during this period were vulnerable targets, in countries where mobilised social movements paved their way to power by unseating previous incumbents and halting neoliberal reforms. Civil society clearly wielded significant influence during that period. Yet as this chapter demonstrates, this influence was contingent on specific circumstances. In particular, this chapter argues in favour of adopting a relational approach to the study of civil society influence. Relations between social actors are highly significant, given the collective nature of their power. Furthermore, the changing nature of power relations between civil society and presidents is of crucial importance to explaining the extent of civil society influence in terms of the realisation of key demands.

## Tense relations: civil society and New Left governments in Latin America

The first decade of the 21st century witnessed a series of electoral wins by leftist presidents across Latin America. Presidents such as Hugo Chavez in Venezuela, Lula da Silva in Brazil, and Evo Morales in Bolivia, took power with mandates to challenge the existing political and economic *status quo*. Even more surprising than their election was the fact that several of them went on to substantively honour their election promises. This unprecedented political phenomenon, often referred to as the 'Shift to the Left', generated a large body of scholarship (Levitsky & Roberts, 2011; Philip & Panizza, 2011).

Much of that attention has come to focus on the influence of civil society on bringing these leaders to power (Lievesley, 2009; Collins, 2014). As Silva (2009) has demonstrated, attempts during the 1990s to install neoliberalism across the region were met with sustained social resistance. In some countries, these waves of contentious collective action ousted presidents and 'ushered in governments inclined to act on mandates' (Ibid: 53). In this way, mobilised civil society was instrumental in preparing the ground for the emergence of these leftist leaders (Lievesley, 2009). The precise nature of that relationship was open to interpretation, however. While Lynch (2017: 97) asserted that these governments were the 'political expression' of social movements, Collins (2014: 61) argued that these presidents 'piggybacked' on these social struggles.

Civil society influence was not limited to creating the conditions for the election of progressive leaders, but extended to effectively setting the electoral agenda, outlining innovative policy alternatives to neoliberalism. Key proposals that emerged from civil society – such as constituent assemblies, sovereign control of natural resources, wealth redistribution and forms of sustainable development – found their way into candidates' manifestos. As Cannon and Kirby (2012: 13) noted, these movements 'generated a discourse critical of the neoliberal project, built movements to challenge it, and provided many of the leading figures that were to win state power'.

Some of these leftist presidents were political outsiders who took power as vulnerable targets, both dependent upon and threatened by civil society. Accordingly, the political influence of civil society was strongest during this period of vulnerability. This was particularly the case in countries where civil society remained mobilised post-election in support of key demands, such as Venezuela, Bolivia and Ecuador (Roberts, 2008). These countries were also notable for the fact that presidents initially governed largely in line with their election offerings, noted to be far from typical in a region where presidents often 'switched' away from their campaign promises (Silva, 2009). Instead, presidents in these countries established stronger national control over strategic natural resources, increased social spending and convoked constituent assemblies to write new constitutions.

Social actors were heavily involved in these processes that overhauled the institutional frameworks and altered the underlying power dynamics of their countries (Ellner, 2012). In the process, social actors incorporated symbols, proposals and alternative paradigms that had emerged during the preceding period of contention. A prominent example is '*sumak kawsay*' (living well), a concept drawn from the indigenous cosmovision that promotes a sustainable relationship with the natural world (Acosta, 2008). Versions of this concept were enshrined in the constitutions of both Bolivia and Ecuador. However, it is also true that this situation was not static. As key shared demands were turned into policy, levels of mobilisation and unity among and between movements declined.

Two further variables stand out. The first is the position of local economic elites. While weakened and delegitimised during the prior period of contention, these groups in time sought to reassert their power and re-establish lost influence (Wolff, 2016). Second, presidents were not content to remain in such a weak position, and attempted to give state form to social demands and in this way enhance their legitimacy (Lievesley, 2009: 34). Indeed, these presidents acquired informal powers due to their extraordinarily high levels of public approval, derived from making good on these promises. Furthermore, the same constitutions that enshrined long-standing civil society demands, also strengthened the formal powers of the executive. These presidents were no longer the vulnerable targets they had been.

This new context presented a new range of challenges for social actors, and many struggled to find an appropriate way to dealt with a 'seemingly sympathetic government' (Becker, 2012: 117). Civil society movements faced a difficult choice between continued confrontation or likely co-optation. Different movements adopted distinct stances, leading to the fragmentation and associated weakening of civil society influence. This situation was hastened by government moves to close associational spaces via the introduction or implementation of draconian laws that sought to delimit civil society to restrict who can 'do' politics. As a result of both these internal and external tensions, the influence of civil society over the policy of leftist governments in Latin America gradually declined, and in some cases transformed into open opposition.

The era of 'New Left' governments in Latin America presents an interesting case for studying the limits of civil society influence. As this overview reveals, mobilised social movements in Latin America created the conditions for the emergence of left-wing presidents across the region through waves of contentious politics. Furthermore, the power of mobilised civil society conditioned the behaviour of some presidents during their early periods in office. Social actors both supported and pressurised leftist presidents to honour campaign promises. Nevertheless, when it came to the actual implementation of alternative development models, tensions arose between presidents and civil society. This chapter considers two such alternatives – food sovereignty and the post-oil development plan known as Yasuni-ITT – and the movements that organised behind them in Ecuador.

## Changing relations: Rafael Correa and civil society

The presidency of Rafael Correa presents a suitable case for studying these dynamics. Correa was elected as a political outsider in 2006, following a tumultuous ten-year period during which three sitting presidents were ousted following sustained social mobilisation. Correa did not have the support of an organised political party, his PAIS (country) movement very much an electoral vehicle made up of 'leftist political operatives and intellectuals' (de la Torre & Conaghan, 2009: 341) and personal contacts. Furthermore, in order to demonstrate his anti-system credentials, Correa refused to run candidates in the legislative elections (Lucas, 2007: 97). While this move is credited with helping him to gain the backing of social actors and the middle class (Ibid), Correa entered office as a highly vulnerable target.

In that context, Correa's failure to establish an electoral pact with Ecuador's most powerful movement, the Confederation of Indigenous Nationalities of Ecuador (CONAIE) was significant in terms of avoiding co-optation. However, while some movements had misgivings about Correa, they supported his electoral offerings (Becker, 2015). This was no coincidence. According to PAIS co-founder Alberto Acosta, at interview on 22 July 2015, the programme for government consciously gathered together the demands and proposals advanced by social movements over previous years, such as participative democracy, pluriculturalism, food sovereignty, environmental sustainability and the solidarity economy.

Once in office, Correa appeared to distance himself from social movements, while proclaiming his intention to forge ahead with some of the progressive proposals in his programme for government (Lucas, 2007). The result was an alliance of convenience between Correa and civil society, united behind a shared demand to convoke a constituent assembly to write a new constitution. In the face of strong opposition from local elites, civil society came together behind Correa. While pressure from civil society undoubtedly played a role in ensuring that Correa followed through with this promise, the assembly also presented him a route to political survival. Ultimately, this combination of state and social power brought about the realisation of this key demand. As noted by former Environment Minister Daniel Ortega at interview on 22 August 2016, the support of civil society was crucial to the survival of the government during its early years in power.

The process of the assembly was highly participative, with civil society playing a central role in producing a draft text that extended rights and enshrined a range of alternative development models (Becker, 2011). If victory in the battle for the constituent assembly worked to the advantage of social actors, it also proved to be a turning point for Correa. The triumph effectively ended elite control of Ecuador's political institutions, and began a series of electoral victories that consolidated the position of the once-vulnerable president (Ellner, 2012). Another key factor was the new Constitution, which along with extending rights and protections, significantly enhanced the formal powers of the presidency (Becker, 2011).

Correa's enhanced legitimacy and strengthened power heralded a significant shift in attitude toward civil society. This change was initially confined to verbal attacks, frequently broadcast via Correa's weekly television show. During this period, Correa utilised plebiscitary tactics to gain more control over state institutions (Sánchez, 2017). In particular, following his re-election in 2013, and having gained an absolute majority in the legislature, Correa moved openly to control civil society. Measures included Decree 016, that obliged social organisations to register and to refrain from political action (Conaghan, 2016: 115–116), and laws designed to criminalise social protest (Coryat & Picq, 2016: 284).

Mobilised civil society played a crucial role in creating the conditions for the electoral victory of leftist outsider Rafael Correa. Social movements produced fresh proposals that effectively set the electoral agenda and remained both broadly articulated and mobilised in support of key demands such as the constituent assembly. Nevertheless, this case also demonstrates the relational nature of that influence. As Correa's position altered, so did his attitudes and policies toward civil society. The next sections will consider how these dynamics played out in the case of two distinct movements that sought the implementation of alternative development models.

## (i) Mobilising for food sovereignty

The desire for fundamental agrarian reform was a long-standing one in Ecuador, with *campesino* and indigenous movements coming to frame this shared demand using the concept of food sovereignty (Intriago et al., 2017). This concept was developed as a response to the impacts of globalisation on small producers (Ibid: 317), and centres on local and sustainable food production. The election of Correa appeared to bring the fulfilment of that demand as Ecuador became one of a 'handful of countries' to institutionalise the concept of food sovereignty (Clark, 2016: 189). Nevertheless, there is consensus in the literature that progress in translating norms into reality was disappointing at best (Ibid; Giunta, 2014; McKay et al., 2014).

It is contended that the uneven nature and progress of these reforms reflects the changing correlation of forces in Ecuador during the course of Correa's presidency. In particular, we can observe the weakening and disarticulation of the movements backing this demand; the re-establishment of elite influence; and the increased strength of the president. In this context, it is possible to observe three distinct phases of development in the proposal for food sovereignty. The first dates from the 2006 elections to Correa's re-election in 2009, during which most progress was made toward significant reform. During the second phase, from 2009 until late 2011, combined a discursive commitment to food sovereignty with an overarching policy direction that directly contradicted its principles. Finally, following Correa's public comments distancing himself from substantive reform in 2011, government discourse finally aligned with policy favouring large agribusiness.

Returning to his election in 2006, Correa's plan for government offered to: diversify production based on *campesino* and indigenous communities; provide access to credit; reducing pesticides; prohibit genetically modified organisms (GMOs); enact land reform; and withdraw from negotiations with the US over the signing of a free trade agreement (FTA). Additionally, Correa signed an agreement with a front of rural social movements known as the '*Mesa Agraria*' ('Agrarian Committee'), that included the Confederation of Indigenous, Peasant, and Black Organisations (FENOCIN; Giunta, 2014: 1210). The agreement included commitments to protect national food production, reactivate the rural sector through increased state funding and 'democratise access to land' (Ibid: 1212). In return, the movements mobilised in support of Correa's candidacy, providing key rural votes.

Following Correa's election, rural movements continued mobilising to pressurise the president to make good on his promises. For example, during a large mobilisation supporting the constituent assembly in 2007, movements presented a list of demands to Correa that included 'comprehensive agrarian reform' (Lucas, 2007: 210). Indigenous and *campesino* movements were also key players in the battle for the constituent assembly, and went on to play roles in the drafting of the new Constitution. The adoption of '*sumak kawsay*' as a framework by Assembly President Alberto Acosta, presented rural movements with a political opening (Peña, 2016). This approach allowed rural actors to frame food sovereignty as transforming the agrarian sector (Acosta, 2008: 43), enabling linkages with a wider group of social actors (Peña, 2016: 223). However, the level of articulation that movements achieved was equally significant. While tensions had long existed between the major indigenous movements CONAIE and FENOCIN, they tended to unite in the face of common threats (Becker, 2015: 78).

This was the case at the constituent assembly, where the combination of their respective forces and methods exerted sufficient pressure to achieve shared goals (Ibid: 178; Clark, 2016: 192). Working closely with the governing coalition, FENOCIN took charge of the committee responsible for the area of food sovereignty. This internal influence combined with CONAIE's use of traditional means to pressure the government from the outside (Sánchez, 2013: 45). This unity proved vital given the level of opposition these movements faced both within and outside the assembly. Lucas details the 'constant pressure' on movements from agribusiness, spanning a spectrum from planted media stories to threats (2015: 158). Opposition also came from Correa, who publicly questioned the proposal to ban GMOs (Ibid: 152).

Faced with pressure from the business sector, and divisions within the governing bloc, the unity of purpose of indigenous and peasant movements proved crucial. The 2008 Constitution reflected many of their key demands. Article 281 established food sovereignty as a 'strategic objective and obligation of the State' to ensure the achievement of 'healthy and culturally appropriate food' for all. The Constitution further committed the state to promoting organic production methods, providing credit, regulating monopolies and the concentration of land; and introduced a qualified prohibition on GMOs. This was to prove the high-water mark of food sovereignty, however. As noted at interview on 16 July 2015 by Luis Andrango of FENOCIN, 'the assembly was a democratic *fiesta*, but then came the hangover'.

In fact, government policy began to diverge from discourse even before the assembly ended. Citing a regional food emergency, Correa introduced measures to boost production, including tax breaks and incentives that favoured agribusiness and pesticides over small producers and organic methods (Ibid: 156). Prior to introducing the measures, Correa consulted with agribusiness leaders but not civil society regarding this 'Agrarian Mandate' (Rosero, Carbonell & Regalado, 2011: 94). The measure was duly passed, in spite of estimates that it would cost the state $415 million, and fears of incentivising agro-chemicals in a way that contradicted food sovereignty (Ibid).

Nevertheless, the second phase presents a somewhat confusing picture, as the Correa government attempted to advance along two contradictory paths: committing to food sovereignty while expanding the agribusiness model. As Correa consolidated power, the main 'enemy of the state' switched from opposition parties to social movements (Sánchez, 2013: 45). For sympathetic movements like FENOCIN there were opportunities, but for those not in agreement, the approach was distinct. When CONAIE made clear its opposition to the proposed Mining and Food Sovereignty laws, Correa responded by labelling them 'infantile' and 'dangerous' (Lucas, 2015: 213). When CONAIE called for a mobilisation FENOCIN refused, heralding the disarticulation of civil society. Nevertheless, Becker (2012: 127) notes that the conflict with CONAIE also came at a cost to Correa, helping to deny him a legislative majority in the 2009 elections.

Following these changes in the correlation of forces, the introduction of an Organic Law of Food Sovereignty (LORSA) proved less contentious than anticipated. Debates around the law saw agribusiness to the fore, with the state now assuming a more 'neutral' role, leaving rural movements as the lone voices advocating radical change (Rosero, Carbonell & Regalado, 2011: 97). As a result, the text approved in February 2009 was a compromise, outsourcing the writing of the laws and regulations to a new independent body, the Plurinational Food Sovereignty Conference (COPISA; Ibid: 98). Nonetheless, Correa exercised his veto over the draft law, modifying a biofuel ban, extending state subsidies to large-scale producers and curtailing the powers of COPISA (Ibid). LORSA was greeted sceptically by movements, and criticised as a concession to 'the pressures of the big agricultural producers' (Acosta, 2009).

During this second phase, however, the government remained discursively committed to food sovereignty. The country's National Development Plan (2009–2013) presented a 'call to action,' proposing a framework for achieving '*sumak kawsay*' (McKay et al, 2014: 1186). Another hopeful sign was the work of COPISA, charged with fostering citizen participation in the formulation of nine supplementary laws (Peña, 2016: 226). Despite initial success, however, at interview on 24 August 2016 a former COPISA delegate from civil society asserted that the body was insufficiently funded and became 'just another public institution with no power'. This dynamic is encapsulated by the fact the government failed to pass even one of COPISA'S bills into law by the end of Correa's term in 2017 (Intriago et al., 2017: 325–326). For some scholars, this failure is attributable to the growing power and influence of the agri-food sector (Giunta, 2014; Clark, 2016).

Other factors also played a role. One of these was the disunity between and within social movements. The decision by FENOCIN to align with Correa came to be heavily questioned within the organisation when their main policy goal – radical land reform – failed to materialise (McKay et al, 2014: 1188). This split further weakened collective power, and contributed to ever-lower levels of mobilisation after 2009 (Giunta, 2014: 1210). With civil society movements divided and weakened, and his own legitimacy and power consolidated, Correa was free to question the more radical aspects of his own plan for government. This is what occurred on 1 October 2011, when Correa used his television show to equate small-scale farming with low productivity, labelling it 'disastrous'. The final blow to food sovereignty came at the end of Correa's term in 2017, when he exercised his presidential discretion to lift the prohibition on GMOs.

In summary, the institutionalisation of food sovereignty in Ecuador's Constitution and national law were significant victories for the rural social movements, but ultimately proved pyrrhic. Changes in the correlation of political forces over time gradually saw these movements lose influence. This weakening can be explained by adopting a relational approach: as movements lost articulation and became divided, agribusiness regained lost influence. In particular, the growth in power of the president – both in terms of formal powers and public legitimacy – saw policies favouring food sovereignty halted and subsequently reversed.

## (ii) Mobilising for post-oil development

On the surface, there is little resemblance between the rural movements promoting food sovereignty as a means of preserving traditional livelihoods, and the *Yasunidos* movement made up predominantly of middle-class urban youth that sought to defend part of the Amazon rainforest many had never visited. However, the movements also exhibit similarities that are worthy of attention. First, both movements set out to pressurise the government into honouring the terms of its own programme for government. Second, these movements were inspired by a civil society agenda that sought to move Ecuador away from natural resource extraction toward 'post-oil development' (Martínez, 2009: 16–17). Third, these movements sought to articulate a broad civil society front, and framed their demands with regard to '*sumak kawsay*', environmental sustainability, indigenous rights and traditional livelihoods.

Nevertheless, *Yasunidos* emerged in a very different context to rural and other social movements in Ecuador. The movement originated in 2013, following Correa's second re-election – this time with a legislative majority – and the introduction of Decree 016. The government's formal powers and public legitimacy were at their peak (Sánchez, 2017). By that time many pre-existing social movements had been effectively tamed through a combination of internal divisions, co-optation and criminalisation. For this reason, *Yasunidos* came to be viewed as an important and powerful social force (Coryat & Picq, 2016).

In order to analyse the *Yasunidos* movement, it is necessary to briefly consider the broader environmental movement in Ecuador. Among its most prominent actors is the environmental collective '*Accion Ecologica*', known for its 'uncompromising position on oil drilling' (Rival, 2012: 159). The Yasuni-ITT Initiative was formulated by a member of this collective, NGO Oilwatch (Martínez, 2009: 13). At interview on 15 July 2015, Oilwatch Coordinator Esperanza Martínez explained that the original idea was for a moratorium on new oil exploitation, reference to which was contained in Correa's plan for government. Upon taking power, Correa initially favoured plans for drilling, but was persuaded by then-Energy Minister Alberto Acosta to back an alternative approach, albeit confined to three oil fields within Yasuni National Park: Ishpingo, Tambococha and Tiputini (ITT).

The choice of Yasuni was based on a combination of factors. First, the park houses extremely high levels of biodiversity, and was declared a World Biosphere Reserve in 1989. Second, the park contained several 'uncontacted' indigenous groups in voluntary isolation, whose survival was threatened by oil activity. Finally, there was the issue of climate change, and the levels of carbon that would be 'saved' by not burning the oil (Acosta et al., 2009). According to estimates, the value of the oil within those fields to the Ecuadorian state would amount to US$7.2 billion over a 13-year period. The Yasuni-ITT Initiative proposed leaving that oil under the ground if Ecuador was paid half that sum. While the plan was light on detail, it was approved by Correa in early 2007 (Martínez, 2009: 14). According to Rival (2012: 153), the initiative opened up new possibilities of government and civil society allying to 'rethink economy, ecology and political commitment' to development alternatives.

While response to the Yasuni-ITT Initiative within Ecuador was muted, the proposal was well-received internationally (Acosta et al., 2009). Martínez (2009: 35) notes that the proposal became the centrepiece of Correa's speeches at international fora, earning him praise and recognition. Correa framed the issue openlyas one of climate justice, asking why under-developed countries should be the ones to pay the price of combating climate change (Ibid: 20–21). Ecuador proposed issuing a kind of government bond that reflected the value not only of the deforestation avoided, but also of the carbon not released into the atmosphere. This scheme was perhaps too innovative for its time, and when the idea was rejected at the COP 15 conference in 2009, the initiative was in trouble (Rival, 2012: 164).

There were issues closer to home also, and in particular a perceived lack of state commitment. The government's initially lethargic approach to promoting the initiative contrasted sharply with campaigning efforts by civil society. In particular, an education programme run by *Accion Ecologica* helped engender pride in the initiative (O'Connell, 2016). Nevertheless, when the government did finally launch its campaign, it had an immediate impact on public awareness (Ibid). Most concerning, however, was the government's refusal to rule out drilling. Indeed, the option to extract the oil continued to advance in step with moves to promote Yasuni-ITT, ready to be called upon 'at any moment' if it failed (Martínez, 2009: 37–38).

This 'dual strategy' was accompanied by ongoing verbal attacks by Correa on the groups behind Yasuni-ITT (Ibid). This changed attitude toward civil society coincided with a resurgence in the influence of economic power groups and transnational capital. Domestic elites had long enjoyed the fruits of service contracts linked to oil production in Ecuador, and increasingly brought pressure to bear on Correa to open new fields (Ibid: 97; Lucas, 2015). With time, social actors also came to identify the role of China – Ecuador's primary creditor – in driving demand for oil (Martínez, 2014). Nevertheless, it was not until after the 2013 elections that Correa finally moved to officially cancel the Yasuni-ITT Initiative.

Given the strength of its position relative to civil society at that stage, the government was taken by surprise when the announcement of the cancellation of the Yasuni-ITT Initiative was met by what senior *Yasunidos* member Omar Bonilla described at interview on 26 August 2016 as 'an explosion of protests'. The source of the resistance – urban middle-class youth – appeared equally surprising. Yet in truth this outcome was the result of a careful civil society strategy. According to Esperanza Martínez, at interview on 15 July 2015, environmental organisations had realised they needed to build support for the initiative in urban areas, due to the lack of organised local communities within Yasuni National Park. Campaigns and education programmes targeted young people, laying the foundations of the *Yasunidos* (O'Connell, 2016).

While the initial response was spontaneous and incoherent, vigils soon gave way to street demonstrations in cities across Ecuador's highland region (Coryat, 2015). Confronted by the first significant protest in years, the government reacted with a mixture of verbal and physical aggression (Ibid: 3747). The *Yasunidos* collective was formed as a response to state actions, openly positioning itself as a heterogenous coalition that was 'not only peaceful, but pacifist' according to Bonilla. The collective described itself as 'non-partisan, autonomous and self-organised', and opposed to extractive activities that threatened the climate, water, biodiversity and indigenous peoples (Coryat, 2015: 3747).

From its inception, *Yasunidos* drew on a broad repertoire of contentious actions, mixing established methods like public debates and conferences, with innovative forms, such as the revival of the Andean tradition of '*zapateadas*' – cultural events featuring music and dance – street theatre, and the temporary occupation of buildings (Gálvez & Bonilla, 2014: 91–92). *Yasunidos* recognised the importance of both visibility and sustained action. At interview on 26 August 2016, Bonilla stated that it was this realisation that led to the establishment of the 'Guardians of Yasuni', a sub-group that camped out opposite the presidential palace every week for over a year. *Yasunidos* also made heavy use of technology, creating videos and music for sharing on social media, while also engaging with mainstream media (Coryat, 2015: 3750).

Faced with contention in the streets and in the media, the Correa government responded in kind. Demonstrations were met with increasingly repressive tactics by police, including the use of teargas, paintballs, arbitrary detentions and infiltrations (Vasquez, 2015). These physical assaults were accompanied – and arguably encouraged – by constant verbal attacks from Correa. In particular, the president used his weekly television show to criticise the collective, even naming individual activists. This campaign of delegitimisation was maintained for months, and extended to the closure of an environmental NGO – *Fundacion Pachamama* – that supported the collective (Ibid; Conaghan, 2016).

Nevertheless, it was the *Yasunidos'* plan to seek a plebiscite (*consulta popular*) on the issue of oil drilling in Yasuni that crystallised the movement's political influence. At interview on 26 August 2016, Bonilla asserted that from the start movement members realised that protest alone would not succeed, and that they needed a 'Plan B'. A political opening was provided by the Constitution, Article 104 of which provided for the initiation of a plebiscite by citizens on an issue of 'national importance', provided 5 per cent of those on the electoral register signed in support. Within days of forming, *Yasunidos* lodged formal notice of a public consultation with Ecuador's Constitutional Court (Vasquez, 2015).

At first, the government appeared relatively unconcerned, with Correa dismissively chiding *Yasunidos* not to be 'lazy' and to collect the signatures required (Ibid: 27). The task was indeed significant, with the collective requiring 583,324 signatures to trigger a plebiscite, a situation made more challenging by civil society fragmentation. As Bonilla noted at interview on 26 August 2016, early hopes that the labour and indigenous movements would provide the bulk of the signatures were quickly dashed. Instead the collective was forced into a 'steep learning curve' of surveys and marketing, and of high dependence on human capital. In that regard, the movement's grounding in popular education paid dividends, enabling members to engage with older generations to promote the consultation (O'Connell, 2016: 51).

It came as a huge shock to the government when, in March, 2014, *Yasunidos* held a press conference to announce that they had gathered almost 90 per cent of the required signatures. As noted by Esperanza Martínez at interview on 15 July 2015, 'that was when the war began'. Members of the collective began to receive threatening phone calls, others were summarily detained and Correa stepped up his verbal attacks (Vasquez, 2015). Most notably, the government launched a rival public consultation in an attempt to sow confusion and obstruct the gathering of signatures (Ibid). In spite of the considerable formal and informal powers available to the government, however, these tactics 'backfired', according to Bonilla. Instead Correa's image was damaged, and public support for the consultation was strengthened. In April 2014 *Yasunidos* delivered 757,623 signatures to the offices of the National Electoral Council (CNE), far exceeding the required amount and all expectations.

While the *Yasunidos* won this battle, the 'war' was not over. The Correa government had failed to delegitimise the consultation, with opinion polls at the time showing 70 per cent support for a referendum. Nonetheless, Correa consistently refused to rule out drilling, with leaked documents indicating that the oil had been pre-sold to China (Martínez, 2014). Furthermore, unlike during his first years in office, Correa's hold on state power was absolute, and included the 'capture' of the CNE (Sánchez, 2017: 133). Accordingly, it came as no surprise when, amid irregularities, the CNE summarily disqualified 60 per cent of the signatures (Coryat, 2015: 3755). Not content, the government utilised the legislative branch to rule out future popular consultations (Conaghan, 2016: 115).

On the surface Correa had won and *Yasunidos* had been defeated. At interview on 26 August 2016, Bonilla acknowledged the negative impact the outcome had on the movement, with membership contracting and mobilisation gradually receding. Nevertheless, the movement had a surprising amount of success in confronting Correa at the height of his power. The movement's tactics, media savvy and membership profile meant that Correa's attempts to demonise them were not persuasive, and damaged his own image. The government suffered a serious setback in the 2014 local elections, losing mayoral races in all the major cities. This outcome was attributed by some to the influence of the movement (Coryat, 2015), and explains why some commentators viewed the *Yasunidos* as a significant social actor (Coryat & Picq, 2016).

## Conclusion

This chapter has considered the issue of civil society's political influence in the context of the Left Shift in Latin America. In particular, it has considered two social actors – rural movements and the urban *Yasunidos* collective – that came to prominence during the presidency of Rafael Correa in Ecuador. While these civil society movements were very different in terms of their organisational structures, membership and tactics, both were mobilised in support of forms of alternative, post-oil development. Furthermore, while the two movements varied in terms of the success they had in translating demands into policy, in both cases their political impact was significant. There are three main points that arise from this analysis of civil society movements in Ecuador under Correa.

The first point is the importance of adopting a relational approach to the study of civil society influence on government. This point includes relations between social actors and the need to maintain unity, given the collective nature of civil society power. The case of food sovereignty illustrates this point: when the two main movements, CONAIE and FENOCIN, worked together at the constituent assembly they were successful in enshrining the concept in the Constitution; however, when old divisions reappeared subsequently, the movement was divided, resulting in a watered-down food sovereignty law.

A relational approach also provides a lens through which to analyse movement relations with government, particularly presidents. The cases studied demonstrate the importance of the vulnerability of presidents. Correa took power without legislative or organised party support, and so depended heavily on civil society support during his first years in office. This support was conditional, and came at the price of the translation of key demands into policy, such as the adoption of the Yasuni-ITT Initiative and enshrining of food sovereignty in law. However, as Correa cemented his position through the acquisition of formal powers, high public legitimacy and wider control over democratic institutions, the level of civil society influence declined sharply.

A second and related point centres on the challenge for movements in engaging with governments that espouse a leftist ideology and adopt as their own demand and initiatives that originated in civil society. This difficulty is particularly evident in the case of the movements supporting food sovereignty. While FENOCIN was co-opted and ultimately absorbed into the ruling party, CONAIE chose the path of confrontation and saw its leaders openly delegitimised and subsequently criminalised. Interestingly, while *Yasunidos* faced a similar dilemma, the collective emerged when Correa was already hegemonic, and attempted to take a different path. Through its use of new media, culture and the arts, and a creative and participative approach centred on the campaign for the public consultation, they managed to avoid the pitfalls of previous movements. In both cases, even though Correa was able to negate the movement's demands, the fallout from doing so had an electoral cost.

Finally, the cases provide some answers with regard to the democratic impact of civil society. While social movements have been criticised as antidemocratic, and for a perceived failure to properly engage with institutionalised democracy. An example is the phenomenon of presidential ousters, and their uncertain relationship to institutions. However, as these cases demonstrate, social actors are capable of working very effectively within democratic institutions provided they are the right institutions. One example is Ecuador's constituent assembly, which was organised as a participative and deliberative space. Rural movements made full use of this space to produce significant portions of the final constitutional text, including sections relating to agriculture and food sovereignty, overcoming business and government opposition. Similarly, *Yasunidos* utilised a mechanism designed to encourage civil participation, the popular consultation, to great effect in its campaign to prevent drilling for oil in Yasuni National Park. A more deliberative approach to institutional design might help to open spaces for a more complete incorporation of social movements into formal politics.

In conclusion, the influence of civil society is contingent on the prevailing relational and institutional context. Nevertheless, movements are dynamic in nature, and as these cases demonstrate, this can present as both a strength and a weakness.

## References

Acosta, A. (2008) El Buen Vivir, una Oportunidad para Construir. *Ecuador Debate*. 75, 33–48.

Acosta, A. (2009) Ecuador: Sobre la ley de soberanía alimentaria, *Rebelión*, 5 May. Available from: http://www.rebelion.org/noticia.php?id=84851, [18 December 2019].

Acosta, A., Gudynas, E., Martínez, E. & Vogel, J. (2009) *Leaving the Oil in the Ground: A Political, Economic, and Ecological Initiative in the Ecuadorian Amazon*. Centre for International Policy.

Amenta, E. (2014) How to Analyse the Influence of Social Movements. *Contemporary Sociology*. 43(1), 16–29.

Becker, M. (2011) Correa, Indigenous Movements, and the Writing of a New Constitution in Ecuador. *Latin American Perspectives*. 38(1), 47–62.

Becker, M. (2012) Social movements and the government of Rafael Correa: confrontation or cooperation? In: Prevost, G., Oliva Campos, C. & Vanden, H. (eds.)

*Social Movements and Leftist Governments in Latin America*. London/New York, Zed Books.

Becker, M. (2015) *¡Pachakutik! Movimientos Indígenas, Proyectos Políticos y Disputas Electorales en el Ecuador*. Quito, FLACSO/Abya-Yala.

Cannon, B. & Kirby, P. (eds.) (2012) *Civil Society and the State in Left-Led Latin America: Challenges and Limitations to Democratisation*. London, Zed Books.

Clark, P. (2016) Can the State Foster Food Sovereignty? Insights from the Case of Ecuador. *Journal of Agrarian Change*. 16(2), 183–205.

Collins, J. (2014) New Left Experiences in Bolivia and Ecuador and the Challenge to Theories of Populism. *Journal of Latin American Studies*. 46(1), 59–86.

Conaghan, C. (2016) Ecuador under Correa. *Journal of Democracy*. 27(3), 109–118.

Coryat, D. (2015) Extractive Politics, Media Power, and New Waves of Resistance Against Oil Drilling in the Ecuadorian Amazon: The Case of Yasunídos. *International Journal of Communication*. 9, 3741–3760.

Coryat, D. & Picq, M. (2016) Ecuador's Expanding Extractive Frontier. *NACLA Report on the Americas*. 48(3), 280–285.

de la Torre, C., & Conaghan, C. (2009) The Hybrid Campaign: Tradition and Modernity in Ecuador's 2006 Presidential Election. *International Journal of Press/Politics* 14(3), 335–352.

Ellner, S. (2012) The Distinguishing Features of Latin America's New Left in Power: The Chávez, Morales, and Correa Governments. *Latin American Perspectives*. 3(1), 96–114.

Escobar, A. & Álvarez, S. (1992) *The Making of Social Movements in Latin America: Identity, Strategy and Democracy*. Boulder, CO, Westview Press.

Foweraker, J. (1995) *Theorising Social Movements*. London, Pluto Press.

Foweraker, J. (2001) Grassroots Movements and Political Activism in Latin America: A Critical Comparison of Chile and Brazil. *Journal of Latin American Studies*. 33, 839–865.

Gálvez, E. & Bonilla, O. (2014) Yasunidos: Los Limites de la Devastación. *Aportes Andinos*. 34, 85–94.

Giunta, I. (2014) Food Sovereignty in Ecuador: Peasant Struggles and the Challenge of Institutionalisation. *Journal of Peasant Studies*. 41(6), 1201–1224.

Hochstetler, K. (2006) Rethinking Presidentialism: Challenges and Presidential Falls in South America. *Comparative Politics*. 38(4), 401–418.

Hunt, S. (2016) Rethinking the Politics of the Shift Left in Latin America: Towards a Relational Approach. *Bulletin of Latin American Research*. 35(4), 437–451.

Intriago, R., Gortaire, R., Bravo, E. & O'Connell, C. (2017) Agroecology in Ecuador: Historical Processes, Achievements, and Challenges. *Agroecology and Sustainable Food Systems*. 41(3–4), 311–328.

Levitsky, S. & Roberts, K. (eds.) (2011) *The Resurgence of the Latin American Left*. Baltimore, MD, The Johns Hopkins University Press.

Lievesley, G. (2009) Is Latin America moving leftwards? Problems and prospects. In: Lievesley, G. & Ludlam, S. (eds.) *Reclaiming Latin America: Experiments in Radical Social Democracy*. London, Zed Books.

Lucas, K. (2007) *Rafael Correa: Un Extraño en Carondelet*. Quito, Editorial Planeta.

Lucas, K. (2015) *Ecuador Cara y Cruz: Del Levantamiento del Noventa a la Revolución Ciudadana. Tomo III: Luces y Sombras de la Revolución Ciudadana (2007–2015)*. Quito, Ediciones CIESPAL.

Luders, J. (2010) *The Civil Rights Movement and the Logic of Social Change*. New York, Cambridge University Press.

Lynch, N. (2017) *Populismo: Dictadura o Democracia?*Lima, Universidad Nacional Mayor de San Marcos.

Machado, F., Scartascini, C. & Tommasi, M. (2011) Political Institutions and Street Protests in Latin America. *Journal of Conflict Resolution.* 55(3), 340–365.

Marsteintredet, L. & Berntzen, E. (2008) Reducing the Perils of Presidentialism in Latin America Through Presidential Interruptions. *Comparative Politics.* 41(1), 83–101.

Martínez, E. (2009) *Yasuni: El Tortuoso Camino de Kioto a Quito.* Quito, Abya-Yala.

Martínez, E. (2014) *Yasuní: democracia en extinción.* In: Cuvi, J. (ed.) *La Restauración Conservadora del Correismo.* Quito, Montecristi Vive.

McAdam, D., McCarthy, J. & Zald, M. (eds.) (1996) *Comparative Perspectives on Social Movements: Political Opportunities, Mobilizing Structures, and Cultural Framings.* Cambridge, Cambridge University Press.

McAdam, D. & Tarrow, S. (2010) Ballots and Barricades: On the Reciprocal Relationship Between Elections and Social Movements. *Perspectives on Politics.* 8(2), 529–542.

McKay, B., Nehring, R. & Walsh-Dilley, M. (2014) The 'State' of Food Sovereignty in Latin America: Political Projects and Alternative Pathways in Venezuela, Ecuador and Bolivia. *Journal of Peasant Studies.* 41(6), 1175–1200.

Naim, M. (2004) From Normalcy to Lunacy: New Latin American Activists Embrace the Politics of Rage, Race, and Revenge. *Foreign Policy.* 141, 104–105.

O'Connell, C. (2016) Yasuni-ITT and Post-oil Development: Lessons for Development Educators. *Policy & Practice: A Development Education Review.* 22, 35–58.

Peña, K. (2016) Social movements, the State, and the Making of Food Sovereignty in Ecuador. *Latin American Perspectives.* 43(1), 221–237.

Pérez-Liñán, A. (2007) *Presidential Impeachment and the New Political Instability in Latin America.* Cambridge, Cambridge University Press.

Petras, J. & Veltmeyer, H. (2005) *Social Movements and State Power: Argentina, Brazil, Bolivia, Ecuador.* London, Pluto Press.

Philip, G. & Panizza, F. (2011) *The Triumph of Politics: The Return of the Left in Venezuela, Bolivia and Ecuador.* Cambridge, Polity Press.

Rival, L. (2012) Planning development futures in the Ecuadorian Amazon. In: Bebbington, A. (ed.) *Social Conflict, Economic Development and Extractive Industry.* London, Routledge.

Roberts, K. (1998) *Deepening Democracy? The Modern Left and Social Movements in Chile and Peru.* Stanford, CA, Stanford University Press.

Roberts, K. (2008) The Mobilisation of Opposition to Economic Liberalisation. *Annual Review of Political Science.* 11, 327–349.

Rosero, F., Carbonell Y., & Regalado, F. (2011) *Soberanía Alimentaria, Modelos de Desarrollo y Tierras en Ecuador.* Quito, CAFOLIS.

Sánchez, O. (2017) Classifying Ecuador's Regime under Correa: A Procedural Approach. *Journal of Politics in Latin America.* 9(3), 121–140.

Sánchez, P. (2013) Resistencia, consenso y disputa; reflexión sobre el conflicto social en el Ecuador (1990–2012). In: Morán, N. (ed.) *A Quien le Importa los Guayacanes? Acumulación, Gobierno y Conflictos en el Campo.* Quito, IIE/CDES.

Silva, E. (2009) *Challenging Neoliberalism in Latin America.* Cambridge, Cambridge University Press.

Smulovitz, C. & Peruzzotti, E. (2000) Societal Accountability in Latin America. *Journal of Democracy.* 11(4), 147–158.

Van Cott, D. (2007) Latin America's Indigenous Peoples. *Journal of Democracy.* 18(4), 127–141.

Vasquez, E. (2015) *Estrategias de Represión y Control Social del Estado Ecuatoriano: Informe Psicosocial en el Caso Yasunidos.* Colectivo de Investigación y Acción Psicosocial.

Weyland, K. (2004) Neoliberalism and Democracy in Latin America: A Mixed Record. *Latin American Politics and Society.* 46(1), 135–157.

Wolff, J. (2007) (De-)Mobilising the Marginalised: A Comparison of the Argentine *Piqueteros* and Ecuador's Indigenous Movement. *Journal of Latin American Studies.* 39, 1–29.

Wolff, J. (2016) Business Power and the Politics of Postneoliberalism: Relations Between Government and Economic Elites in Bolivia and Ecuador. *Latin American Politics and Society.* 58(2), 124–147.

Zamosc, L. (2007) The Indian Movement and Political Democracy in Ecuador. *Latin American Politics and Society.* 49(3), 1–34.

# 9 Shifting landscape in Morocco

## The case of civil society activism in post 2011 uprisings

*Mohammed Yachoulti*

## Introduction

Civil society is an expression heavily present in the daily conversation of people, politics and medina in Morocco. However, despite the aura it always enjoys, it is undeniable that civil society actors and organizations are trapped within a web of hurdles that impede their free activism to develop a strong democratic state with strong political institutions and a vibrant civil society (Yachoulti, 2012). Some of these hurdles are traced to the era of colonial periods while others are the result of the contemporary era. Some are associated with the actors themselves whereas others are the outcome of an environment that still is unable to embrace plurality and rid itself of traditional ways of government based on garnering powers (Ibid). This chapter addresses the specificity of Moroccan civil society and traces its journey of development and metamorphosis with special focus on the post Arab Spring era. Of special importance is the contribution of the 2011 constitutional reforms in strengthening civil society's role and engagement in the process of change. The discussion centres itself on different impairments that prevent the growth and development of Moroccan civil society.

To achieve the objectives of the chapter, the author traces the dynamics and growth of civil society in Morocco from the pre-protectorate period to the post Arab Spring era. He also looks at the different phases of its development and change with some focus on the contemporary era. The first section traces the dynamics of civil society from the pre-protectorate to the eve of the Arab Spring in Morocco. It mainly tracks the four main phases that characterized its development during this era. The second section reveals the story of the Arab Spring in Morocco as a momentum in the growth and life cycle of Moroccan civil society activism. The third section considers the metamorphosis of civil society activism by focusing on cases of activism that emerged as a reaction to the loss of trust in the existing political actors. Finally, the chapter finishes with a discussion and concluding remarks.

## The dynamics of Moroccan civil society before the Arab Spring

In Morocco, civil society should not always be thought of as a "mélange of associations, clubs, guilds syndicates, federations, unions, parties and groups" [that stand as a] "buffer between the state and the citizen" (Norton, 1995, p. 7) but an amalgam of cultural values, practices, beliefs, and institutions that are specific to the Moroccan history, culture, and people. These institutions and cultural values have their origins in the dawn of Moroccan history (Yachoulti, 2012). More explicitly, civil society in Morocco dates back to the pre-protectorate era and has ever since taken different forms and shapes depending on the changes that have affected the Moroccan state.

In pre-colonial Morocco, informal associations such as *Touiza, Djma'a* and *Mowzara'a* existed throughout Moroccan rural areas, out of state control, to deal with or facilitate the normal daily-life difficulties at the level of the local community, namely in rural villages. These traditional associations usually had a fairly homogeneous membership since they were limited to the inhabitants of rural villages or towns. They were spontaneous and pragmatic associations that constituted forms of community ad hoc self-help in areas such as agriculture, irrigation, food stocks, and even religious teachings (Laayachi, 1998). Nowadays, with the evolution of Moroccan society, these associations have started to disintegrate and disappear except from some very remote rural areas. They are altered by new modern forms of organizations which are centred in the urban areas (Yachoulti, 2012).

At the urban level, highly associative organizations were developed. In Fez for instance, artisans and other workers were grouped by the type of activity into corporations called locally as *hannatin.* Tanners, shoemakers, and weavers are examples of these groups in which membership was compulsory. These groups:

> were guided by the notion of just price and the principle of the quality of work. The corporation often accepted collective responsibility for fraud, for bad workmanship, and for injuries suffered on the job. Entry into a corporation was controlled by its leader, called *amin*; and it was to him that customers carried their complaints against a member. He was elected by the membership for a life term [...]. The *amin* had an assistant, or *khalifa* who assumed the duties in his absence.
>
> (Stewart, 1967, p. 31)

Interestingly enough, above the *amin* was an authority called *mouhtassib* appointed by the *sultan* to head all corporations. The most important function of the *mouhtassib* "was to set the prices for goods sold by the corporations; he also served as court of appeal from the decisions of the *amin*" (Stewart, 1967, p. 31). Indeed, the importance of the corporations was very great and not negligible. But what is worth observing is that the election of the *amin* for a life-term suggests the existence of hierarchy and vertical relations within the structures of these organizations. Also, the *sultan*'s appointment of *mouhtassibs* as higher authorities to these groups connotes that the latter worked under the direct supervision of the *sultan,* a fact which suggests their lack of independence (Yachoulti, 2012).

Indeed, tracing Moroccan political history before the protectorate shows the existence of an *ulema* (religious scholars) category standing as a buffer between the sultan and his subjects. This category acted both as a guardian of *Shari'a* (Islamic law) and representative of citizens. It also legalized and legitimized the status or rule of the sultan through signing the act *bay'a* (allegiance; Sater, 2007). The *ulema* stood also as a counterbalance to the *sultan* in times of his unjust ruling. Their role is summarized as follows:

> If the sultan rules justly, preserves order and the safety of the roads, keeps his officers under control so that they do not 'tyrannise', the people, raises taxes in a fair way in accordance with *shari'a,* and protects the country against attack by outside forces, particularly the Christian, then they have a duty to obey him. If he does not, and fails so manifestly that justice and order are replaced by tyranny, then he can be removed from office. Indeed, on occasion it was argued that it was not only the right of people – led by the *ulema*- to remove him, but their duty to do so.
> (Pennel, as cited in Sater, 2007, p. 28)

Still, despite this apparent power represented by *ulema* and heads of some *Zawayas* (congregations) scattered all over the country, their power remained very limited. The Moroccan scholar and political scientist, Mohamed Tozy, emphasizes this fact when he says "what is sure is that despite the real weight that the *ulema* represented, their power remained limited and one should not exaggerate their importance" (Tozy, as cited in Sater, 2007, p. 33). Indeed, the failure of *ulema* to stand as a counterforce to the *sultan* may be attributed to the prevalence of illiteracy and therefore the absence of an educated mass that would help the *ulema* in their pressure; the absence of a strong administrative organization; and most importantly, the continuous unrest of the country that was usually divided by *bled el-Makhzan* (lands of government) and *bled es-siba* (lands of dissidence). *Bled el-Makhzan* are the lands that surrounded immediately the urban areas; "[T]hey paid taxes to the sultan and provided the backbone of the army. The *bled es-siba*, however, refused taxes to the *sultan*, yet they accepted him as the spiritual head of the region" (Daadaoui, 2011, p. 54).

During the protectorate period (1912–1956), the development of Moroccan civil society started to take a different shape. In other words, the right to found an association was "guaranteed by the *dahir* [decree] of May 24, 1914, modeled after article 291 of the French penal code and the Association Law of July 1, 1901" (Halstead, 1961, p. 58). Also, "public meetings other than religious were prohibited by the state of siege order of 1914, reinforced by *dahir* of June 29, 1935" (Ibid). However, the right to organize labour unions was granted only to the French and not to the Moroccans (Ibid). Until 1934, all organizations founded and run by Moroccans were operating clandestinely (Ibid).

As for the role of *ulema,* though they were alienated, along with the clergy and traditional local leaders, by the French authorities, they

> turned to a conservative Islam, one "purified" of distortion, to liberate the country in general and the Sultan in particular from foreign influence. This turn to Islam became *Salafisme,* which influenced heroic nationalist leaders such as Abderlkrim al-Khattabi, who led the rebellion in the mountainous Rif region (1919 to 1926) and Allal al-Fassi, who became one of the leaders of the nationalist Istiqlal party. Resistance against colonialism took the form of restoration of Muslim Arab Identity, and law.
>
> (Cohen & Jaidi, 2006, p. xiv)

After independence, two sub-phases could be recognized. The first extends from 1956 to the early 1980s and it is always described as the oppression phase. During this period, Moroccan civil society was as an amalgam of urban associations and rural notables representing the colonial tribal construct. Therefore, "[I]t proved relatively easy for king Mohammed V to play upon the divisions within the *Istiqlal* [Independence political party] and to encourage other parties and associations in rural areas where the *Istiqlal* was weak" (Clement, 1999, p. 18). Also, after two coup attempts in 1970 and 1972, the Moroccan regime feared not only the possibility of being dethroned, but also the possibility that different independent groups with different ideologies and political orientations would undermine national unity. Therefore, independent civic activity, namely Marxist-Leninist movements were brought under tight state control either through transforming them into state-dominated institutions or just repressing them. This period was known as the 'Years of Lead'[1] as it was marked by state violence against dissidents and activists. Sater (2007) summarizes this period when he reports:

> The antagonism between the monarchy and the Nationalist movement on the one hand, and between rural and urban elites on the other, resulted in the establishment of monarchical power and the duality of exclusion and co-optation of the opposition. The evolution of associative activities and the establishment of a public sphere accompanied this development, which was also marked by close patron–client relationships. As a result, political parties and labour unions became power bases, and not zones free of power beyond administrative manipulation. The same applies to organizations of civil society that started to operate.
>
> (pp. 33–34)

The second sub-phase started in the early 1980s to the late 1990s. During this period, Morocco started to witness an unprecedented growth and diversification of associative life. This growth has come as a result of many external and internal factors and developments. First, the Moroccan regime started to recognize the necessity to implement economic and political liberalizations as a way of staying in power (Yachoulti, 2012). Therefore, it allowed new civil society organizations to be created and expanded the operating space for the existing groups. Second, state officials found in civil society a new political language to promote projects of modernization and development and reinforce notions of pluralism and democracy. This new attitude of Moroccan state officials encouraged citizens to join "civil society" activism (Ibid).

Third, the increase of foreign aid from international institutions and organizations such as the National Endowment for Democracy (NED), European Instrument on Democracy and Human Rights (EIDHR), and the US Agency for International Development (USAID) channelled to civil society organizations also encouraged their growth. Fourth, the state's disengagement from providing basic needs opened the gates widely to civil society organizations to revive the tradition of corporation and solidarity in the country and try to work out their legitimacy based on the proximity, participation, and adaptation to local needs (Yachoulti, 2012). These included basic infrastructure and services (providing drinking water, irrigation networks, and environmental conservation), social services (health, schooling, and adult literacy), and a range of income-generating projects (such as female cooperatives for embroidery and weaving, planting of fruit trees, beekeeping, and tourism). As for the upper and middle classes, the needs were mainly cultural, provisional, and political. Finally, the expansion of the educated population has a share in the development of Moroccan civil society. Though lacking in quality in the policy, the mass education the state has followed has nevertheless created high levels of consciousness, expectations, and organizational skills. Such attributes have been instrumental in building formal associations.

To note, the new urban groups have always drawn the suspicion of the state and the monarch and aroused the interest of political and urban notables. The largest increase in these civic formations was registered in the mid 1980s and 1990s; the number exceeded 40,000 associations (Laayachi, 1998). Many of these associations were highly influenced by the political and social environments in which they evolved, and this often contributed to their inefficiency as independent aggregators and articulators of grass roots demands (Ibid). They also often served as top-down relays between the political sphere and society, and many of them were used by the state as instruments of ideological integration (Ibid).As for the role of *ulema* after independence, it has been confined or undermined. Cohen and Jaidi (2006) report that

> the control of the state over society operated through other channels besides politics, for instance, through religious institutions (the official Conseil de Oulémas) and the surveillance of zaouis, tombs of Muslim saints and spaces for the practice of sufi Islam (or moraboutisme, so prevalent in Morocco). Through the mid-1970s, those in leadership positions remained intensely loyal to the regime out of necessity. Only sectors in need of technical expertise, such as finance or agriculture, enjoyed a degree of independence from central authority.
>
> (pp. 57–58)

In addition to the obstacles, there has been a number of barriers that prevented the development of strong civil society that could have been able to counterbalance the state's hegemony since the early 1980s to the eve of the so-called 'Arab Spring'. These include, among others, the existence of judicial hurdles, the nature of the existing political system, the divide and rule strategy, and the policy of boundary setting and co-optation that the Moroccan state has always adopted.

### *The existence of juridical hurdles*

The establishment of any CSO requires carrying out certain legal formalities. The law on associations (law no. 75.000, dahir 1.02. 206 of 23 July 2002) dictates through its Article 5 that every association has to submit a declaration of its constitution to local representatives of the Ministry of Interior, being usually the *Caid* (District Sheriff). The founding members of the association would receive a date and a stamped receipt right away. The *Caid* sends a copy of the declaration to the tribunal and issues a definite receipt to the association after the period of two months (60 days). The law also includes some bureaucratic control measures that the founding members of this association still have to face. This involves that they have to submit their national identity card and an extract of their criminal record, pay fees for the legalization of copies, and have to be granted permission for any public gathering of the association. Failure or indifference to these procedures would risk imprisonment and fines.

### *The nature of the existing political system*

Under the previous constitution (1996–2011), the king garnered absolute power for the royal family in matters of the state and in the interpretations of what is best for the community (Smith & Loudiy, 2005). For instance, the parliament initiated legislation and the king had to sign it before it became law. The king also had the capacity to dissolve parliament by decree and call for new elections and propose his own legislation for popular consent by way of referendum. He could declare a state of emergency, rule by decree, and sign and ratify international treaties. Further, the king acted as a referee in national matters and delegated authority to others in the executive, legislative, and judicial branches; he appointed the prime minister and cabinet and presided over meetings of the cabinet and that of the Supreme Judicial Council; this restricted the proper functioning of institutions.

### *Divide and rule strategy*

In times of social tensions and hot debates in Morocco, civil society actors and groups were played off against each other. The state manipulated, manoeuvred, and played off one group against the other to blur the image and borders between 'enemies' and friends. This strategy enabled the state to maintain an upper hand over all the decisions and prevent any networking that could undermine its authority.

### *Boundary setting and co-optation*

Vibrant civil society groups were usually met with a state's policy that set boundaries to their activism, and established 'red lines'. For instance, rights and liberties of expression and opinion were sometimes criminalized. Opinions, assemblies, and expressions were subject to censure and interdiction, especially when the king and members of the royal family were insulted, criticized, or accused of malfeasance publicly, when the legitimacy of Islam as a state religion with the king as its tutelary head was questioned or undermined and when Morocco's territoriality was defied. In addition, the state usually appropriated their discourse and made it part of its agenda of reform, and hijacked the leading figures and appointed them supervisors of its reforms.

Despite all these changes, Moroccan CSOs that flourished during this phase are numerous and diverse in terms of their agenda, their objectives, and the impact they have made in the public sphere. These include basic rights defence associations (including human rights associations, Amazigh associations, and women's associations); unions (including the Moroccan Labor Union, General Union of Moroccan Workers, and Democratic Labor Confederation of Workers, among others); state associations, or what are also called government non-government organizations (GONGOs, such *as Angad el Maghreb Acharqi* Association, *Dukkala* Association, *Haoud Assafi* Association, and *Fes-sais* Association); youth and students' associations (Associations of Unemployed Youth and National Union of Moroccan Students), and Islamic associations (*Da'wa*, or preaching association).

## Arab Spring: a turning point in Moroccan civil society history

The winds of change that swept the MENA region in early 2011 did not exempt Morocco. Indeed, in the early days of January of the same year, a number of virtual activists created a Facebook group called 'Moroccans converse with the king'. The group invited the public to address Mohammed VI with questions, concerns, and comments. This mode of addressing the king directly stemmed from the loss of trust in elected institutions, as well as in politicians and political parties. The majority of the activists who launched the group were brought up in an environment characterized by both radicalization and democratization; they did not experience the fear of the 'Years of Lead' that still haunt the older generations (Skalli, 2011). Further, these younger activists grew up with the new king, have witnessed his reforms, and have become part of the youth's political expectations (Ibid).

When President Ben Ali fled from Tunisia on January 14, 2011, the act had a profound impact on the group as they seized the opportunity to fill the group's page with daring demands addressed to Morocco's king. They asked the king to change the constitution, fire the cabinet, dissolve the parliament, and put those who steal public money on trial. On January 25, 2011, when the Egyptian people started gathering in Tahrir square, the Facebook page administrators changed the site's name to 'Freedom and Democracy Now' and then published a call for nationwide protests on February 20 (Benchemsi, 2012). It was clear the group wanted their activism and actions to have an impact on real life. Targeting the same effect, two-minute YouTube videos were launched showing young men and women each stating that "I am Moroccan and I will take part in the protest with the February 20 movement" and then going on to explain why. The unifying demands and claims of the activists were "freedom, equality, an end to corruption, better living conditions, education, labor rights, Amazigh rights and many others" (Benchemsi, 2012).

Despite the attempt of the official national media to discredit the campaign, the YouTube videos were widely watched by internet users. This encouraged the creation of multiple Facebook groups in different cities like Rabat, Casablanca, Fez, Marrakesh to mention but a few. These local groups decided to meet, discuss, prepare, and urge citizens to demonstrate on February 20. Interestingly, on February 18, *Al Adl wa lIhsan* (Justice and Charity Association)[2] published a communiqué stating that its youth section would join the protest throughout the country, a fact which boosted the courage of all the activists and proved, once again, that their claims and demands reflect the demands of all ideologies in Morocco. All this helped to launch the February 20 Movement.

The success of the first protests that swept through all Moroccan cities and villages not only set the ball rolling for subsequent rallies but received an immediate response from the king and resulted in many political reforms. On March 9, 2011, the King announced the creation of the Consultative Commission for the Revision of the Constitution (CCRC) to propose amendments to the constitution. The ultimate aim was to limit the power of monarchy and strengthen the roles of the prime minister and the parliament. In this regard, the reforms aimed to give voice to all actors in the political arena. Dozens of human rights organizations were invited to make recommendations on constitutional reforms and were consulted by the CCRC. On July 1, the constitutional reforms were subject to a referendum and were followed, on November 25, by parliamentary elections which brought the Justice and Development Party (PJD) to power.

Importantly, unlike the previous constitutions, the newly approved one has come with unprecedented reforms. Tamazight has become an official state language along with Arabic. The king has the obligation to appoint a prime minister from the party that wins the most seats in the parliamentary elections and he is no longer sacred but the integrity of his person is inviolable. The prime minister is the head of government and president of the council of government. The judiciary system is independent from the legislative and executive branch; the king guarantees this independence. Women are guaranteed civic and social equality with men. Previously, only political equality was guaranteed, though the 1996 constitution grants all citizens equality in terms of rights and before the law. All citizens have the freedom of thought, ideas, artistic expression, and creation. In the previous constitution, only free speech and the freedom of circulation and association were guaranteed.

As far as some civil society provisions are concerned, the general provisions of Part I of the constitution preamble, Article 12 explicitly states that "The associations of civil society and the non-governmental organizations are constituted and exercise their activities in all freedom, within respect for the Constitution and for the law" (Ruchti, 2011). Article 13 states that public authorities should create consultation bodies in order to involve the different social actors in the preparation, activation, implementation, and evaluation of public policies. Further, Articles 14 and 15 expand the scope of civil society action to include all citizens and guarantee them the right, in the field of legislation, to present petitions to public authorities under the conditions and clauses prescribed by a subsequent regulatory law.

In Part II of the constitution entitled: 'Fundamental Rights and Freedoms', Article 27 stresses the right of all citizens to access information held by public administration, elected institutions, and public service agencies. Article 33 creates *Conseil consultative de la jeunesse et de l'action associative* (Consultative Council of Youth and of Associative Action), while Article 170 specifies its function as "a consultative instance within the domains of the protection of youth and of the promotion of associative life" (Ruchti, 2011). It is also charged to study and follow the questions of interest to these domains and to formulate the proposals on any subject of economic, social, and cultural order of direct interest to youth and associative action, as well as the development of the creative energies of youth, and their inducement to participation in the national life, in the spirit of responsible citizenship (Ruchti, 2011).

Part IX of the constitution entitled 'regions and local governments' includes Article 139 which stipulates that Regional Councils and other local government entities should develop participatory mechanisms for dialogue and consultation for the sake of facilitating the contribution of citizens and associations in the preparation and tracking of development programmes (Ibid). The same article re-iterates that citizens and associations have the right to make petitions, the goal of which is to demand from the councils to include in their agenda points falling under their jurisdiction (Ibid).

Indeed, the 2011 reform of Morocco's constitution was a historical moment that activated a dynamic dialogue and change in the state–civil society relationship in Morocco. Also, the 2011 constitutional provisions were assumed to facilitate the task of civil society actors to go beyond the traditionally defined boundaries of activism, re-emerge as strong interlocutors or actors that would instil the democratic practices and work to develop laws that would allow them the capacity of watchdog vis-a-vis state institutions.

Unfortunately, the subsequent developments in the political arena have proved otherwise and made Morocco overheat at all levels. In other words, because of the failure to implement the true heart of the new constitution not to mention the intensity of exploitation, widespread grievances and violations suffered by the masses, and deficiency in policymaking, a series of protest movements and other extreme self-sacrifice forms have started to take place as resistance or refusal to the status quo. These forms of activism are tracked in the subsequent section.

## Morocco after 2011: a metamorphosis of civil society activism

Though Morocco adopted one of the most advanced constitutions in its political history in 2011, the reforms have not led to real democratic practices and changes. The institution of the monarchy still garners religious powers, and still takes all major decisions that concern the nation both nationally and internationally. Abdelilah Benkirane, the ex-head of the Moroccan government, has repeatedly acknowledged that his government's role is to implement royal orders and instructions. Added to this, the claims that the February 20 Movement activists and demonstrators have advanced and fought to end corruption, achieve equality, freedom, and better education are gone with the wind. The official promises of restructuring and radically changing the socio-economic and political conditions of the citizens have remained ink on paper (Yachoulti, 2019).

Actually, the only gain of the February 20 Movement is the psychological therapy it has provided to all fractions of Moroccan society to get rid of the fear of the 'Years of Lead' that haunted them for decades and therefore re-engage them in their battle for more rights and equality. This may be traced to the emergence of a number of spontaneous protests, solidarity movements, and other forms of self-sacrifice to fight against *Al-Hogra*,[3] injustice, and the deterioration of living conditions. These forms of activism have gone beyond the traditional forms of activism to express a new culture of resistance in the making (Maghraoui, 2016). This culture is ideology-free, distrusts political parties, unions, and civil society groups, celebrates both the individual and the group as the main actors in the process of resistance, and even delegitimizes the February 20 Movement for not being able to achieve its political objectives.

### *The rise of self-sacrifice and self-immolations phenomena: Fadwa Laroui and Mmi Fatiha*

Cases of protest suicides and self-sacrifice are the first extreme ways of showing anger, dissatisfaction, and refusal of deteriorating living conditions and the prevailing of injustice and *Al- Hogra*. Two cases are included here. This choice, among others, is made based on the discussion they raised in the public sphere and the huge media attention they received.

In February 2011 amid the Arab turmoil, Fadwa Laroui, 25 years old, set herself on fire in front of the town hall of *Souk Sebt* (*Tadla Azilal* Region), in central Morocco after being excluded from a social housing scheme because she was an unmarried mother. Criteria of eligibility set by local authorities do not consider divorced, single women, and single mothers as heads of households as they live with their parents. Therefore, they are illegible to benefit from the government development plan of housing schemes for low-income households. On the day Fadwa set herself on fire, she had visited a local official one final time after having registered six complaints, none of which was taken into consideration. Added to this, Fadwa had discovered that part of the land reserved to the low-income households would go directly to businessmen with connections. She felt *Al-Hogra* and humiliation especially that her family's makeshift housing had already been destroyed and she and her family had nowhere to live. When in flames, Fadwa's last plea, as recorded on camera phone, was to make people "take a stand against injustice, corruption, and tyranny." Also, in the same month Fadwa set herself on fire, more self-immolations took place in Morocco. These concerned five unemployed graduates who set themselves on fire in the capital Rabat as part of their demonstrations over the lack of jobs. Of the three who were hospitalized, two passed away, while the other two just had their clothing singed.

Similarly, in April 2016, a 60-year-old street vendor, named *Mmi* (means 'mother', also used to address any elderly woman to show respect) Fatiha selling *Baghrir* (Moroccan pancakes) committed self-immolation after a Kenitra *Caid* confiscated her stall because she refused to move it. "*Mmi* Fatiha set herself on fire because of *Al-Hogra*; the *Caid* of the district scolded the woman, using verbal abuse and physical harassment against her to force her to leave the place" (*Albawaba News*, 2016) where she was selling her pancakes. After she refused his orders to leave the place, the *Caid* violently shoved her, publically threatening her in front of all. The video disseminated on social media shows *Mmi* Fatiha sitting in front of the *Caid*'s district building, in front of the *Caid*'s assistants who ignored the incident. *Mmi* Fatiha's self-immolation is but a clear message to the rest of society to stand against the tyranny, oppression, and *Al-Hogra* of some local government authorities.

Though these cases of self-immolations have sparked demonstrations and strong solidarity in the social media, they have not led to any reaction on the part of the government. The reason may be traced to the idea that the Moroccan government avoided giving the impression to the Moroccans that Fadwa Laroui and *Mmi* Fatiha are symbols of sacrifice. Indeed, Bouaziz's self-immolation in Tunisia was the first flame of the Tunisian revolution, but the Moroccan state managed to avoid the duplication of his case in Morocco at the beginning. Furthermore, in the absence of official support of civil society organizations, the state has worked on normalizing this kind of protest and used religion to delegitimize them (Yachoulti & Lachhab, 2018). The Moroccan state used the Friday sermons in the mosques to prohibit and even condemn the act of self-immolation, a fact which led only to sympathy behind the screens of the computer.

Also, as Yachoulti and Lachhab (2018) argue, these cases of self-immolation have resulted in two contradictory results. On the one hand, there has been no punishment of the government authorities responsible for their cases, a fact which reflects the yawning gap between the reality and principles of the new constitution which affirms in the first article the importance of "the principles of good governance and of the correlation between the responsibility for and the rendering of accounts" (Ruchti, 2011). Indeed, the non-implementation of this principle encourages many authorities in different sectors to go on violating the basic rights of ordinary people. On the other hand, their resistance has led to the reappropriation of the street and the public space after decades of indifference and political apathy to contest both the political and the economic status quo. This reflects the emergence of a new political culture which has legal and democratic dimensions. In other words, the sacrifice of the abovementioned victims has managed to give a voice to the marginalized (disfranchised groups) and made the weak able to revolt and fight against *Al-Hogra*, and humiliation and ask for justice (Yachoulti & Lachhab, 2018).

### *The rise of protest movements: medical students and teacher trainees*

In 2015, the Health Minister drafted a law called 'mandatory civil service project'. The project requires medical graduates to work for two years in remote areas of Morocco, but it neither counts this two-year period as part of the years of service (seniority) nor guarantees permanent employment in the public sector. This fact has outraged the students and their families, and pushed the students to engage in organized protests and struggles to dismantle the draft. The students also boycotted both theoretical and practical lessons in provincial hospitals and public clinics. This resulted in the disruption of work at public hospitals. In November of the same year, because of this chaotic situation, the government was forced to withdraw the draft law and freeze the decision. To note, the students' struggle and protests were led by general assemblies in which all decisions were taken democratically after long collective discussions away from any political or civil society institutions. Moreover, the students' protests took place in all cities that include medical schools: Marrakech, Casablanca, Fez, Oujda, and Rabat.

Similarly, in July 2015, the cabinet council approved two decrees of the Ministry of National Education regarding teacher trainees in provincial centres for the professions of education and training, the most important of which separates training from recruitment. In other words, the new decree stipulates that the state disengages from guaranteeing jobs to teacher trainees at these state centres of training. The aim of this decision is to provide abundant and cheap labour to the schools and institutions of the private sector which are known to be notorious for exploitation and harsh working conditions. This pushed teacher trainees to mobilize to dismantle the two decrees and defend the 'Moroccan Public School'. Away from the exiting unions that are known for their strength and presence in the education sector, the teacher trainees started by creating a network of organizations called 'coordination committees' at the local level and which have representatives and delegates in the National Coordinating Committee for Teacher Trainees.

The fact that this National Coordinating Committee of teacher trainees is made up mostly of ex-militants in the National Moroccan Student Union and then movements or associations of unemployed youth in addition to the fact that many of them belong to *Al Adl wa lIhsan* (Justice and Charity Association), the movement of teacher trainees engaged in fierce battles to dismantle the two ministerial decrees. The coercive interference of the state did not stop the teacher trainees from engaging in long boycotts of the theoretical and practical lessons, sit-ins in front of the parliament, and mass demonstrations in both local cities and the capital Rabat. After five months of blockage, liberal personalities, famous civil society activists, and some union leaders suggested a mediating role between the state and the teacher trainees. The purpose was to bridge the communication gap and solve the problem. Indeed, this mediation initiative paid off. The government reconsidered the decision and retreated from applying the two decrees at least for the school year (2015–2016) and agreed to appoint at once the teacher trainees.

### *The rise of solidarity movements: El Hoceima and Jerdaa Hiraks (popular uprisings)*

In October 2016, after confiscating and destroying his swordfish, on the grounds that he is not permitted to catch swordfish at that time of the year, the fisherman, Mouhcine Fikri, from Imzouren in El Hoceima city, jumped into a garbage truck to retrieve his 500 kilogrammes of fish, but unfortunately he was crushed to death by the truck's compactor.

Fikri was harshly treated by the local authorities. The verbal assault and command "crush this mother(fucker)!" sandwiched his body instantly in the garbage truck. In less than 48 hours, protests were taking place throughout Morocco denouncing Fikri's horrible death and have been ongoing since then. Fikri's funeral in El Hoceima drew large crowds with the procession led by hundreds of cars and marchers. Then a series of protests followed the incidents denouncing, among many other things, the spread of corruption, the marginalization of the north-west region, and the lack of hospitals and universities.

The protest wave escalated into a 'popular movement' far beyond the Rif region. It was called *Hirak El-Shaabi* (Popular Movement). Indeed, Mohcine Fikri's death has triggered a strong and unprecedented national solidarity to the extent that many observers and political analysts considered it the second phase of the Moroccan Spring. Moreover, the influence of Fikri's case has had its echo in other cities and towns of Morocco which went in demonstration against all kinds of marginalization (the case of Zagoura in the South, and Jerada in the North). Because of the peaceful nature of the protests, the state remained passive. Governmental attempts to negotiate with the local inhabitants and protestors were fruitless because of the inability to respond to *Hirak's* demands.

After one year of mobilization, exactly in May 2017, when *Hirak* leader Nasser Zefzazi interrupted a sermon in which an *imam* (preacher) claimed the social movement was tantamount to a *fitna* (chaos), the government took it as a pretext to clamp down on *Hirak*. Many activists were jailed and demonstrations are now systematically broken up. Zefzazi was arrested on 29 May and was sentenced to 20 years. On the other side, the protests in El Hoceima pushed the government to organize meetings with their representatives and spokespersons to El Hoceima and resulted, as described by Moroccan media, in a 'political earthquake', namely when the King dismissed several ministers and top officials for failing to improve and implement economic and infrastructure projects in the Rif region.

A similar story repeated itself in Jerada town in north-eastern Morocco. The region of Jerada is one of the poorest in the country. It was known for coal mines; however, after their closure in the 1990s, the regions deteriorated socially and economically as hundreds of former miners were forced to leave their jobs. Now, unemployed youth risk their lives in the so-called 'mines of death', extracting coal in dangerous conditions, and smuggling it for a handful of dirhams. Accordingly, in December 2017, two brothers, Houcine and Redouane, died in a disused underground coal well. Two weeks later, two other young people died in similar circumstances. The two incidents have incited people in the region to mobilize and revolt against economic marginalization, poverty, and mass unemployment. After the first wave of mobilization which involved daily demonstrations and sit-ins, the state proclaimed an 'emergency plan' for the city in February. This included a ban on illicit mining permits, the creation of new agricultural projects, and free medical care for ailing retired miners. However, the demonstrators were dissatisfied and saw this just as a kind of tranquillizer to the population and therefore went back to daily strike actions, a fact which angered the state and made it respond violently to the protestors and criminalize their mobilizations.

On 13 March, the Minister of Home Affairs banned all 'unauthorized' public gatherings. The state also resorted to massive arrest of activists and leaders of the *Hirak*, some of whom, along with others for El Hoceima *Hirak* Activists, were pardoned by the king in 2019. Worth noting in this regard is the fact that all the protests were spontaneous and no political unions or parties have been involved.

### *The boycott campaign: Afriquia, Sidi Ali, and Centrale Danone*

In April 2018, anonymous cyber activists launched on social media a boycott campaign that targeted three large companies in Morocco: *Afriquia* gas stations, *Sidi Ali* bottled water, and dairy products *Centrale Danone*. Because of the rise in prices and deteriorating living conditions, the cyber activists opted for the boycott as a form of pressure to ask for a drop in the high price of these products. The choice of the three companies was not innocent as these latter "symbolize an economy dominated by large groups linked to a business and political elite, or foreign brands" (Masbah, 2018). Also, the lessons learnt from El Hoceima and Jerrada *Hiraks* made the activists choose the boycott as "a risk-free tool for social and political mobilization that allowed [them] to be politically engaged and influential without risking the threat of state repression" (Masbah, 2018). Indeed, the 2018 boycott campaign was more popular than any previous calls for protest. Salah reports that "[w]ithin two weeks of its launch April 20, 2018, more than 90 percent of Moroccans were aware of the campaign and almost three quarters of citizens participated in some way. Among those who supported the campaign, 95 percent targeted *Central Danone*, 78 percent targeted *Sidi Ali*, and 52 percent targeted *Afriquia*" (Salah, as cited in Masbah, 2018).

The campaign persisted for several months and resulted in two interesting results. The first result was that one of the companies – *Centrale Danone* – decided to reduce its prices and launched an advertisement campaign to reconcile and apologize to the consumers. The second result was that the campaign managed to avoid modes of repression used by the authorities to contain the aforementioned *Hiraks*. Added to this, the boycott showed its efficiency to mobilize a large portion of society around an organized cause away from any conventional political institutions.

## Discussion and conclusions

A look at these new forms of activism show that they have distinguishing characteristics that make them different from any other previous struggles and activism in the political history of Morocco. First, they are the product of social and political change engendered by the 2011 turmoil in both North Africa and the Middle East. Second, they are instigated and directed by the same cause and agenda fight against poverty, unemployment, injustice, *Al-Hogra*, corruption, and despotism. Third, some of them are extreme, radical and revolutionary in their form.

First, the new forms of activism are the product of the February 20 Movement per se. In other words, if this movement has left any legacy, it has resulted in a radical shift in the relationship between the governments and the governed. The pro-democracy calls that swept Morocco were instigated by a group of young activists who were brought up in an environment endowed with both radicalization and democratization. These young activists were born and raised during and after the political and economic liberalization Morocco has undergone since the early 1990s and most if not all of them did not experience the fear of the 'Years of Lead ' that the old generation is still haunted by (Skalli, 2011). Further, these youngsters and activists grew with the new king and have witnessed his reforms and have become part of the political expectations (Skalli, 2011). The area is also characterized by the appropriation of the public space and street that resulted out of "more tolerance for different forms of protest and civil resistance as long as they were directed against veneer institutions such as the government or the parliament" (Maghraoui, 2016). This means that Moroccans' aspiration is not to overthrow the king or seek absolute revolution, but rather to implement constitutional and democratic reforms that would insure more transparency and less corruption in government. For example, in the hectic days of the February 20 Movement in Morocco, the slogan raised was 'down with corruption' and not 'down with the monarchy'. Therefore, unlike some other countries in the Maghreb, namely Tunisia and Libya, "Morocco underwent a peaceful transformation that left the monarchy in place" (Ennaji, 2012). After February 20 Movement' protests, "the Moroccans voted overwhelmingly to approve a new constitution that shifts executive power from the king to the prime minister, who will now be fully responsible for the cabinet, the civil service, and the implementation of government policies" (Ibid).

Second, because the 2011 reforms did not lead to any democratic changes, the new forms of activism have emerged to fight against corruption and against the expropriation of resources for the benefits of a few. That said, the new forms of activism are basically the result of the emergence of deep social inequalities, the growth of corruption, shortage in social and health services, and difficulties in finding housing (Thierry, 2012). They are the result of the widespread feeling of '*Al-Hogra*' and a strong sense of dignity, the contempt for people that is frequently shown by local government authorities in various social, political, and administrative institutions or through, for example, the excessive use of force, verbal humiliation, and the confiscation of their goods in public.

Third, in terms of form, these new forms of activism are endowed with a number of distinguishing characteristics. They are spontaneous and voluntary and "the individual has become a player who maintains a central importance within the collective action" (Thierry, 2012, p. 33). This shows that citizens sacrifice themselves to stand up as guardians of the constitutional principles, democratic values, and accountability. People from the margins have started to look for other forms of mobilization outside formal institutional groups such as civil society and political parties. That is to say, the weakness of civil society groups and the fragmentation of political parties and their inability neither to adopt nor to defend citizens' causes "gradually channelled social activism into a new public sphere, [where different individuals sacrificed themselves]to contest both the political and the economic status quo" (Maghraoui, 2016, pp. 197–198). Another aspect is that most activists, if not all of them, come from the margins and belong to different age and gender groups; their target is the dismantling of corruption, *Al-Horga*, humiliation, and poverty . This is totally different from the resistance led by civil society groups who emerged during the liberalization process (1980s–1990s) whose activism and ability to mobilize remained rooted in specific and separate issues such as human rights, gender rights, or cultural rights.

Amid this discussion, one should not deny the role of social media in communicating these new forms of activism to the rest of the world. In Morocco, the decreasing cost of mobile phones and their dimension from the point of sharing materials such as video and photographs in addition to the rapid proliferation of the internet and social networking sites such as Twitter, Facebook, and YouTube has not only facilitated communicating these forms of activism but has also, compared to other mass communication tools, helped the new activists and actors to produce the content of the media themselves and make others including the government aware of their grievances. Despite its limited impact on the ground and specifically in terms of political changes and reforms, social media served as a megaphone for these forms of activism and helped in inspiring other Moroccans scattered all over the world to join in virtually and on the ground.

## Notes

1 The Years of Lead is the term used by opponents to the rule of the former King Hassan II to describe a period of his rule (from the 1960s to the beginning of the 1980s). This period of Moroccan history was marked by state violence against dissidents and democracy activists.

2 This is an association founded by Cheikh. The association is not legal but is tolerated by the Moroccan authorities. It advocates mainly the transformation of Morocco into an Islamist state ruled by its interpretation of the *Shari'a* (Islamic law).

3 The word *Al-hogra* comes from the Arabic *ihtiqaar*, meaning disdain, contempt, humiliation, and deprivation. In Morocco, *Al-hogra* is an overloaded term when used in Moroccan *Darija* (Moroccan colloquial Arabic) as it expresses a number of negative feelings and moods (injustice, outrage, inequality, inferiority, disempowerment, frustration, feelings of contempt). In this chapter, the word is used mainly to express the feeling associated with exclusion and the feeling of the loss of dignity one experiences after being treated inequitably or unfairly in the provision of public services or in the protection of civil or human rights. This is usually manifested in different situations such as excessive use of force by the police, inability and denial to benefit from a public service, confiscation of one's goods and the contempt shown by some local government authorities in various administrative institutions because of one's poverty or social background.

## References

Benchemsi, A. (2012). *Feb 20's Rise and Fall.* Retrieved May, 2012 http://ahmedbenchemsi.com/feb20s-rise-and-fall-amoroccan-story/.

Clement, M. H. (1999). Postcolonial dialectics of civil society. In Y. H. Zoubir (Ed.). *North Africa in transition: State, society and economic transformation in the 1999s* (pp: 11–28). Florida: Florida University Press.

Cohen, S., & Jaidi, L. (2006). *Morocco: Globalization and its consequences.* London: Routledge.

Daadaoui, M. (2011). *Moroccan Monarchy and the Islamist Challenge: Maintaining Makhzen Power.* New York: Palgrave Macmillan.

Ennaji, M. (2012). The Maghreb's Modern Islamists. *The Project Syndicate*. Retrieved from https://www.project-syndicate.org/commentary/the-maghreb-s-modern-islamists?barrier=accesspaylog.

Halstead, J. P. (1961). *Rebirth of a nation: The origins and rise of Moroccan nationalism, 1912–1944*. Cambridge: Cambridge University Press.

Laayachi, A. (1998). *State, society and democracy in Morocco: The limits of associative life*. Washington, DC: The Center for Contemporary Arab Studies and Georgetown University.

Maghraoui, D. (2016). Morocco: Obedience, civil resistance, and dispersed solidarities. In A. Roberts, M. J. Willis, R. McCarthy & T. Garton Ash (Eds.). *Civil resistance in the Arab Spring: Triumphs and disasters* (pp. 194–222). Oxford: Oxford University Press.

Masbah, M. (2018). "Let it spoil!": Morocco's boycott and the empowerment of 'regular' citizen. *Al Jazeera Centre for Studies*. Retrieved June 2019 from https://studies.aljazeera.net/sites/default/files/articles/reports/documents/0f024583209a467dab4e2f8cd08055f2_100.pdf.

Norton, A. R. (1995). Introduction. In A. R. Norton (Ed.). *Civil society in the Middle East* (pp. 1–16). Leiden: E. J. Brill.

Pennell, C. R. (2000). *Morocco since 1830: A history*. London: Hurst.

Ruchti, J. (2011). *Draft text of the constitution adopted at the referendum of 1 July 2011*. Retrieved from: www.ancl-radc.org.za/sites/default/files/morocco_eng.pdf.

Sater, J. N. (2007). *Civil society and political change in Morocco*. London: Routledge.

Skalli, L. H. (2011). Generational politics and renewal of leadership in the Moroccan women's movement. *International Feminist Journal of Politics*, 13 (3), 329–348. https://doi.org/10.1080/14616742.2011.587366.

Smith, A. R., & Loudiy, F. (2005). Testing the red lines on the liberalization of speech in Morocco. *Human Rights Quarterly*, 27 (3), 1069–1119.

Stewart, C. F. (1967). *The economy of Morocco: 1912–1962*. Cambridge, MA: Harvard University Press.

Thierry, D. (2012). Moroccan youth and the forming of a new generation: Social change, collective action and political activism. *Mediterranean Politics*, 17 (1), 23–40. https://doi.org/10.1080/13629395.2012.655044.

Yachoulti, M. (2012). *Civil society women's movement and the Moroccan state: Addressing the specificities and assessing the roles*. Saarbrücken: LAP Lambert Academic.

Yachoulti, M. (2019). Moroccan civil society after the 2011 constitutional reforms: The case of the women's movement. In I. Natil, C. Pierobon & L. Tauber (Eds.). *The power of civil society in the Middle East and North Africa: Peace-building, change, and development* (pp: 76–96). New York: Routledge.

Yachoulti, M., & Lachhab, M. (2018). Moroccan women's resistance to Al-hogra in the aftermaths of Arab spring patterns and outcomes. *Feminist Research*, 2 (1), 22–28.

# 10 A case study of two Irish faith-based CSOs

*Youcef Sai*

## Introduction

Given the changing landscape at a time when civic and political spheres are faced with populism and divisive identity politics, charities play an important role in contributing towards sustainable societies by forging some cohesion and joint purpose. In order for civil society to grow and develop, the public sphere ought to be a space whereby freedom is guaranteed by the state. Habermas contends in his book *The Structural Transformation of the Public Sphere*, that the public sphere is made up of private individuals who come together as a public body that articulates the needs of society to the state, and enjoys basic freedoms of expression and opinion (1991: 176). To a large extent, Irish society provides such a public space whereby individuals can, and have the right to, establish CSOs that operate autonomously. The Constitution of Ireland provides fertile ground for Muslims to engage in Irish civil society. It is therefore no surprise that the minority community have availed of their constitutional right, as expressed in Article 44.2.5, to form associations and unions for various causes, including charitable purposes.

The Article stresses that: "Every religious denomination shall have the right to manage its own affairs, own, acquire and administer property, movable and immovable, and maintain institutions for religious or charitable purposes" (Constitution of Ireland, 1937).

In Ireland, the Charities Regulatory Authority (CRA) is an independent authority whose key functions are to establish and maintain a public register of charitable organisations operating in the country. Established in 2014, they are considered the national statutory regulator for charities in the country and serve to ensure compliance by organisations with the Charities Act 2009. Their mission is to "regulate the charity sector in the public interest so as to ensure compliance with the law and support best practice in the governance, management and administration of charities" (Charities Regulator, 2020). Furthermore, their functions are to increase trust and confidence in the management and governance of charitable trusts and organisations in Ireland by encouraging transparency in operations. The Charities Act 2009 outlines charitable purposes as including "the prevention or relief of poverty or economic hardship; the advancement of education, the advancement of religion and any other purpose that is of benefit to the community" (Article 3.1).

According to the Charities Regulator annual report in 2017, there has also been an increase in the establishment of charity organisations in Ireland with more than 9,000 officially registered (Farrelly, 2018). In Ireland, since the early 1990s, the Muslim population has increased exponentially from approximately 4,000 in the nineties to over 60,000 according to the latest census in 2016. It is therefore not surprising to witness an increase in the establishment of CSOs by Muslims to cater for their religious commitments and cultural needs. Although an exact number is not officially known, it is estimated that there are at least 50 registered charities established by Muslims in the Republic of Ireland out of approximately 9,000 (Farrelly, 2018).[1]

## Data and methods

This small-scale qualitative case study aims to gain insights and perspectives from two established faith-based charities, Islamic Relief Ireland (IRI) and Muslim Sisters of Éire (MSOÉ). Both are based in Dublin, in the Republic of Ireland and are examples of two CSOs that operate and exercise their constitutional freedom, as well as contribute to Irish society in different ways through their purposes, operational practices and engagement with their communities. The former is an international CSO with affiliates around the world established for the sole purpose of prevention or relief of poverty or hardship, whilst the latter is a small indigenous CSO with several purposes, including promotion of community and providing welfare to those in need. For the purpose of this study, data was collected via semi-structured interviews with members of each organisation. A questionnaire was also administered to one member of each charity. The questions related to different areas of enquiry such as their: history; current activities; impact and influence on society; current challenges; funding and sustainability and future plans.

Adopting two methods of data collection, firstly by questionnaire then semi-structured interviews, allowed for participant responses to be clarified, if needed, and checked to ensure accuracy of information. This method was suitable as it focused on collecting and analysing sensitive data and its meaning in context. The purpose of selecting these two particular CSOs is not to compare them but rather to understand and gain knowledge of how different charity organisations in contemporary Ireland are operating and their impact on society. Furthermore, the case studies aim to contribute to the literature on faith-based charities in general and deepen our awareness of the issues they are engaged in, as well as highlight some of the work and challenges they face. As evaluative case studies involve description, explanation and judgment (Merriam, 1998), the data and content gleaned from this study was analysed inductively to gain greater understanding of the phenomenon.

## Islamic Relief: background

Generically, the term 'Islamic Relief' (IR) refers to any member of the Islamic Relief worldwide family of charities who share the common vision, mission and identity of the organisation. Islamic Relief Worldwide (IRW), based in Birmingham in the United Kingdom (UK), specifically refers to the charity organised under UK law that serves as a catalyst and coordinator for many relief projects around the globe, in which members of the Islamic Relief family of charities collaborate (IRW, 2020a). This is regarded as the main headquarters that overseas global standards. IRW started its work in 1984 in the UK and has since expanded to many parts of the world. Inspired by Islamic principles and values, this faith-based organisation aims to help people in need across the world irrespective of their background. The universal vision of IRW, which is motivated by their religious convictions and values and will to empower communities worldwide, is to ensure that "social obligations are fulfilled and people respond as one to the suffering of others" (IRW, 2020b). The CSO was co-founded by Dr Hany El Banna OBE in response to the famine in the Horn of Africa, with a donation of "20 pence" (IRW, 2020b) and has since then, established itself in over 40 countries with over 100 offices worldwide. It is one of the largest Islamic NGOs (non-governmental organisations) in the world and the first Islamic European humanitarian organisation (Barylo, 2017).

In the early 1990s, IR established independent branches across many European countries and North America. The international operations of Islamic Relief operated with each other on a consensual basis in accordance with a loose international association. Islamic Relief operates through separate legal entities in the UK (IRW), USA, Switzerland, Germany, Sweden, Canada, Malaysia, South Africa, Pakistan, India, Kenya, the Russian Federation, Australia and Spain. In other countries where Islamic Relief family members operate, the legal registration is such that IRW is the foreign NGO registered in that country. The operations in Ireland, for example, were registered as a branch of the UK entity IRW (IRW, 2020a).

## The case of Islamic Relief Ireland (IRI): a brief history

In 2007, IRW considered opening a branch in Ireland. However, after carrying out a feasibility study at the time the organisation was advised not to proceed. Economic shifts can play a major factor for CSOs and their ability to expand operations. According to Mudafar Al Tawash, the Chair of IRI, there were several reasons for not setting up an office then, however one of the main reasons was that "due to the economic recession that hit Ireland around that period and the international financial crisis, it was not an appropriate time to set up IRI" (Al Tawash, 2020).

It was not until 2010, that IRI officially became an incorporated branch of IRW. With the assistance and expertise of Al Tawash, who worked previously with IR in various African counties including Kenya, South Sudan and Somalia, the establishment of the first IR branch had begun. Although not established officially as an independent charity prior to 2010, Al Tawash's engagements and individual fundraising initiatives, on behalf of IRW, throughout various mosques "by collecting funds for Ramadan food packs for the poor in Muslim countries" (Al Tawash, 2020) helped to prepare the ground for the future of the organisation. This initial connection with the Irish Muslim community provided them with knowledge of the work IRW were enagaged in, as well as information on their various charity projects. In 2013, IRI set up their first office in Dublin, by renting an office within the premises of the Muslim Association of Ireland (MAI), who are based in an industrial estate in the south of Dublin. By 2014, they rented a nearby warehouse to begin their clothing collection operation. This initial move assisted IRI to gain a notable presence in the Muslim community, particularly in the south Dublin region.

In 2019, the office relocated to the heart of Dublin city. Al Tawash believed it was an appropriate time to relocate to a more centrally located premises as it was "a bit isolated and it was difficult for general public people to access us, so in order to increase our exposure and accessibility we decided to locate in the city". As of 2020, IRI is located in Clanbrassil Street, a busy multi-ethnic area with numerous halal shops and restaurants as well as mosques and churches. It is also close to Ireland's oldest and well-known university, Trinity College Dublin, as well as other third-level institutions. Historically, the area was known as part of Little Jerusalem, from 1900 to the 1950s, and was considered the heart of the Jewish community in Ireland, to where many Jews fled persecution from east Europe (Keogh, 1998). Al Tawash asserts that moving location has been a positive one and added that "people from the general public, even non-Muslims, come into the office to inquire about our work … so the response and support from the local community has been welcoming" (Al Tawash, 2020).

## Challenges and opportunities

CSOs can be vulnerable to change in regulation and the need for trustees and directors to be abreast of all new charity laws and legalities. The CRA was established in 2014 to restore public confidence after a series of scandals to some high-profile Irish charities (Murphy, 2015). However, the CRA faced their own challenges including a lack of funding and inability to perform its various functions. The Wheel, Ireland's largest representative body for charitable organisations asserted that this led to the inability of the CRA to conduct an appropriate public awareness campaign of the various new requirements and registration procedures (Murphy, 2015). In 2016, due to sudden changes in Irish charity regulations and procedures, that were of an unprecedented nature, IRI operations, along with a number of charities who were at the early stage of formation, were temporarily suspended until revised applications under the newly formed CRA were completed.

In 2018, after having successfully fulfilled and negotiated the newly implemented CRA application process and received approval from the Charity Commissioner to recommence operations, IRI trustees contend that this was a challenging yet exciting period for the organisation. Doyle recalled, in reference to the recommencement of operations and the relaunch of fundraising activities just prior to the beginning of Ramadan that year, that IRI had to "hit the ground running … due to the keen interest from the Irish Muslim community to channel their zakat donations to those most in need across the globe" (2020).

Despite increased regulation and compliance requirements imposed upon Irish charities, the IRI team did not consider the legal frameworks or regulations to be much of a burden, rather they viewed this as something positive and even "necessary to effectively operate" (Atique, 2020). For IRI and IR, in general, their commitment to transparency is one of their key characteristics which they aim to demonstrate as an international charity with a faith-based ethos. One of their aims in the future is to move beyond minimal expectations to the highest level of transparency. Referring to SORP (Statement of Recommended Practice, Accounting and Reporting by Charities) by the Charity Commission of England and Wales, Doyle (2020) asserts that although it is not a requirement for charities in the Republic of Ireland at this present moment, IRI are already "adopting these recommendations, beyond minimal standards, demonstrating the highest level of accountability and transparency for all our stakeholders and donors which improves our reputation in the community".

Before committing to any project, IR conducts a needs assessment on the ground which aims to determine and address the gaps between current conditions, with the assistance from a local team of experts to communicate their requirements. Once this has been carried out and an implementation plan set in place and achieved, it is then audited to ensure transparency and to verify that the objectives of the projects have been fulfilled and the impact has been reached. This involves a service-level agreement (SLA), a formal contractual collaboration between IRW and IRI on the details and purposes of the project (Doyle, 2020).

## IRI: Impact and influence

The impact of IRI activities is often measured through the response and the amount of donations from the general public, as well as the number of beneficiaries from the collection. Apart from collecting donations, the social activities arranged surrounding a funding project aim to bring local community members together, such as through family entertainment or dinners, in order to integrate with the wider public. IR view their role in Irish society as a positive one whereby their charity fundraising work prevails but aim, in addition, to facilitate opportunities for people to come together socially and "providing people with an avenue to fulfil their duty as Muslims by giving charity, but also enjoying themselves by making a fun day out of it" (Atique, 2020). In 2019, the international nasheed artist Zain Bhikha was invited by IRI to Dublin to perform, which included fundraising to sponsor orphans worldwide. In 2020, IRI organised a sponsored cycle where about 50 volunteers from different IR affiliates across the world travelled from Cordoba to Alpujarra to raise money and awareness for the Water for Life project in Africa. Atique admits that while the sponsored cycle is not groundbreaking in terms of the funds collected it has other benefits such as "building camaraderie among volunteers from different countries and creating an awareness about the project in a creative and fun way" (2020).

At a local level, another initiative which young IRI volunteers are involved in is bagging shopping items for customers at local supermarkets. Visibly recognizable wearing distinct Islamic Relief tee-shirts, their representation may be seen as a kind of empowerment and loyal commitment to changing negative perceptions of the public towards Islam. Interaction and engagement with general public through simple actions and awareness campaigns demonstrate a growing sense of activism and perhaps a "form of participatory democracy" amongst young Muslims, most of whom are born and raised in Ireland (Aragonès & Sánchez-Pagés, 2009).

IR encourage their team and trustees to visit the sites, where charity projects are being implemented, to experience and feel the impact of the donations on the ground. Reflecting on a trip to a refugee camp in Lebanon in 2014, Doyle described the salience of "professional distribution in charity work" and that this "leads to greater impact and over-achievement in many cases due to proper planning and organisation" (2020). By witnessing the impact of charity work on the ground, this affects the hearts of those involved, who can speak reliably and with confidence, having experienced and been close to the project site. In 2013, one of the IRI team went to Mali to help and witness the completion of water wells in some of the country's poorest areas. For many, the closest access to water required locals to make a journey of at least five miles. Projects like this and others were described by Al Tawash as, "really a life changing experience for the people but also for the member who went to participate … it really created a real sense of empathy and an intrinsic motivation to continue to work harder for the less fortunate in the future" (2020).

## IRI: Partnerships and relationships

Since its inception, the main concern of IRI has been to raise funds and collect donations to support a variety of humanitarian projects around the world in places such as Yemen, Syria and Myanmar, including non-Muslim-related projects in Haiti, the Philippines and USA. In 2018, funds were raised for the delivery of urgent medical supplies to hospitals and health centres in Syria. In 2018, the Irish Muslim community funded 1 million US dollars' worth of medical aid for the Syrian people (Doyle, 2020). Furthermore, IRI supported emergency responses in Yemen and also in Myanmar, where homes were built for refugees fleeing persecution.

One of the strengths of IRW is their ability to access remote and challenging areas. It is widely known in charity circles that Islamic Relief provides emergency aid and assistance and initiates development projects in countries in Africa, Asia, Europe and the Middle East. Islamic Relief employ people locally because they believe that they will understand the nuanced needs of their own communities. With the constant social and political shifts that occur, matched with conflict and tensions around the world, IRI receive updates regularly of incidents and events that take place globally.

In 2018, during the Yemen conflict which led to the spread of cholera, Trócaire, which is the official overseas development agency of the Catholic Church in Ireland, attempted to provide life-saving care to people. However, without a direct presence in the area, they decided to partner with Islamic Relief and avail of their 'on the ground' expertise for this project, highlighting the international reputation of the organisation. Trócaire provided IRW and Islamic Relief Yemen with €300,000 in response to the Yemeni crisis, to provide families with hygiene supplies and water (Jansen, 2018; Gallagher, 2018).

Furthermore, Al Tawash (2020) recalls his experience working with IRW in South Sudan during the famine in 2005 and the collaboration efforts at that time by saying,

> we had an agreement with World Food Programme (WFP) to provide food packs for children under 5 years old and also in Kenya in 2006, we worked with the UN to distribute specific food nutrient packs for those under a certain weight and their mothers over a period of time, which lasted around six to eight months.

Similarly, IRW has worked with the Irish government for international development. In 2010, the Irish government donated funds towards the Pakistan floods emergency appeal. Al Tawash asserted that "the Irish government is well-known for its generosity despite being a small country, and there is lots of potential for us now, as IRI, to build strong partnerships in the future". Since establishing its branch in Dublin, IRI have tended to focus on building relationships with the local Muslim communities by networking and collaborating with various organisations, including mosques, Islamic student bodies, as well as other Muslim-led charities who focus on feeding the poor, supporting refugees or tackling women's issues. In 2018, IRI also supported the homeless on Dublin streets, through Muslim Sisters of Éire's 'Bag for Life' appeal. Furthermore, in 2019, IRI and IRW collaborated with Heartship, a non-profit organisation based in Northern Ireland, to send containers of medical supplies and equipment to Syria.

During my interviews, all members of the IRI team expressed their intention to expand their collaborative efforts both nationally and internationally. Atique summarised the sentiments of the organisation by stating that "it is very much an area of work we are interested in and we are welcome to the idea of partnering with other organisations from different backgrounds" (2020). IRI assert that, from their base in Ireland, they intend to continue and build on those relationships established previously by IRW with various well-known international charities such as the United Nations International Children's Emergency Fund and WFP, as well as local charities such as Human Appeal Ireland, Muslim Sisters of Éire and Tasnuva Shamim Foundation Ireland.

## The case of Muslim Sisters of Éire (MSOÉ): from humble beginnings

Muslim Sisters of Éire (MSOÉ) was established in 2010. This grassroots civil organisation, which was set up by two Muslim women, Lorraine O'Connor, Irish born and raised, and Jasmina Kid from Australia, was initially established with the primary objective of providing a 'safe space' for women. Their aim was focused on breaking down stereotypes about how Muslim women were represented in the media, as well as building bridges between Muslim and non-Muslims across Ireland. This small women's group began as a weekly social gathering where mothers and their children met to form new friendships and general support. Within a few years, the organisation attracted migrant women from diverse social and ethnic backgrounds. According to Kid (2020), "many Muslim women in our group shared their experiences of racism and Islamophobic attacks and this was one of the reasons for us to establish a Muslim women's organisation that would serve society and breakdown stereotypes at the same time". During the recession period, MSOÉ began to prepare sandwiches to be distributed to the needy and it was soon afterwards that they realised "a greater commitment would be required in the future to help alleviate this growing social crisis" (O'Connor, 2020).

## Local societal impact and influence

For MSOÉ, social activism and positive engagement with Irish society is the most effective way to break certain stereotypes and to demonstrate their salient and participatory role as Muslim women in the local community. In 2017, they began, what has now become their longest and ongoing project, the feeding of the homeless in the heart of Dublin city. This project takes place every Friday night outside one of Ireland's most famous historical buildings, the General Post Office (GPO) in the centre of O'Connell street, which historically served as the headquarters of the leaders of Irish Republicans who fought against British rule. Ironically, in 2020, MSOÉ are fighting a different cause. With the recent housing crisis in Ireland, MSOÉ assert that the homeless community are "being failed by the system" (O'Connor, 2020). The organisation often shares live videos through social media of the team serving food, most of whom are wearing hijab. Commenting on this further, Kid

(2020) emphasised that "this project addresses many challenges facing Ireland today including integration, poverty relief and building community cohesion … elevating the poor and their sense of dignity and belonging and showing that we, as Muslim women, are in solidarity with the misfortunate". On an operational level, the team of volunteers, who meet at least once a week and communicate via the social media application, WhatsApp, decide the weekly cooking rotation and collection of supplies across Dublin and beyond as they aim to prepare food for "up to 300 to 400 people a week" (Kid, 2020).

This regular contact with the Irish community has increased their exposure and reputation. In 2019, although unsuccessful, MSOÉ were shortlisted for The Wheel's Community Impact 'Community Hero Award', for their contribution to feeding the poor, which is a charity organisation that supports community and voluntary organisations, charities and social enterprises to assist them "in changing Ireland for the better" (The Wheel, 2019a, b).

The Irish media took particular interest in MSOÉ in 2019, in celebration of 'World Hijab Day' on the first day of February, where its members were interviewed by the national broadcaster, Raidió Teilifís Éireann (RTÉ), about their work and a segment of a speech delivered at the event by a Muslim student was also broadcast (Little, 2019). The organisation views their team of eight core committee members, from Ireland, Australia, Scotland, South Africa, India and Pakistan and Malaysia, including over 50 volunteers from mixed backgrounds and origins, as one of their significant strengths, which allows them, it seems, to work seamlessly across a variety of platforms. One of those ways is through the school outreach programme, 'This Is Me' project. In this educational outreach initiative, members of MSOÉ attend Irish secondary schools to present a talk to students about their charity work. For the founders, this is an important avenue to foster community integration and to connect with the future generation about their work which "provides secondary students with the opportunity to ask questions and learn more about Muslim women and activism in Irish civil society" (O'Connor, 2020). In addition, they have also featured in the religious secondary school textbook *Inspire*, and are currently collaborating with Veritas [another Irish religious publication house] to discuss their inclusion in the upcoming secondary textbook *Soul Seekers* (Kid, 2020).

## Challenges

As a not-for-profit organisation, MSOÉ runs solely on grants, local fundraising initiatives and public donations. As an indigenous CSO, which in 2020, celebrated ten years of operation, it faces challenges for sustainability and this is their main concern. Without any paid employees working in the organisation they face similar challenges to other CSOs. The founders expressed this by saying that whilst preparing and serving food for the homeless and those in need is "rewarding, it is also very challenging at times as there is always the constant pressure to be self-sustaining … generate funds, apply for grants and be reliant on donations and volunteers to help us out with our bucket collections and organisation of fundraising events" (Kid, 2020).

Without secure financial backing either from the Irish government or private sources, the future of MSOÉ remains tentative. There is a constant pressure to secure funds to maintain activities for the forthcoming year. Unlike some CSOs who depend on mostly foreign aid and support, this indigenous organisation relies on the support and generosity from the local public.

Despite financial constraints, they continue to raise donations to support a variety of campaigns to assist the less fortunate in Irish society. Some of these projects consist of the 'Bag for Life' annual campaign in December which consists of purchasing 'survival kits' and supplies for the homeless to assist them through the winter period (Filaih, 2019). Within the Irish Muslim community, during the month of Ramadan, MSOÉ aim to provide support to fasting Muslim families living in emergency accommodation, as well as promoting a toy drive appeal for children to assist financially struggling families during the festive Eid religious celebration (MSOÉ, 2019a). They also collaborate with other organisations, such as Human Appeal International Ireland, to hold fundraising events such as the 'Summer community family festival' and a yearly 'Ladies Winter Charity Ball' to support their campaigns (MSOÉ, 2019b).

## Interfaith dialogue and advocacy initiatives

According to the MSOÉ website, the independent organisation also aims to promote "social integration, diversity and empowerment of women" as well as "promote a better understanding of Islam" (MSOÉ, 2020). In 2018, MSOÉ held an interfaith conference during Ramadan where they invited people from different faiths such as the Archbishop of Dublin, Diarmuid Martin; Helen Marks, President of Dublin Jewish Progressive Congregation (DJPC); and Michael O'Sullivan, a member of Dublin City Interfaith Forum. MSOÉ has also engaged in other social and political contexts that have taken place in Ireland through non-violent peace activism and grassroots initiatives, including anti-hate campaigns. After an attack on some Muslim girls in Dublin in 2019, MSOÉ established a petition to put forward an anti-hate campaign after the violent attack where they had their headscarves ripped off in Dublin city (Schiller, 2019), which "received much support from the wider Irish public as well as from various organisations who signed this petition in support" (Kid, 2020). In 2019, Glencree Centre for Peace and Reconciliation, a non-profit, non-governmental organisation invited MSOÉ to meet with the President of Ireland's wife, Sabina Higgins and Lord Mayor Nial Ring to discuss and share a panel discussion on the importance of dialogue in the community (Ali, 2018).

Aside from feeding the poor in Dublin city, MSOÉ have participated in demonstrations to campaign against the government to solve the homeless crisis in Ireland. In 2018, they participated in a march organised by the National Homeless and Housing Coalition, raising their banner '#NoToHomelessness', where they joined thousands of protestors, charities and activists to show their advocacy and solidarity for the cause (Filaih, 2018).

Although on a small scale, MSOÉ are conscious of playing their role in preserving the environment and in ecological change and its impact on civil society. They collaborate with Tesco and others via FoodCloud, which is an Irish social enterprise that connects businesses with surplus food to charities in their local communities that need it via a software platform. This initiative aims to build a business around a shared interest in the elimination of food waste, pollution and food poverty. For MSOÉ, being able to avail of such an initiative "shows the multi-faceted benefits that our work is having, in that we can contribute to the preservation of our environment and at the same time serve our people" (O'Connor, 2020).

## *Conclusion*

In the last decade there has been an increased prominence and recognition of Muslim charity groups in the Republic of Ireland which demonstrates their valuable social and civic contribution to society. The Irish constitution and current regulatory and legislative framework have enabled minority communities, including the Muslim community, to avail themselves of the opportunity to establish CSOs that aim to serve their various purposes. It is clear that the two organisations in this study have made a positive impact at a societal level and beyond. As the population of Muslims increases in Ireland, as well as the number of CSOs, more research is desired to understand their purposes, challenges, contributions and impact in Irish society and transnational links. As far as both the organisations in this study are concerned, their development and growth has been, for most part, due to the sacrifice and dedication of their volunteers. Exploring their voices, their experiences, challenges and rationale for choosing to volunteer their time and energy to their respective charities is a desirable avenue for future research.

The two organisations in this study, although established and operating in different ways, share a similar world vision based on Islamic values and principles. Moreover, neither of the charities discriminate in religious terms, either with regard to beneficiaries, nor to their employment policies and principles where they continue to have workers and volunteers from different faiths and backgrounds. They both wish to represent their faith through civic duty and service towards society. Apart from fundraising, they both play an increasingly important role in their advocacy for human rights, dialogue and harmonious community relations, empowerment of youth and women through education and capacity building.

In a globalised world, where political, social and economic shifts are constantly in a state of change, the salient roles of CSOs, like IRI and MSOÉ, cannot be underestimated as they strive for the betterment of society. The case studies provide valuable lessons for other faith-based CSOs, who may choose to operate in isolation and deprive themselves of social recognition and impact, by demonstrating how cooperating with others can add real value and strength to an organisation. With a greater concern shown by faith-based CSOs to engage and work with each other on common goals and purposes, by promoting shared universal values that contribute positively towards society at large, then their future in Irish society looks bright.

## Note

1 This figure is based on a basic search for the term 'Islamic' or 'Muslim' in the list of registered charities in the Republic of Ireland.

## Bibliography

Ali, A. (2018) 'Mansion House – 21st November 2018', *Muslim Sisters of Éire*, Available at: https://MSOÉ.ie/index.php/latest-updates/110-report-21st-november-2018 [Accessed 19 February 2020].

Aragonès, E., and Sánchez-Pagés, S. (2009) 'A theory of participatory democracy based on the real case of Porto Alegre'. *European Economic Review*, 53.

Barylo, W. (2017) *Young Muslim Change-Makers: Grassroots Charities Rethinking Modern Societies*. UK: Routledge.

Constitution of Ireland. (1937) *Bunreacht na hÉireann*. Article 44.2.5.

Charities Act. (2009) 'Charitable Purpose, Section 3'. *Irish Statute Book*. Available at: http://www.irishstatutebook.ie/eli/2009/act/6/section/3/enacted/en/html#sec3 [Accessed 20 February 2020].

Charities Regulator. (2020) 'What We Do', Available at: https://www.charitiesregulator.ie/en/who-we-are/what-we-do [Accessed 10 February 2020].

Farrelly, J. (2018) 'Over 9,000 charities registered at end of 2017 following Charities Regulator's busiest year to date', 6 June, Available at: https://www.charitiesregulator.ie/en/information-for-the-public/our-news/2018/june/over-9-000-charities-registered-at-end-of-2017-following-charities-regulators-busiest-year-to-date, [Accessed 14 February 2020].

Filaih, B. (2019) 'Distributing Bags for Life', *Muslim Sisters of Éire*, Available at: http://MSOÉ.ie/index.php/latest-updates/113-distributing-bags-for-life [Accessed 1 February 2020].

Filaih, B. (2018) 'Raise the Roof – Dublin Protest to End Homelessness', *Muslim Sisters of Éire*, Available at: https://MSOÉ.ie/index.php/latest-updates/111-raise-the-roof-dublin-protest-to-end-homelessness [Accessed 12 February 2020].

Gallagher, C. (2018) 'Yemen Crisis: Millions Facing Famine', 17 October, Available at: https://www.trocaire.org/news/millions-face-famine-yemen [Accessed 19 February 2020].

Habermas, J. (1991) *The Structural Transformation of the Public Sphere: An Inquiry into a Category of Bourgeois Society*, translated by T. Burger and F. Lawrence. Cambridge, MA: MIT Press (Originally published in 1989).

Islamic Relief Worldwide [IRW]. (2020a) 'Governance', Available at: https://www.islamic-relief.org/family-governance/ [Accessed 1 February 2020].

Islamic Relief Worldwide [IRW]. (2020b) 'History', Available at: https://www.islamic-relief.ie/about-us/history/ [Accessed 1 February 2020].

Jansen, M. (2018) 'Saudi-led war in Yemen risks plunging half population into famine'. *The Irish Times*, 18 October. Available at: https://www.irishtimes.com/news/world/middle-east/saudi-led-war-in-yemen-risks-plunging-half-population-into-famine-1.3668323 [Accessed 18 February 2020].

Keogh, D. (1998) *Jews in Twentieth-Century Ireland*. Cork: Cork University Press.

Little, J. (2019) 'Muslim community in Ireland mark World Hijab Day', *RTE News*, 1 February 2019, Available at: https://www.rte.ie/news/ireland/2019/0201/1027042-muslim-community-in-ireland-mark-world-hijab-day/ [Accessed 15 December 2019].

Merriam, B. (1998) *Qualitative Research and Case Study Applications in Education*. San Francisco, CA: Jossey-Bass.

Murphy, S.J. (2015) 'Charities Regulatory Authority needs more staff – support group'. *The Irish Independent*, 27 July, Available at: https://www.independent.ie/incoming/charities-regulatory-authority-needs-more-staff-support-group-31406081.html [Accessed 28 February 2020].

Muslim Sisters of Éire [MSOÉ]. (2019a) *Facebook*, 'Toy Drive for Children in Direct Provision'. 12 April, Available at: https://www.facebook.com/muslimsisterofeire/posts/2211841648904460 [Accessed 3 February 2020].

Muslim Sisters of Éire [MSOÉ]. (2019b) *Facebook*, 'Ladies Grand Charity Winter Ball', 9 November, Available at: https://www.facebook.com/events/hilton-dublin/ladies-grand-winter-charity-ball/537778923652220/ [Accessed 6 February 2020].

Muslim Sisters of Éire [MSOÉ]. (2020) 'This Is What We Do', Available at: https://www.msoe.ie/ [Accessed 20 April 2020].

Schiller, R. (2019) 'Gardaí probe assault on Muslim teen who allegedly had hijab ripped off and was pelted with eggs', *Irish Independent*, 20 August, Available at: https://www.independent.ie/irish-news/news/gardai-probe-assault-on-muslim-teen-who-allegedly-had-hijab-ripped-off-and-was-pelted-with-eggs-38420156.html [Accessed 15 February 2020].

The Wheel. (2019a) 'Shortlists for the Charity Impacts Awards 2019 Announced'. Available at https://www.wheel.ie/news/2019/10/shortlists-charity-impact-awards-2019-announced [Accessed 17 February 2020].

The Wheel. (2019b) 'About us/projects'. Available at: https://www.wheel.ie/about-us/projects [Accessed 10 February 2020].

### *Interviewees*

Al Tawash, M. (2020, 19 February). Chairperson and Trustee, *Islamic Relief Ireland*.

Atique, M. (2020, 3 February). General Manager, *Islamic Relief Ireland*.

Doyle, B. (2020, 6 February). Trustee, *Islamic Relief Ireland*.

Kid, J. (2020, 10 January). *Muslim Sisters of Éire*, Vice-Chair and Co-Founder.

O'Connor, L. (2020, 10 January). Chair, *Co-Founder*.

# 11 Conclusion

## Implications and future direction

*Ibrahim Natil*

This volume brings various experiences, challenges and contributions of CSO engagement into complicated shifting contexts that are the result of limited political space given by some governments, emerging new social dynamics and funding constraints or conditions. It explores the barriers faced by civil society organisations (CSOs) and their power to cope and function despite the shifting political landscape, restrictive social context and the complexity of funding conditions and requirements. By addressing not only the challenges but also the power of civil society organisations to function, it increases our understanding of their contribution, interaction and engagement in countries of high social and political complexity such as Iran, Cambodia, the Gaza Strip in the Palestinian Occupied Territories (oPt), Egypt, Ecuador and Morocco. The countries identified in this volume have been influenced by enormous shifts and complicated challenges, owing to social, political and economic influences. The capacity of CSOs within these countries is reflected in their ability to function and achieve their values, missions and visions despite barriers from the political landscape, social and cultural dynamics and context, and unstainable financial sources.

In order to provide a holistic understanding of challenges facing CSOs, the engagement of western CSOs is introduced and discussed in Chapter 10 which examines the relatively stable economic and political context in Ireland, providing a comparison between this and civil society from the south. Cultural dynamics and social cohesion have been crucial elements for CSOs working for Muslim communities in a Western country like Ireland. This edited volume delivers up-to-date research and analysis of civil society organisations as an important actor within society, while challenging these shifts. As highlighted by Natil in this volume, civil society organisations are not typical in coping with the various changes hitting their societies, which have been influenced by at least three different shifts – political, social and financial. Natil also introduces the reader to some of the barriers of effective civil society organisations. These are impacting their power to fulfil significant contributions in the field of development, human rights, civic engagement, development, democracy, social cohesion and legal reform.

The volume then provides an in-depth analysis of CSOs as a significant actor to foster development and change at all levels, despite the overwhelming social, financial and political shifts characterising these countries. In particular, it shows how CSOs are not only influenced by various and sudden shifts but are also able to engage as a development actor with societal changes. The contributors whose different cultural, social and scholarly backgrounds from around the globe (south–north exchange) enrich this volume through in-depth analysis, insightful views, new knowledge and expertise. Expertise in civic space in Africa interacts with the limitations of political freedom that CSO activists encounter in Iran. Nationalism and patriotism reclaimed and exploited by the government to undermine the way CSOs receive foreign aid and their scope of work in a shifting political landscape in Egypt is further considered. In order to overcome these barriers, foreign NGOs had to localise, indigenise and nationalise their own operations and scope of work to accommodate new shifts and policy changes in Colombia; while local Ecuadorian CSOs failed to influence the powerful leftist government.

These shifts made the attempts by CSOs to develop and change processes very limited in these contexts. However, the contributions in this volume raise legitimate questions. For example, how can local CSOs find strategies, tactics and techniques to accommodate and survive sudden, rapid and unexpected changes? How will CSOs strengthen their own 'local ownership' away from international donors or foreign aid? How will CSOs find new civic spaces to create opportunities for change?

## Civic spaces and opportunities

CSOs need to come together to create an active network and effective local partnerships, thus increasing their networks to avoid any duplication in delivery and become resilient to sudden shifts. CSOs need to engage with other CSOs from their own field to share local resources in terms of planning, implementation and evaluation. This promotes CSO engagement to create civic spaces and opportunities for policy change and development processes in closed contexts. CSO operations have increasingly become restricted and in some instances closed. While the traditional media had gone some way in supporting the efforts of CSOs in their accountability work, this is largely no longer possible because of their inability to carry out critical investigative journalism. Traditional media also played a negative role in attacking CSOs that received foreign aid. For example, in the case known as 'Case 173' before the judicial system, as El Assal and Marzouk discuss in this volume. Governments are no longer accountable for their inefficient and ineffective policies and lack of service delivery. Proper venues and spaces are closed and prohibited from holding them accountable. All stakeholders in civic space, including the traditional media and CSOs are unable to manoeuvre and function in proper spaces. CSOs have already shifted by using social media as a possible alternative to newspapers, television and radio to overcome restrictive regimes in African contexts, as Malila shows in exploring the perspectives of CSOs on the way in which media has changed across Africa.

CSOs, however, have been unable to change policies from within the existing structures managed by the Islamic regime of Iran; as discussed by Moheimany and Najafinejad in their chapter on shifts in the status of civil society across two political periods, namely the reformist (1997–2005) and conservative (2005–2013) eras. However, in the reformist period where shifts have taken place, a number of modern CSOs emerged and operated to improve human rights status and policies. The reformist government created a civic space when it amended the legal and administrative procedures and utilised the financial resources and mechanisms in the state to allow modern CSOs to function and operate. Modern CSOs are supported by the reformist class or groups, taking a liberal–secular approach. This has contributed to a state of rift and division among CSOs affiliated to reformists and conservatives. However, Ahmadinejad's presidency made an explicit shift by not accepting CSOs in a spontaneous religious context. CSOs are unacceptable in the conservative Iranian context as they represent a Western model and approach of engaging, delivering and intervention. The conservative leaders of 'associations' or 'CSOs' in Iran are connected to or part of the regime, serving its policies, philosophy and doctrine. CSOs are monitored by security to ensure operations are in accordance with the Iranian Islamic revolution framework.

This shift imposed a new challenge on CSOs already functioning or operating in limited spaces during reformist governments. Reformist CSOs were accused of playing a part in a Western plot against the Iranian revolution. Conservative policies aimed at limiting CSOs from a policy role and from advocating volunteer activism and associated with mass movements in support of the Islamic revolution were introduced. The civic space given by the reformist government no longer existed. CSOs had to shift and cope with new social and political contexts as the number of CSOs has already reduced drastically, owing to closures, bans and restrictions on their activists. A few moderate CSOs were able to operate, but with very limited resources from members and activists themselves; additionally, their impact, efficiency and effectiveness were also limited.

## Funding challenges

The controversial and crucial relationship between CSOs and the government has been an open issue for debate and research for many scholars and activists. The question of foreign aid, however, is the most complicated and dangerous question for CSOs and civil society activists in Egypt. How CSOs respond, engage and cope with political shifts in their relationship with the government is also discussed by El Assal and Marzouk in this volume. The regime, however, proclaims 'patriotism' and 'nationalism' to promote its own legitimacy and credibility. Local CSOs are not entitled to share this claim as long as they receive Western or foreign funds. The political shift or transition in Egypt challenged CSOs' scope of work and operations, where social dynamics and grassroots engagement were influenced by the media campaigns. The media intervention influenced the public against the judicial 'Case of 173', without engaging or providing a sufficient platform for CSO activities to contribute to the debate. However, Egyptian society is open by its nature for engagement and cooperation with other cultures and societies. There have been a number of international companies and organisations operating in Egypt and the Egyptian government has already signed international agreements and protocols to allow CSOs and international donors to engage in human rights and democratic activities. CSOs have to get the government's approval to receive foreign aid; however, approval is often slow or never comes at all, as El Assal and Marzouk discuss in Chapter 5.

Channels of foreign funds to the Gaza Strip must also be approved by the Israeli government, despite the fact that it has no physical presence on the ground there. However, it controls all single access to goods, people, money, health and even technology. The Gaza Strip is under full control, monitoring and surveillance by the Israeli occupation forces by digital and cyber security. Post the 2014 war, all international humanitarian donations to the Gaza Strip must be coordinated with Israel, including the Qatari humanitarian aid discussed in Alkahlout's chapter. Qatari humanitarian deliveries have been essential for a significant segment of Palestinian society in the Gaza Strip, and the continuity of some CSOs' existence in terms of assisting people in various areas including electricity, health and salaries to the Hamas government. Qatari assistance is still conditional to engage and influence Hamas' commitment to the ceasefire imposed after the war in 2014. Qatar will shift or cease channelling aid to the Strip if the political landscape is changed, due to the conflict that might erupt between Gaza's factions and Israel. CSOs in the Gaza Strip have no power or any influence over the distribution of aid to Palestinians. Civil society activists, however, use their social media networks to criticise the mechanisms of aid distribution, including the Qatari one. Social media is a space where Palestinians overcome the shortcomings of a representative democracy that has failed to achieve good governance, ending occupation, ending violence and internal division.

CSOs in the Gaza Strip, however, need to find an alternative to increase 'local ownership' and promote networking to share limited resources and increase the spirit of volunteerism by replacing dependency on foreign aid, despite the dire economic and social circumstances since 2007. Activists in the occupied Palestinian territories, for example, have been challenged at all levels by violence, by their social context, foreign occupation and conditions, requirements and shifts by international donors since 1967. Dalia Hatoqua discusses why some Palestinians are shunning foreign aid. There have been a number of critics and activists who argue that depending on international aid is unsustainable after USAID shifted its policies in 2019. Besan Abu Joudeh, CEO and co-founder of BuildPalestine, says "After USAID left, many organisations had to shut down. Our local non-profits should be sustainable, such that the changing political interests or international donors won't cause them to close up shop" (Hatoqua, 2019).

CSO interventions should be based on existing networks or on building new coalitions, which include grassroots organisations, both active and working on civic engagement, and active community participation at grassroots level. CSOs also employ partnerships to promote the local ownership of activities on the ground and to introduce change. CSOs sometimes use an integral policy to establish a steering committee of all partners and independents, aimed at creating a process of collective decision-making. The use of networks aims to ensure the implementation of effective methodologies to interact with participants and to encourage them to share their thoughts, and engage in role-play and simulations based on real-life experiences. Each activity is used to facilitate the engagement of participants in a discussion on how they can best apply their skills. Participants also engage in discussion groups to identify how best to work together to improve the social situation in their locations. This includes a natural process of identification of promising and talented young people, who help in empowering networks and cooperation between CSOs working for active participation and engagement in civic actions.

The cultural, political and social discourse of civil society through social media was also introduced as some of the volume's contributors reviewed various publications produced by CSOs in which representatives, speakers and experts tackled different issues and problems affecting activists. The contributors also addressed a variety of issues and needs of disempowered people, increasing their local intervention opportunities and their ability to help solve the problems of civic space limitations and the lack of freedom. The examination of the above tools and themes of CSO interventions during contextual shifts includes aiming to understand whether or not CSOs continue their operations as promoters of activist participation within society after the completion of advocacy campaigns. The public campaigns were accompanied by a series of supporting activities including live radio programmes, discussions and debates on a number of sensitive issues, as well as the writing of articles and production of newspapers.

These constitute popular techniques and tools of advocacy for people's engagement in decision-making processes and public transformation, regardless of any negative or destructive criticism from the media (as happened in Egypt against the 'Case 173'). Within this framework, the contributors assess the approaches of CSO interventions in terms of active participation in community actions and engagement in decision-making processes at all levels. O'Connell's chapter, however, criticizes the limits of civil society influence over left-wing governments in Latin America, despite the fact that civil society assisted Correa to power and influenced policies, but ultimately failed. The relationship changed and Correa shifted to control all systems and enacted social organisations to register and limit engagement in politics. CSOs also attempted to contribute to the community efforts that were influencing the political establishment, but the power and popular legitimacy of government was stronger and more deeply rooted than expected at this stage. Social mobilisation, however, presented a real threat to presidential or government survival in Latin America. These cases conclude, however, the significance of a relational approach to identify civil society influence on politics and policies, but also reveal the importance of creating transparent institutions to allow for deeper and more sustained social engagement.

## Social dynamics and shifting landscape

CSOs have to engage grassroots leaders and member organisations in mutual work in order to facilitate hosting meetings and to promote people's civic engagement, community participation activities and economic development. They should cooperate with their international networks to secure cooperation/platforms for future activities and to make CSOs an integral part of their own activities. This approach of engagement will have a direct impact on project sustainability and, in particular, citizens' active engagement in community participation. Yachoulti identifies the shifting social landscape by investigating some changes that have already challenged civil society activism and the role of CSOs in Morocco after the 2011 constitutional reform. The importance of Yachoulti's investigation resides in the fact that it sheds light on a different understanding of the dynamics of civil society in Morocco and helps in foregrounding the state's politics and strategies of governance in Morocco. Yachoulti indicates the cultural values, practices, beliefs and institutions that are specific to Moroccan history, culture and people. These institutions and cultural values have their origins in the dawn of Moroccan history. However, the absence of the willingness to change has made the reforms simply ink on paper, thus, taking things back to their point of departure. In other words, though the constitutional reforms have been revolutionary in terms of content, they have not pushed for clear democratic paths and practices. A fact which resulted in the emergence of new forms of activism that are spontaneous and sometimes radical and extreme in their forms and legal in their dimension and messages.

A different type of culture and values encompass Irish community participation modes, including the strategies of small NGOs in Ireland, that reflect their power in civic engagement and social contribution, and their ability to generate local resources. Sai identifies and maps keys challenges facing operational practices of two non-profit charities within the shifting landscape and influences of CSOs in Irish society. Both CSOs succeeded in building successful partnerships and networks with other organisations. For example, Islamic Relief Ireland (IRI) cooperated with Trócaire, which is the official overseas development agency of the Catholic Church in Ireland, to fight the spread of cholera in Yeman. The grassroots contribution and engagement of the Muslim Sisters of Eire (MSOÉ) with Irish society also reflected its success in maintaining sustainability and being able to cope with social changes, despite the changing Irish context during the last few decades. MSOÉ's full dependence on local volunteers and funding without support from paid staff is a crucial challenge. This indicates, however, a success example of 'local ownership' for sustainability, credibility and legitimacy to engage with their own communities and generate resources to render services for the homeless, women's empowerment and community dialogue.

To this end, and in keeping with these principles, CSOs are careful to ensure that the implementation of programmes remains inclusive and as broad-based as possible. Focussing on empowering networks and collective work amongst civil society actors, as a base for sustainable action. Civil society partnerships ensure their actions are successful. It also ensures inclusivity and the active civic engagement of activists with participatory approaches. This strategy uses a principle methodology of process, network, education, communication and change. CSO involvement in the community is not only based on a holistic approach combining discussions, training, dialogue and coalition-building, but also on interviews and various interactions with grassroots groups and other stakeholders. The process is need-based and responsive to the changes taking place and is, thus, able to adapt itself to the requirements of the socio-political contexts.

The scope of this book also examines whether CSOs working to increase civic engagement and participation also attempt to secure coordination and cooperation amongst partners during the implementation of activities within shifting landscapes. CSOs should also seek to determine whether the outcomes and implications of internationally sponsored civil society empowerment activities will go beyond the target groups in participatory activities. This sometimes includes public opinion-makers, decision-makers and universities but mainly involves professional media personnel. CSOs, therefore, seek to identify whether young people's civic engagement activities, conducted by CSOs in particular, strengthen cooperation, communication and cross fertilisation between the CSO groups, media and participants in the activities on the one hand and local/national authorities on the other. Many programmes, however, allowed participation in empowered activities by CSO staff and network members to conduct and implement future projects. Their capacity for lobbying, networking and organisation, in order to influence decision-makers, is now much more powerful and able to achieve sustainable impact and change.

## Way forward

This volume has indicated that this sector is significant for researching political shifts in different locations all over the world. The contributors, through the case studies, deliver explicit results that the political landscape shifts do not only influence the regimes or governments, but also CSOs and their own scope of work and intervention, which have been the main themes for research and academic studies in different social and political backgrounds and contexts. In fact, CSOs have the legitimacy and credibility to function, deliver and influence despite the failures and setbacks in different countries.

The contributors and editors hope to encourage scholarly debate on the importance of the scope of work of CSOs, as a main actor and partner for change and development, in cooperation with other sectors. This will encourage scholars in the field to re-examine existing CSOs to determine their mechanisms of shifting, accommodating and ensuring sustainability. Considering the political, funding and social landscape of the country case studies, CSOs' commitment to their resolute drive for change is in itself powerful and revolutionary. This volume has shown that there is value in understanding CSOs, not only as a precursor to democratic advances, but as an influential sector in its own right to exist, develop, expand and sustain.

This volume assists to understand various social, political and funding challenges, shifts and barriers to effective CSO work, operations and deliveries. These barriers influence CSOs' sustainability and ability to intervene and renew their legitimacy and credibility during periods of shifts and the resultant challenges. This volume concludes that CSOs are always required to work under pressure to meet their own funding, conditions, quality of work and reporting. In the meantime, they are required to meet and accommodate their scope of intervention to sudden challenges and emergencies to keep their current operational practices and strategies for future development. It also assists researchers to explore the factors, circumstances and historical changes that influence the development of CSO activities, and the organisational, financial and political challenges facing them today. Therefore, the editors will expand their investigation to explore various development themes in the sector as follows:

## Local ownership and social capital

Relationships between CSOs and for-profit businesses
CSOs and service delivery
CSOs and social accountability

## Partnership, cross-cultural relations and sustainability

Negotiating the big CSOs versus small CSOs divide
CSOs versus populism
CSOs versus the North/South divide

## Local funding and networking

Mechanisms for sharing information, resources and expertise
Challenges to networking and strategies for overcoming those challenges
CSOs and advocacy

## Reference

Hatoqua, D. (2019) *Why Some Palestinians are shunning foreign aid.* Accessed February 25, 2019. https://www.thenewhumanitarian.org/analysis/2019/05/14/why-some-palestinians-are-shunning-foreign-aid.

# Index

Printed in the USA
CPSIA information can be obtained
at www.ICGtesting.com
LVHW011149150324
774517LV00041B/1757

9 780367 512590